Stephen L. Atlas is a member of Parents Without Partners and Montgomery County (MD) Single Parents. He has been a guest speaker at the Family Therapy Practice Network's Symposium, a single parenting seminar held by the National Chapter of the Black Women's Consciousness Raising Association, and the Parents Without Partners Regional Conference. Mr. Atlas is a previous non-custodial parent who now enjoys a joint/divided custody arrangement of his two children.

SINGLE PARENTING

A PRACTICAL RESOURCE GUIDE

STEPHEN L. ATLAS

foreword by
Connie Manfrada
President of Parents Without Partners (1979–1980)

A SPECTRUM BOOK

PRENTICE-HALL, INC., Englewood Cliffs, New Jersey 07632

Library of Congress Cataloging in Publication Data

ATLAS, STEPHEN L
  Single parenting.

  (A Spectrum Book)
  Bibliography: p. 222–234
  Includes index.
    1. Single-parent family—United States. 2. Child-
ren—Management. 3. Parenting—United States.
4. Parent and child—United States. I. Title.
HQ777.4.A74   306.8   80-25939
ISBN 0-13-810622-3
ISBN 0-13-810614-2 (pbk.)

Editorial/production supervision and interior design by Suse L. Cioffi
Cover design by Ira Shapiro
Manufacturing buyer: Cathie Lenard

PRENTICE-HALL INTERNATIONAL, INC., *London*
PRENTICE-HALL OF AUSTRALIA PTY. LIMITED, *Sydney*
PRENTICE-HALL OF CANADA, LTD., *Toronto*
PRENTICE-HALL OF INDIA PRIVATE LIMITED, *New Delhi*
PRENTICE-HALL OF JAPAN, INC., *Tokyo*
PRENTICE-HALL OF SOUTHEAST ASIA PTE. LTD., *Singapore*
WHITEHALL BOOKS LIMITED, *Wellington, New Zealand*

Table of Contents

82 354

Foreword

Many books, articles, and publications are written every day about the trauma a person experiences when he or she faces the loss of a mate through death or through the death of a marital relationship. For years the experts have studied which loss has a greater effect on the survivors. Child psychologists, too, have been addressing the effects of death and divorce on the mental and physical stability of children. Little, if anything, has been written about the rehabilitation period that the single-again must experience in building a brand new life. When children are involved, the adjustment is far more complex, requiring the individual to expend immense energy and creativity in establishing the single-parent home.

Steve Atlas, through his own experiences as well as through the experiences of others, has captured a true picture of the well-functioning, well-established single-parent family. Their collective experiences have attested to the difficulties that the single parent encounters. Through support groups such as Parents Without Partners, Inc., these single parents have learned to cope, support, and encourage one another. They have discovered that they can be a single-parent family—a well-functioning unit providing security, caring, discipline, and sufficient psychological nourishment for the optimal development of children.

Single Parenting clearly points out that single-parent families are more close knit and more democratic than two-parent families, as children share in the responsibilities of running a household. This cooperative spirit seems to build the strength in our children that will help them later in life. This book portrays how to become a successful single-parent family: how to balance responsibilities and how to share heavy workloads and still have a rewarding personal life open to growth and social relationships. Single parenthood is no longer a transitional state but a chosen lifestyle full of endless opportunities and countless open doors. With its practical advice and comments from those who are living the single-parent experience, *Single Parenting* is worthwhile reading for anyone who wants to improve the quality of their single-parent family life.

Connie Manfreda, President (1979-1980)
Parents Without Partners, Inc.

Introduction

Hello. My name is Steve Atlas, and like many of you, I am a single parent. My son, Nick, is now ten years old; my daughter, Alia, is nearly eight. From December, 1974 until June, 1977, I was a noncustodial single parent. From June, 1977 to July, 1980, my children have lived with me full time under a special joint-custody agreement giving my former wife and me the option to modify the custodial arrangements—without going to court—if we agree that the change will benefit the children. (For practical purposes, I had custody of my children from June, 1977 to July, 1980.) Since July, 1980, we have had a joint/divided custody arrangement. During the week my son lives with me and my daughter with her mother. Weekends and holidays the children are together, alternating between their mother and me.

When I became a single parent, I found excellent books about coping with divorce and about being a single person, but nothing that discussed single parenthood as a distinct and valid way of life. As I joined single-parent organizations—such as Parents Without Partners (PWP) and the Montgomery County (Maryland) Single Parents (Montcosps), I found that these groups' single-parent discussions gave me a better understanding of how other single parents had dealt with fears and concerns such as those I was experiencing. Also, the groups' family activities to which I have taken my children have given all three of us a special sense of community.

As I came to know other members of PWP and Montcosps as friends and single parents who seemed content with their single-parent families, I began to realize that for many of these people, their single-parent family was a *positive* influence on their children and on themselves. It was not the "broken home" I would so often read of in books, newspapers, and magazines. I asked myself, "Why is there such a difference between the single parents I see and the media's set view?"

In recent years, there have been several worthwhile books about single-parent families. While many of these books have been written by psychologists, social workers, and counselors (individuals whose frame of reference is generally limited to their clients—who usually have problems), a number of good books have been written by single parents. Two things concerned me, however, about most of these books.

First, they typically dealt only with one group of single parents (noncustodial fathers or joint custody, for example). I have found that there are concerns common to many groups of single parents, even though the specific situation may differ. (For example, problem solving involves any parent who has children. Thus, a noncustodial father may need to deal with problem solving and other custodial-parent concerns when the children visit him for a weekend or summer.) It has helped me, and other single parents with whom I have talked, to gain a variety of perspectives and opinions on a given problem or concern. Also, it can help you as a custodial or noncustodial parent to be aware of the problems and concerns faced by the "other type" of parent.

Second, to this day I have seen no book that makes use of the wealth of positive and practical experiences and insights to be found in the members of single-parent groups, such as PWP and Montcosps. Most books, if they even mention PWP, quote briefly from PWP's brochure, or discuss the organization's dances and other social events. I have seen little, if anything, about the group's discussions, which help new members (and older members) to understand, accept, and build on the positive aspects of their lives as single parents. Why is it, I wonder, that we do not read about PWP's (and Montcosps') family activities, such as picnics or trips, that offer members and their children a special opportunity (usually free, or at little cost) to feel part of a special community while also having a good time?

I believe omissions such as the two just mentioned contribute to the popular view that single parenting is difficult and undesirable, creating a family in which the parent is isolated from any meaningful support. According to this viewpoint, the best to be hoped for is that a single parent and his or her children can learn to cope with, or accept, their unfortunate situation.

When I examined the available books and other resources relating to single-parent families—with the notable exception of single-parent groups such as PWP or Montcosps—I was struck by the fact that virtually all of these focused on the first stage of single parenthood, the stage of shock, disbelief, and fear. The "ideal" family portrayed was that of the traditional two-parent, or nuclear, family, and most books and counselors tried to "help" single parents model their families after nuclear families. I was forcefully reminded of this when I was invited to lead a discussion for family therapists concerning "Making It as a Single Parent: The Experience of Successful Single Parents." After my initial talk, in which I described seven ways that a single-parent family can be *beneficial* to both its children and parent, one family therapist commented in real surprise, "You make it sound as if a single parent can be a healthy environment for both children and parent."

That *is* exactly what I am saying. The main point of this book is that *Single-Parent Families Can Be Healthy and Satisfying, and They Offer Unique Opportunities for Personal Growth for Each Family Member—Provided We Understand and Base our Efforts on the Single-Parent Family, Rather Than Try to Make Our Families Identical to Two-Parent Families Either Through Imitation or Remarriage.*

Here, I will make no apologies for single parenthood. Rather, I will discuss the single-parent family and your life as a single parent as a complete way of life (*not* limited to the period from separation to divorce, or as a way station to remarriage), which can offer both you and your children an opportunity to satisfy your needs in a warm, supportive family environment.

These are some of the reasons why I felt a book such as *Single Parenting* was necessary. Here, I have based my information on the positive experiences of successful single parents. (By *successful*, I mean those who seem to enjoy and feel good about themselves, their children, and the relationship they have with their children. As single parents, these people have been able to help their children to accept themselves and grow in ways that are beneficial to the children's overall development.) Most of these are members of either PWP or Montcosps. I have used many of the ideas that were shared in single-parent discussion groups held by these and other organizations (while disguising names and being sufficiently vague about other details to ensure the confidentiality of these discussions), personal interviews, and answers to a questionnaire sent to single parents throughout the United States (see Appendix B).

Where they would be helpful, I have also included some of my own experiences as a single parent. I have interviewed single parents at work and in my local community, and have also asked the advice of family therapists and counselors, educators, and others who work with single parents and/or their children.

Additional information was obtained by identifying and contacting resource groups and other organizations and by reading many books and articles relating to the concerns of single parents. (Especially helpful was *The Single Parent*, the magazine of Parents Without Partners.) I am particularly grateful to Barbara Chase, editor of *The Single Parent*, who included my request for help from other PWP members in an issue of the magazine, and Ann Parks, information specialist for Parents Without Partners Inc. Ann is a walking treasure of information, publications, and resources relating to single parents and their children. Her help, cooperation, and assistance in utilizing PWP's extensive library has been a real inspiration to me.

This book does not attempt to isolate individual groups of single parents. Rather, it deals with concerns of single parents in both everyday and special areas of concern. I believe that any single parent can be most effective when he or she understands not only his or her individual type of custodial situation but also those experienced by single parents in other types of custodial situations. For this reason, any single parent—whether custodial, noncustodial, joint, or divided custody—or person who is concerned about single parents and their children, can benefit from reading the book.

This is a practical resource guide—by single parents, for single parents—about both everyday and special concerns of single parents. If you are a single parent, seeing how other single parents have succeeded, and reading their ideas and suggestions, may help you develop your own ideas and realize that you *can* succeed as a single parent.

If you are not a single parent, this book will give you a better understanding of how single-parent families can *and do* succeed in meeting the needs of their individual members. It is incorrect to view a single-parent family as a broken home. It is more accurate to say that the single-parent family is a type of family. Like any other type of family, it has its own strengths and weaknesses. For too long we have heard about just the weaknesses. This book will show you the strengths. It will provide the positive information that will enable you to understand and help single parents and their children build on the positive aspects of their single-parent family and so achieve meaningful, fulfilling lives and personal growth.

ACKNOWLEDGMENTS

This book could not have been written without the help of many people.

I want to thank Parents Without Partners, Inc. (an organization of which I am proud to be a member) for the exceptional assistance I have received. I especially want to thank the following staff members and officers: Ann Parks, Barbara Chase, Virginia Martin, Elizabeth Hormann, Jean Teeter, Hugh Cole, Nancy McGrath, Lynn Maggio, Betsy Kelley, Bob Campbell, and Connie Manfreda. My own PWP chapter (Chapter 1, in Baltimore, Maryland) was especially helpful by giving me permission to take notes during selected discussions. Three other PWP chapters were exceptionally helpful: both in distributing and returning my questionnaire, and in arranging telephone interviews when necessary; I want to offer them my special thanks. These chapters are in Baraboo, Wisconsin; Belen, New Mexico; and Binghamton, New York.

I want also to express my appreciation to my friends and fellow members of the Montgomery County Single Parents (Montcosps). I am particularly grateful to Barbara Van den Arend and Murray Stein, Codirectors of Montcosps' Dialogue (Discussion) Program, for allowing me to take notes during selected dialogues, and for arranging several special dialogues to help me obtain material for this book. Murray and Barbara also put me in touch with Montcosps members with personal experience in such areas as noncustodial motherhood and the living-together arrangement (LTA).

Thanks to everyone who took the time to complete my questionnaire. I know it took *a lot* of your time, but the quality and depth of your responses have been the major reasons why this book can be as thorough as it is.

Thanks also to Paul Shoffeitt, Ph.D.; Muriel S. Karlin; Carolyn Males; Julie Raskin; Joanne Small, M.S.W.; A. Billy S. Jones; Missy Zane; Judith Latham; Vanessa Brooks; Carol Callendar; Charlotte Staub; George Mikulskis; Marie Mayor; Mark R. Lohman, M.D.; Joyce Shemer Keating; Patricia Nurse, M.Ed.; and all the other individuals whose insights and suggestions have been invaluable to this book.

Special thanks to Janey McCauley and Paul Ephross, who reviewed each and every chapter and to Linda Brown and Sharyn Nesselhauf for typing my book—and deciphering my handwriting into a manuscript.

My sincere gratitude to Kathy Aversano for giving me the perspective, practical advice, encouragement, and support necessary to write this book.

I want to thank Mary Kennan, Suse Cioffi, Beverly Fulton, Dean Karrel, and the other staff members at Prentice-Hall whose support, practical suggestions, cooperation, and belief in the value of this book have been invaluable.

Also I would like to thank Nancy McGrath for preparing the study guide.

And, finally, to my children: Alia and Nick. Their understanding and cooperation, support, and willingness to work with me so that we could each satisfy our needs while I worked on this book has been my inspiration. I still marvel at Alia and Nick's patience and willingness to respect my privacy and need to work—especially since I know that when I was seven or nine years old, I would never have had the patience that they have had. I can truly say that Alia and Nick have helped me make it as a single parent.

Author's Note

With the exception of a few professionals who have given me permission to use their full names, I have used only first names throughout this book. In those cases where people requested that their names not be used, I have invented other names. In those cases where more than one person had the same first name, I have used the first letter of the individual's home town as the first initial of their last name.

Chapter 1

From Marriage to
the Single-Parent Family

How did I get here? If you are presently a single parent, or are experiencing a life crisis which might result in your becoming a single parent, you have probably asked this question at least twice in your life: when you asked your parents how you were born, and when you became single again. Indeed, for most single parents, becoming single again is similar to being born again.

Traditional roles and expectations are changing in many areas. This is particularly true of family life today. When we grew up, we were taught to believe that life followed a predictable pattern. We went to school and made friends. After high school, a man either went to college or got a job. After a few years of being a bachelor, he was expected to marry, "settle down," and raise a family. Traditionally, he was expected to be the breadwinner and family disciplinarian. Although he supported his wife in raising the children, his main area of responsibility was providing the financial support.

Women, too, followed a predictable life pattern. After school, a woman might get a job, but only until she was married, which was supposed to be a woman's major goal. After marriage, perhaps she and her husband would have a few years without children. In any case, upon pregnancy, she quit her job and stayed home full time to super-

1

vise the house and child(ren). (If, due to financial burdens, a woman had to work, her husband generally saw this as a negative reflection on his masculinity; and both parents saw this as an unfortunate necessity to be endured temporarily.)

It can be very upsetting to us, as single parents, to feel that we have failed at what we have been taught is one of life's most important responsibilities: providing a stable two-parent family in which our children can grow up. This sense of failure is reinforced by widespread beliefs in our society, such as the term *broken home* to describe a single-parent family, and the view that parents who divorce are indulging themselves at the expense of their children.

According to the United States Bureau of the Census, in 1978, 9.3 percent of all families in the United States were headed by a single parent. This does not include noncustodial parents (those not living with their children) or those whose children have grown up and are no longer with them. According to the National Center for Health Statistics, in 1977 there were 1,090,000 divorces as compared to 2,200,000 marriages. This is over two and a half times as many divorces as in 1960. Why do so many people get separated or divorced?

One major factor in this changing pattern is the growing discontent of many women with the limitation of their traditional roles as housewives. The women's liberation movement has produced many consciousness-raising and support groups, where women have learned that they are not necessarily crazy to feel trapped and discontent in their marriages. Some of their desires include wanting jobs and promotions, pay and job opportunities, and career advancement based solely on their ability; wishing to be taken seriously, listened to, and treated as equal partners by their husbands; and having their needs and concerns taken seriously and responded to, rather than being limited to responding to the needs and concerns of their husbands and children. Although women may well have had these concerns previously, the support of their fellow group members and the availability of assertiveness training presently makes them more willing to confront their husbands.

Sometimes these problems can be resolved within the marriage. Frequently, however, this is not possible. In the past, women ignored their feelings of discontent because they needed their husbands' economic support and desired their community's social acceptance of their role. Today, women are learning that they can support themselves economically. The availability of women's groups, singles' groups, and single-parent groups offers a woman increased support if she decides to leave her husband and strike out on her own. For example, Beatrice, a single parent I met, said, "All my life, I've lived for others. First, I was my father's daughter; then, I was my husband's wife and my children's mother. I've always been somebody's daughter, wife, or mother. Now I need to be *just somebody*, and think of my own needs and desires."

Men, too, have come to realize that they have their own problems. As the film *Men's Lives* vividly demonstrates, boys and men are supposed to be as strong as rocks, never showing weakness or emotions, always competing—rather than cooperating—for the best prize, the most attractive woman, and the best paying and most prestigious job, regardless of whether or not these are what they really want. Their human and emotional needs and their ability for nurturance have also been ignored.[1]

In the past few years, several men's consciousness-raising and support groups have developed. They encourage men to reaffirm their bond with other men and, consequently, to share their emotional needs and skills with other people. Just as women have been accepted and respected in the work world, men have finally begun to be accepted as fathers who are fully capable of raising their children—with or without a partner. For a truly inspiring book about a man raising his children alone, read Michael McFadden's *Bachelor Fatherhood* (Ace Paperback, 1975).

Another factor in the growing divorce rate has to do with the length of people's lives. Parents used to marry in their late teens or early 20s and have children shortly thereafter. They were generally so busy fulfilling their traditional roles and raising their children that they had little time or need to really know each other as individuals. Inevitably, people change and grow, develop new values and approaches to life, and relate to each other in new ways. Because of demands of work and home, however, married couples did not usually have to deal with these changes or spend any length of time alone together until their children were grown. By this time, the parents were usually 40 or 45 years old. As a matter of fact, "at the turn of this

[1]Josh Hanig and Will Roberts, *Men's Lives* (Franklin Lakes, NJ.: New Day Films, 1974), 16mm, 43 min.

century, menopause occurred during a woman's forties, her life expectancy was forty-nine years."[2] Since men and women considered themselves old when they were in their 40s and their lives were nearly over, why make a change? The overwhelming belief was that even if negative feelings developed between the parents while the children were growing up, a parent should subordinate his or her personal desires to the needs of the children. After all, everyone knew that children were far better off in any nuclear (two-parent) family—even if there was strife, tension, and hostility between the parents—than in a broken home.

The change in society's attitude toward single-parent families also contributes to the rise in separations and divorces. In the early part of this century, society in the United States consisted primarily of small communities where nearly everyone knew everyone else. While there was a warm feeling of belonging, there was a tremendous stigma, or public shame, in being a single parent. Single parents (whether never married, divorced or separated, or widowed) were, at best, regarded with sympathy. More often, other people ignored them or thought little of them because of their being "unnatural parents." Of course, everyone knew that if you really loved your children, you stayed married for their sake, regardless of your personal feelings about your spouse. Children of broken homes were also regarded with professional sympathy by teachers and other adults who worked with them, and were frequently shunned or ridiculed by other children their own age. In such an atmosphere, was it any wonder that couples seldom divorced?

In the last 30 or 40 years, we have changed from a rural, small-town society to one based in urban and metropolitan areas. Although this has, unfortunately, eliminated much of the close feeling of belonging to a community where people knew and cared about each other, there have also been some benefits to the change. Our change to a more urban and metropolitan society—with the development of mass media and communication—has made people more aware of, and tolerant of, life styles different from their own. People no longer have the time or interest to worry about how others live their lives. While this indifference often causes people to feel alone and uncared about, it also removes the stigma from life changes such as divorce

[2]Paula Weideger, *Menstruation and Menopause* (New York: Knopf, 1976), p. 198.

and separation. People are no longer subject to public embarrassment or shame in the same way that they were 40 or 50 years ago.

In the past 25 years, there have been dramatic changes in both the length of people's lives and their relationship to their marital partner, their children, and society. "Today, the typical woman in the United States has menopause at the age of 50 and a life expectancy of seventy-five years."[3] Men, too, can expect to live about 20 years longer than at the turn of the century. Labor-saving devices and the increase in vacations and leisure time have given husbands and wives the opportunity to spend more time together and enjoy their relationship. This has been combined with an increased emphasis on personal satisfaction and the gratification of one's own needs. Rather than waiting until their children are grown, women and men are recognizing the legitimacy of fulfilling their own needs and desires. People want fulfillment and satisfaction *now*.

Research has shown that women in unhappy marriages experience a far higher degree of mental and physical health problems than women who are happily single or divorced. This was vividly explained by Jessie Bernard, in *The Future of Marriage* (Bantam paperback, 1973), when she found that married women have the greatest amount of physical, emotional, and mental health problems and never-married women, the least.

There has been a growing recognition by psychologists, social workers, and society that divorce or separation does *not* have to be terrible for children. A study by Ivan Nye, in 1957, found that children were actually healthier and more stable in a single-parent home where there is love, consistency, and opportunity for parent and children to fulfill their personal needs than in a two-parent family where there is tension and hostility between the parents.[4]

In his book *Helping Troubled Children*, Michael Rutter makes the point that in homes broken by separation or divorce, the discord and disharmony preceding the break, rather than the separation or divorce itself (which may actually provide much needed relief from the family tension), causes the main stress in children.[5] He found that

[3]Ibid., p. 199.
[4]F. Ivan Nye, "Child Adjustment in Broken and in Unhappy, Unbroken Homes." *Marriage and Family Living*, 19 (1957), pp. 356–61.
[5]Michael Rutter. *Helping Troubled Children*. New York: Plenum, Harmondsworth, Penguin Books Ltd., 1975, p. 174 © 1975 by Michael Rutter.

"although there are ill-effects stemming from being brought up in a one-parent family, the effects are probably less uniform and less severe than is widely assumed. In general, the number of parents in the home is probably less crucial to the child's development than the relationships and behaviour provided by whoever is present. Furthermore, family life is determined not only by the peculiar characteristics of the individual family members, but also by the social circumstances and environment within which the family live."[6]

The factors discussed (more leisure time, recognition of the legitimacy of one's own needs. and the growing public awareness that a single-parent family is not the worst possible environment for raising children) have contributed to the willingness of parents to undergo separation and divorce. This is reinforced by the development of a single-parent and singles' community which offers both single parents and their children an opportunity to feel part of a community, make new friends, develop new relationships, and be accepted as individuals rather than as stereotypes.

The best-known group for single parents and their children is Parents Without Partners (PWP), an international organization with chapters throughout the United States and headquarters in Bethesda, Maryland (a suburb of Washington, D.C.). In addition, there are local single-parent groups, singles' discussion groups, clubs for single people, and organizations designed to meet the needs of special groups (such as widows and widowers).

The availability of these groups helps ensure that people considering separation or divorce do not have to feel alone or isolated. As a matter of fact, Esta Lee, a member of the Montgomery County Single Parents (Montcosps)—a single-parent group in the Washington, D.C., area—told me, "Montcosps is like an extended family. When I was married, I was home all day and isolated from people. Now I know more people, have friends, places I can go, and things I can do. People call me frequently. My children and I are part of a real community. When I had a personal crisis in my family, people called and came over to show they cared. That really means something!"

As mentioned earlier, over five million families in the United States are headed by single parents. This figure does *not* include single parents who do not live with their children full time or those

[6]Ibid, p. 174.

whose children have grown up and left home. Therefore, as a single parent you are hardly alone!

COPING WITH BEING A SINGLE PARENT

Single parenting offers you an opportunity to know and value yourself more fully than before. Single parenthood does not have to be escaped from or fought: It can be an experience to be appreciated, savored, and embraced for what it can offer. The self-awareness, communications skills, and freedom to base your life and relationships around your own needs can enable you to gain the maximum benefit from this stage of your life—simultaneously increasing the likelihood of a satisfying remarriage should that be what you desire.

As in any new experience, there are good and bad times. From the many single parents I have come to know both personally and through my research, from articles in PWP's *The Single Parent* magazine, from books concerning separation and divorce, and from discussions with family therapists and counselors, I have found that there are several stages through which single parents progress.

The first stage is largely one of shock, disbelief, and fear. At this point we, as single parents, feel cut off from our married friends and associates, possibly estranged from our parents and extended family, and not yet comfortable with the single or single-parent community. It is easy to feel as if we are all alone. New challenges such as finding a new job, handling responsibilities, coping with the demands of our children without the help of a partner, trying to find new friends, and developing a new identity as a single person can make life seem pretty discouraging. There is also the almost inevitable hostility and tension between you and your former spouse.

However, even in this first stage, we can see positive signs. There is usually less tension in our home, since our former spouse is no longer present. Angela, a single parent from Baltimore, Maryland, remembers that "after the divorce, the children were relieved of tension and felt more comfortable. Our home was filled with their friends." At a single-parent discussion group in Washington, D.C., one woman recalled that after she and her husband separated, she found that it was a tremendous relief to be free from his constant criticism.

Being completely responsible for ourselves can be frightening but also exhilarating. We begin to seek out resources to help us progress in our new life as a single parent. At a PWP discussion, one woman expressed amazed joy at finding other single parents—particularly men—who really cared about their children.

In the second stage, we begin to identify resources and organizations that can help us in our new life as single parents. Counseling, returning to school, job training, and involvement in singles' clubs and single-parent organizations are just some of the available resources. It is terrifying at first to attend parties and socials and "get back into the dating game." It can feel really good to realize that our former spouse is not the only partner we can find. Being seen as attractive, interesting, and desirable by single people of the opposite sex can give us a feeling of incredulous delight.

Another aspect of this second stage is the opportunity to get to know other single people of both sexes as individuals and friends. As single people, we can pick our friendships without having to consider the wishes of anyone else. We can enjoy a depth and quality in our friendships that is frequently unavailable to married couples, since their primary relationship can make it difficult to devote much time to other friendships, especially if the friendship only involves one member of the couple.

As we begin to know ourselves and build a new life, one danger can be the feeling of conflict between our own needs and those of our children. As we become more comfortable with our life, though, we increasingly feel a sense of self-worth, accomplishment, and peace of mind that make it easier to communicate with our children and work out family problems in a way that satisfies each family member. The communications and active-listening skills gained from single-parent discussions and workshops can be invaluable here. Betty, for two years a single parent of two teenagers, from Lincoln, Nebraska, found that the solution for her family was to "talk out the problem and discuss what can be done to solve it. We are more of a unit now, not just separate people going our separate ways."

In the third stage, we have come to grips with ourselves and our single-parent life. We have usually found what we enjoy doing and do it without feeling strange or uncomfortable. We have developed a life with our children that allows for both their needs and ours, while no longer blaming ourselves completely for the failure of our marriage.

Perhaps we have already experienced an intimate, on-going relationship. We are aware of the singles' and single-parent community, and the support of our single friends reminds us that it is not necessary to be isolated and alone. We know and accept ourselves, realize our limitations, and have built a new life for ourselves, with its joys and problems.

As single parents, we are of course concerned with how divorce, separation, or becoming widowed affects our children. For this reason I talked to Marie, a junior high school student who is a leader of her local International Youth Council (IYC)—PWP's group for teenage children of single parents. According to Marie, young people also go through three stages when their parents become single: "At the beginning, it really hits hard. However, they eventually get used to it; even though they don't understand it, they stop asking questions. When they reach high school age, they usually start asking why the separation or divorce occurred. The parent's attitude can make a huge difference to their children. If the parent is understanding, does not pressure their kids to be more open than they feel, consider the kids' concerns and feelings, and gives straightforward, but not long and drawn-out, answers, the young people can do just fine. Above all, don't make too big a deal about being 'different' from 'normal' families." Marie also suggested that the International Youth Council can be a major support to young people with single parents: both in helping them realize they are not alone in their family situation and in letting them feel part of a community where they can make new friends and enjoy both social activities and discussions relating to their concerns as children of single-parent families.

Many of us remarry, and many of us don't. Those who do frequently find that the insights they have gained as single parents, along with their greater ability to assert their needs, work together with their partner to anticipate and resolve problems, and their general willingness to give of themselves make their second marriage far more rewarding than their first.

Single parents who do *not* remarry (and there are many) find that they, too, can have fulfilling lives. They can enjoy friends, children, and interests, and share an involvement in *their* community of single parents and their children.

The three steps described are quite simplified, but they should make you aware that single parents *can and do* have rewarding and fulfilling lives. While marriage has real advantages, and remarriage is a satisfying life style for many people, being a single parent can be a viable and positive alternative. In this book, I will be discussing ideas and strategies that might help you and your children. I will also show you some ways that other single parents have dealt with problems that most of you have experienced.

Chapter 2

Seven Ways Your Children Can Benefit From a Single-Parent Family

Being a single parent can feel a lot like being shipwrecked on a strange island. Like the lost traveler who would prefer to be somewhere other than the island where he or she is trapped, most of us single parents initially find our single-parent status an undesirable situation for which we have had little or no preparation. Fears, including loneliness, a sense that we are cut off from normal society, feeling overwhelmed by the responsibility of being the *only* full-time parent in our family, and our concern that we may be destined to live the remainder of our lives alone without a partner can make it difficult for us to see and achieve a positive family environment for ourselves and our children. The traditional view that single-parent families are not beneficial to children can, all too easily, cause us to give up in despair.

However, to carry our shipwreck analogy a step further, if shipwrecked travelers wanted to survive, they had to stop lamenting that they had not reached their destination, discover what resources their new environment could offer, and then utilize these effectively to make their lives as pleasant and rewarding as possible. Frequently, the shipwrecked discovered new abilities and inner resources they never realized they possessed. Often, they got to enjoy their island, some-

11

times choosing to remain there rather than return home. Even if they did return, they were usually happier and more aware of their strengths than if they had never been forced into their island existence. What distinguished the survivors from those who died or were miserable on the island was their positive attitude and willingness to work to achieve their goals.

From my personal experience and comments from other single parents, I have found that a healthy single-parent family can offer its children many benefits. In fact, from discussions with my friends who are married parents, I have come to realize that both two-parent and one-parent families can offer a healthy living environment—*provided that each type of family realizes its own strengths and resources and builds on these to create an effective family.*

I am reminded of a childhood experience. When I was a boy of ten, my father and I enjoyed hiking and climbing mountains. I had also been fortunate in having had a safety clinic the previous spring, where I learned, among other things, how to give artificial respiration. I was very excited, both about my new skill and the satisfaction I was deriving from hiking up Mount Snow in New York State's Adirondack Mountains with my father. As we were puffing and panting our way up the trail, my father suddenly turned to me and said, "Steve, if I were to fall and injure my leg, what would you do?" My instinctive response was "I'd give you artificial respiration." There was a moment of silence; then my father replied, "I hope I never get hurt when we're on a hike together."

Just as artificial respiration was not the best solution for an injured leg, so the two-parent family is an unrealistic and inappropriate model for single parents. As single parents, we need to discover the positive side of single parenting and realize that, as in any type of family, there are both problems and rewards. While being a single parent is not always easy, single parenthood offers special opportunities for personal growth that can enable you to develop a happy and secure family.

From my own experience and what I have learned from other successful single parents, I have come to realize that there are at least seven benefits that children *can* receive from a single-parent family.

These seven benefits are not automatic. They require work, flexibility, and a willingness to ask the advice and help of others when necessary. In the following chapters of this book, you will have a chance to learn about strategies, ideas, and experiences that have worked for other one-parent families, while gaining some helpful hints that can make your job as a single parent and your life as a single person easier, less frustrating, and more rewarding for you and your children.

√ *Benefit 1:*
A Reduction in Tension, Hostility, and Discord within the Family and an Increase in Family Solidarity and Consistency

As single parents, it is easy to idealize the nuclear family—*regardless of how the parents get along together.* Take a second, now, and think back to your own married days. Remember the arguments and tension between your former spouse and yourself. Do you really think that you and your children were better off then? How do you think your children felt? At a PWP discussion in Baltimore, Maryland, Joe recalled that when he was growing up, there was constant arguing and fighting between his parents. Joe told the group, "I was terrified that my parents would separate—even though this never happened—and then, where would I be? As I look back on it now, maybe I would have been better off in a happy, more peaceful single-parent family."

The overwhelming majority of the single parents who have contacted me—men and women both—felt that a major benefit for both them and their children has been the reduction of tension, hostility, and bitterness within their family.

In unhappy, tension-filled nuclear families there are real obstacles to spending *quality time* with our children. By "quality time," I mean the time that you and your children (or other adults) are free to enjoy each other's companionship free from external demands, pressures or expectations. A hostility between partners and the expectation that our needs will not be seriously considered—and what success we do achieve in satisfying these will be due only to a bitter struggle—often leave our children in the middle of our struggle and offer them only a tense and chill, not a warm and supportive, environment. In this type of living situation, we see our family as restrictive and unresponsive to our needs. It becomes easy to use our job (either at home or away from home) as an excuse to be "too tired" for any meaningful involvement with our family. For example, my friend Leonard told me, "When I was married, what did I have to look forward to? Misunderstandings, conflict, and tension. It takes effort to spend time with my children in a meaningful way. Because of my own expectations of a hostile home environment, I experienced a feeling of fatigue and became too tired to deal with my family. I didn't even read to my kids. Sure, I was unhappy about my lack of quality time with the children, but what could I do?

"As a single parent who shares custody of my two daughters, I have only myself and my children to consider. The tension of a hostile partner is gone, and I feel much freer to express my feelings and get closer to my children. I read to them, we have fun together, and we talk to each other. I feel our life together is much better than when I was unhappily married."

Jane, a single parent in the Washington, D.C., metropolitan area, found that a major benefit for her was the reduction in criticism within the home. She explained that since she is no longer being constantly criticized by her ex-spouse, she is better able to pay attention to her 18-year-old son and help him with his problems.

Another way that tension and bitterness within a family can *hurt* children is that in an atmosphere of emotional friction, there is often no consistency in family rules. Children are not sure what the rules are. As a result, although they become experts in manipulating one parent against the other to satisfy immediate desires, they frequently do not learn to respect the desires of others, to live within rules and regulations when necessary, and to work with others openly and cooperatively, rather than manipulatively, to satisfy their needs. In a single-parent family, since there is only one full-time parent, there is usually greater consistency.

This reduction in tension can also be a real help in solving special problems. Suppose your son or daughter has a particular problem for which outside help is needed. What if your husband or wife says, "No, we don't need any help. It costs too much money, and, anyway, we can handle it ourselves." Do you give in and sacrifice your child's welfare? Or do you force your partner to give in? This case is vividly illustrated by Millicent, whose husband refused to let their oldest son receive therapy. This was one major reason why Millicent and her husband separated. As a single parent, Millicent has been able to get her son the help he so badly needed. The result is that the boy has become increasingly able to communicate with other family members. This positive result is also the case with Robin, whose son has a learning disorder. She told the other participants at a single-parent discussion group, "It is easier to handle this as a single parent because I don't have to fight the hostility and negativism of the other parent."

As single parents, with the hostility and tension from our married period reduced, we are free to offer more support, help, and acceptance to our children, at the same time providing the greater consistency and security vital for their growth.

√ Benefit 2:
Flexibility in Planning Quality Time with Our Children

Single parents are not distracted by the expectations or time demands of another adult. We need to consider only our own schedule and needs and those of our children. Although in some ways spending time alone with each child can be more difficult, the flexibility of not having to consult another adult can prove surprisingly rewarding in providing quality time together.

For the past two years, I have been very busy because of the preparations for this book, a full-time job, and the necessity of taking full-time care of my two children. At one of our family conferences, my youngsters remarked that they would like some time alone with me. We worked out an arrangement. Every school day that I have to work, I and one of the children get up 20 minutes earlier than we normally would and spend 15 minutes together doing what the child wants—usually playing a game, talking, or something else that involves just the two of us. This is our "special time." In exchange, the child who has "special time" helps me make breakfast. It's fun for all of us and a great way to start the day. Each child can feel he or she is important enough to me to have a time just for the two of us.

Jean, in Portland, Oregon, has developed her own system for herself and her 13- and 14½-year-old sons: "We all discuss our wishes and feelings and work out our schedules accordingly. We all take turns doing what each enjoys doing."

What do you do if your children want to spend time with you on the weekend but you have job-related work or other things that you must do? Must you choose between your children and your work? Jean's approach offers one solution. On at least one weekend day, my need to write conflicted with my children's desire to take a trip. After a futile argument, we had a brief family council. Finally, we agreed that in the afternoon I would write and they would play outside. In the evening we would have dinner out and play miniature golf. As a result, I was able to work in peace and the children had an enjoyable evening.

Flexibility and a willingness to work together can enable all of you to enjoy and appreciate the quality time that you do have together. Most important, it helps each family member feel that his or her needs and time demands have been considered and taken into account.

Benefit 3:
A Democratic Working-Together Approach to Problem Solving and Daily Living

In recent years, it has been found that the most effective way to obtain the cooperation of another person is to involve him or her in the problem-solving and decision-making process. Frequently, the person involved can find his or her own solution with the help of an empathic listener. Most important, a person (whether a child, employee, or other person) feels a greater moral commitment to carry out a decision that he or she was involved in making. This has been widely recognized in parent-education programs such as Parent Effectiveness Training (PET) and Systematic Training for Effective Parenting (STEP).

Since as single parents we do not have full-time partners with whom to consult, we must depend on the voluntary cooperation of our children to an even greater extent than must the nuclear family. This may be one reason why nearly all the single parents I contacted, when asked how they solve individual and family problems mentioned family councils, talking things out, and letting their children make many of their own decisions. Although a few parents had difficulty in this area, the majority found as Martha (a single parent from Bowie, Maryland) observed, "Joint decisions and compromise usually work out best." Cathy, a mother of two teenagers in North Bend, Oregon, commented, "When there is a problem, I use brain storming and listening. I identify the problem and ask for help." Angela, a single parent in Baltimore, Maryland, recalled that when her children were teenagers, "I had a special time alone with each child every week. We talked; mostly, I listened. They could find their own solutions, usually by having to put their thoughts into words. I suggested solutions if needed. If a conflict in their ideas and mine arose, and others in the family were affected, I had the controlling vote."

From this approach flows a feeling of value for each family member—whether adult or child—as a unique individual whose feelings, needs, and desires are worthy of respect. The ability to listen, empathize, and trust our children to make their own decisions and share with parents the responsibility for problem solving is a valuable skill in today's society, where communications skills, decision making, and individual autonomy are increasingly important. This is an area where successful single-parent families might well serve as a model for two-parent families. Let me close this section with a description by Carol Ann, in Arnold, Maryland, about how she and her son (now 15; 7 when she was newly single) handle problem solving.

"When my son was younger, I encouraged him to select his own clothes, rather than waiting for me to get them together. I tried, then and now, to allow him to take part in major decisions and share with me his ideas, feelings, or fears. I have encouraged him to make choices and offered choices, rather than saying, 'Do it this way because I said so.' "

Benefit 4:
An Opportunity for Growth and Sharing

It is generally necessary for single parents to combine a full-time job with parenting and homemaking. Often, we must learn new skills and obtain additional education. Many of us are involved in organizations, such as Parents Without Partners, which require skills and time commitments not as frequently required in a nuclear family. It is a little like someone being stranded on an island and having suddenly to learn survival skills while providing his or her own recreation. It's frightening, but it can lead to tremendous growth.

Beverly, a never-married single parent from a city in Montana, found that after her now-seven-year-old daughter was born, she was forced to rely on herself, rather than her parents or a husband. In thinking back, she commented that as a single parent, she had a special opportunity to develop her own potential and fulfill her own needs without being confined to a traditional wife-homemaker role. By completing college, finding a job, and developing a satisfying social life for herself, she was freer to devote her attention to the needs of her daughter, without feeling the conflicts that many parents (especially mothers) feel between being a parent and satisfying their own needs. While Beverly was fortunate in having the understanding and help of her parents, there are other resources and approaches that have also worked for single parents. (For a discussion of these, see Chapter 8.)

By allowing our children to know us as "real people"—with strengths, weaknesses, and experiences that can relate directly to their problems—we can frequently help them overcome their own problems more effectively than might otherwise be possible. For example, many of your feelings, experiences, joys, and frustrations with your job might be similar to those your child feels in school. This was true in my family when, a few years ago, my son, Nick, had problems listening to his after-school teacher, Becky. He felt that his desire to read in the media center (library) was not being considered, and he was forced to play games with the other students. I sympathized with Nick and explained that in some ways our situations were comparable, since at my job I frequently felt that my needs were not considered. I explained that both my supervisor and Nick's teacher were in charge, however, and we had to find ways to adjust. In my case, I tried to do a good job and, for relaxation, sang in a chorus after work. Another advantage, I told Nick, was that I had a few friends on the job. I was lucky to have many interests to enjoy when I wasn't working. This I summed up by commenting that work, like school, was a necessity; but I could make the best of it and enjoy my free time. However, since I had to work, it was necessary that Nick be in the after-school program.

Nick said he understood, but what could he do? I asked him "What would you like Becky to do?" He said, "Allow me to read in the media center." We then discussed what Nick could do to make Becky want to allow him this privilege. As a result of our conversation, Nick, Becky, and I had a conference, and made a deal. Nick would be allowed to read in the media center, provided he ask Becky so she knew where he was. In return, Nick would follow Becky's directions and recognize that there would be times when he would have to do things he might not enjoy. A month later, a report from Becky indicated that Nick was much more cooperative. Nick told me that Becky was really much "nicer" and he had helped her clean up several times.

Obviously, one possible problem is that of becoming so concerned with our own needs that we neglect our children. Joan, a single parent in Albuquerque, New Mexico, balances the needs of her different family members by a family discussion of individual versus family needs. When necessary, these needs are arranged by priority and a joint decision is made. While Joan's children are teenagers, Penny, a mother of a five-year-old son, in New Lenox, Illinois, has a different approach: "I try to be very involved with his interests and do things together; and when I have something to do, such as a meeting, he understands."

Being a single parent and heading a one-parent family involves change, frustration, and exhaustion. It can also be exhilarating and stimulating and offer a unique opportunity for us to know—and be known by—our children as real people. The problem solving and working together to balance the needs of parent and children alike can result in a strong and flexible family structure that satisfies the needs of each family member.

Benefit 5:
The Widening Experience: Two Differing Spheres of Influence

A nuclear family, by definition, consists of two full-time parents, each with individual interests and friends. Although differences between the parents can be resolved by compromise, all too often a conflict concerning interests or values can frustrate one or both and create an inability to share these interests or values with the children. The children lose by having an incomplete exposure to each set of values and interests. Although there are many couples who value each other's uniqueness and different interests, many couples, unfortunately, expect to share and enjoy *everything* together, rather than accept and respect each other's need for individual pursuits. When, inevitably, disagreement arises, the togetherness expectation can lead to conflict, hostility, and tension.

A single-parent family has greater consistency than such a nuclear family. The custodial parent can share her or his interests with the children more fully and without conflict from the other parent. The noncustodial parent can also share his or her interest with the children when they are together. In other words, the children are now members of two single-parent families, each offering its own special interests and values. Children are thus exposed to a greater variety of lifestyles than they otherwise might have been.

A good term for the situation where two separated or divorced parents can work together *as parents* to make it possible for their children to gain from what each parent has to offer is the *widening experience*.

Jill, a single parent from a small town in central Pennsylvania, regrets that she and her former husband had been unable to work together for the benefit of their two older children. She believes this is the reason why these children have a poor relationship with their father. However, in Jill's own words, "We have been able to cooperate in the case of our youngest (age 17), and she is equally comfortable with each of us. My husband and I have accepted each other, even though our values are different; and we do get together socially occasionally with the children, his wife, and the man I live with. Most of the negatives went away with time and socialization. We now accept (as a reality) and respect our opposing values."

Mike, a single parent from Wheaton, Maryland, whose daughter has lived with him for about a year, used the term *differing spheres of influence* to describe what he felt were the greater alternatives for his children since he and his former wife had separated. Mike described himself as a home-loving person who enjoys puttering around the house. "With me," Mike explained, "the kids enjoy woodworking and a life centered around the home. By way of contrast, my former wife is dating a man who likes sailing, baseball, and going to the movies. The children now have an opportunity to enjoy types of activities that they would most likely not have done with me. For example, they now enjoy sailing on the bay."

This type of widened influence extends to each parent's family and friends. Sometimes one parent's friends and family members do not get along with the other parent. The natural result is tension and a customary solution is to minimize contact with the people in question. When parents separate or divorce, each is free to rebuild his or her friendships and reestablish family ties. Since we are the only persons determining whom we will spend our time with, our children benefit, both from the lack of conflict and our freedom to associate with people of our own choice. Thus, the children are more fully exposed to differing worlds, each centering around one of their parents and, of course, themselves.

This ideal situation, unfortunately, is not always present in the single-parent family. Two causes of problems are criticism of one parent by the other in front of the children and extreme physical distance between the parents' hometowns. Either problem can make it difficult for the children to receive the full benefit of these diverse influences.

Annelle lives in a small town in Missouri, and her former husband lives 600 miles away. Nevertheless, they have decided to work together. They consult by phone at least once a week and work together to keep him involved and informed. Annelle believes that the widening experience can work even if the parents live far away from each other. According to her, "The key is desire."

Don from Baltimore, Maryland, and his former wife have been able to offer their children a successful widening experience. In a personal interview, Don shared with me some of his suggestions for other custodial and noncustodial parents who want their children to benefit from the widening experience:

"First, recognize what your child is not receiving from the other parent's sphere of influence and determine what you can contribute toward fulfilling those needs.

"Second, if you are the custodial parent, encourage the other parent to develop a special relationship with the children that can meet the desires of both the children and their noncustodial parent.

"Finally, even if bitterness between you and your former spouse exists, recognize that the noncustodial parent is a parent of the children, with an interest in sharing with the children's upbringing. The children's other parent can make your job easier and help your children at the same time. Even if a remarriage has occurred, you and your former mate can still work together for the children's benefit. A remarriage can further expand the available spheres of influence, thus providing an additional widening experience. This can only benefit your children in their present and future growth."

Working together with your former spouse can be extremely difficult and just not seem worth the time or effort. This is one area where counseling, or talking to other single parents who have succeeded in this area, can be worth your time, effort, and expense—both in giving you the courage to try and the support you need. The key for most single parents who contacted me and had succeeded in this area was to completely separate their former marital relationship from their relationship as parents. Only then could they begin to fully expose their children to the positive side of the widening experience.

Benefit 6:
The Extended Single-Parent Community

A popular belief about single-parent families is that they are cut off, isolated, and hurt because of the absence of one of the full-time parents. Through both research and personal experience, I have found that this is not necessarily true. Rather, single-parent families and nuclear families differ in their basis of support.

In an interview, George Mikulskis, a family counselor in Columbia, Maryland, explained, "Nuclear families tend to be self-contained in that they rely primarily on the mutual support and resources of their two parents. The single parent, by contrast, must look to the outside community for support." Fortunately, there are several single-parent organizations such as Parents Without Partners (PWP) and the Montgomery County Single Parents (Montcosps). Many churches and community organizations also sponsor groups for single parents and their children.

These single-parent groups offer their members a sense of community. They also offer other benefits such as understanding and support of other single parents, family activities, and personal growth opportunities.

Single-parent discussions offer PWP and Montcosps members an opportunity to discuss with other single parents some common concerns under the leadership of a trained moderator (also a club member). Topics such as "How Can I Be A Good Parent If I Don't Have Custody?" "Communicating With Teenagers," and "Loneliness" offer an invaluable opportunity to hear how others have dealt with common problems, as well as the chance to share your own feelings in a confidential and supportive (nontherapeutic) group.

Lois J., a single parent from Johnson City, New York, found PWP discussions to be "an opportunity to discuss feelings and problems with others."

Family activities offer single parents and their children an opportunity to share fun activities with others in a friendly setting. At PWP campouts or trips, the parents can relax and the children can make new friends, while realizing that there are many other young people with only one full-time, resident parent. At a single-parent family activity, one can feel a special sense of community. Holiday celebrations provide an alternative to loneliness and offer the very real feeling of being an extended family.

My friend Leonard, who is a member of Montcosps, told me that one summer he and his two daughters shared an oceanfront cottage with seven other Montcosps members and their families. As Leonard put it, "It was nice to know that, on several weekends, we could visit the ocean and share experiences with other families at the cottage. We would never have done this when I was married. Decisions on a mutually acceptable plan were almost impossible."

Single-parent groups also offer their members unique opportunities for personal growth and leadership training. The training required to become a moderator is invaluable not only for leading a single-parent discussion group but also for listening and facilitating communication both on the job and at home. Since PWP is a national organization, a single parent can get involved in his or her local chapter or serve as an officer on a regional or national level. PWP offers numerous leadership training courses and other workshops and resources which can be invaluable to single parents.

Young people can get involved in comparable groups. The best known of these is the International Youth Council (IYC), which is open to teenagers of single parents and is sponsored by PWP. PWP also sponsors "Buddies and Pals" for single-parent children from ages 6 to 12. Here, children of single parents can make friends and obtain peer support, while feeling part of a community of young people in the same situation.

Young people also benefit from the opportunity to know a wide variety of single parents other than their own. Many women who answered my questionnaire commented that they found their children benefited from seeing male single parents in a nurturing context. Children can see single parents in a three-dimensional context and learn for themselves the limitations of traditional role stereotypes. The opportunity to get to know men as nurturing parents while seeing that women can—and do—succeed in the work world can give young men and women confidence in their own ability to actualize and fulfill their potential, while not fearing to ask for help, should it be necessary.

Alice, a single parent from Fort Wayne, Indiana, has five children. At the time of her separation six years ago, two were grown and three were teenagers. When she wrote to me, Alice described what a single-parent group (in this case, PWP) meant to her and her children: "PWP taught my children what men can be like. We made many friends and experienced different situations that we would never have had an opportunity for when I was married. We've made trips, and gone camping. I found out some men *like* their children. It was a shock. The children found other young people in the same boat as themselves, with similar problems."

Liz, a single parent in Baltimore, Maryland, enjoyed "meeting other people in the same situation. It doesn't seem to be unusual when you have friends in the same situation."

Sally, a single parent who belongs to Montcosps, summed it up well when she said: "I feel as if my kids and I are part of a community of friends and family (grandparents, aunts and uncles, for example). My children are part of a network of friends of both sexes, my family, and the larger community. Even my dates are seen as friends who temporarily join our immediate family (which consists of my children and myself). This has immeasurably enriched all of our lives."

Some single parents have discovered inner resources they never knew they had. Their struggles and success in dealing with loneliness, self-identity, returning to school or work, and adjusting to the world of the single parent can be helpful to adolescents who are seeking their own identity and struggling with loneliness and uncertainty. By sharing their personal achievements and their feelings and experiences in their jobs, work, and life, our fellow single parents can help provide our children with a realistic basis for career and life planning. While schools and books can explain what a job involves, there is no substitute for learning how people feel about actually performing a specific type of job: the rewards, the frustrations, and whether or not they would recommend it to someone considering a new job.

The single-parent community is not necessarily the answer for all single parents. Rather, it is a special resource which, by providing support and a sense of community, has helped many custodial and noncustodial single parents and their children develop a new life as individuals and as a family. For this reason, you might find it helpful to contact single-parent organizations in your own area (or start one, if need be), attend a few of their activities, and decide for yourself which groups, if any, might be helpful to you and your children.

√ *Benefit 7:*
The Opportunity for Young People to Mature, Gain Independence, and Feel Needed and Valued as Contributing Members of the Household

In a two-parent family, the parents share the major responsibilities. Consequently, their children frequently do not feel a real sense of being *needed* to ensure the efficient operation of the household. Although this does not have to be the case, frequently a major revision in parental attitudes and approach is required to make the children feel they are vital, valued, and necessary to the family's day-to-day life.

The single-parent family cannot afford this luxury. As single parents, we usually need to work full time and to manage the household. Time commitments, plus a concern with balancing a rewarding life for our children with satisfying our own needs, create a huge number of demands within a short time period. Accordingly, it is appropriate and necessary to ask the help and cooperation of our children. This gives the children a real sense of being needed. Since Mom or Dad doesn't typically have the time to clean up after the kids, it really *does* matter what the young people do and how well they do it. This encourages maturity and a sense of belonging that is so essential for survival in today's society. (This is also true of two parent families where both the parents work.) For example, in a discussion at the Baltimore chapter of PWP, Sonia told how her 18-year-old son helps his 14-year-old sister, spends time with her, and brings problems to his mother's attention. While this is a big help to Sonia, she has found that it has also helped her son's maturity, independence, and stability. Sonia explained, "My son is not involved in drugs, dropping out of school, or other 'normal' aspects of teenage rebellion. When I asked him about it, he replied, 'Helping our family is important. I just don't have the time to mess around with less essential stuff.' My 14-year-old daughter also seems to have benefited from the extra responsibility."

This benefit can be true for children of all ages. When I have to write or attend meetings, I frequently ask my ten-year-old son to prepare dinner for the two of us and his seven-year-old sister. He enjoys helping, and it seems to have increased his resourcefulness and his independence.

Of course, it is especially important not to overload our children with excessive or inappropriate responsibilities. For this reason, it is essential to consider your child's age, maturity level, personality, and temperament when assigning tasks. Whatever the tasks, sharing responsibilities with your children provides a positive experience for all the family members.

Our children are exposed to many negative attitudes concerning single-parent families. To find ourselves living within a single-parent family is often assumed to be a tragedy. However, if we as single parents can make our children more aware of the positive side of our single-parent family, the results can be quite different. We and our children can justifiably hold our heads up high and say to those of our friends who have two full-time parents, "I'm glad you enjoy your family. I have a good family, too. It really makes a difference how we feel and think in my family, since my Mom (Dad) and we kids really work together. We might not have two full-time parents, but we have our friends and the single-parent community." Our children's positive experiences within their own single-parent family can encourage them to question the popular belief that single-parent families are "bad" and "abnormal." Our children can and will find their own answers.

This ability to question and find one's answers is important in modern society, where the complexities of life today demand flexibility and judgment. For example, our society has developed stereotype definitions of the roles of men and women. Men have traditionally been seen as career and money oriented while women are supposedly more emotional and home oriented. While these attitudes are changing, children from single-parent families have a special opportunity to get to know both men and women in achievement/career-oriented and nuturing roles. The men and women friends of their single parent, the frequent "family activities," where men are seen in nurturing roles and the increasing number of women single parents who are developing and succeeding in their own careers offer a varied approach for learning.

By providing a positive single-parent family, based on the special strengths and resources—the benefits—of the single-parent family, we can help our children to be responsible, contributing, perceptive, and informed members of society who will find their own answers to questions and problems, rather than rely primarily on the beliefs and attitudes of others. By helping our children develop this maturity and independence, we will be giving them a priceless gift that they can use throughout their lives.

THE SEVEN BENEFITS IN BRIEF

1. A reduction in tension, hostility, and discord within the family and an increase in family solidarity and consistency
2. Flexibility in planning quality time with our children
3. A democratic working-together approach to problem solving and daily living
4. An opportunity for growth and sharing
5. The widening experience: two differing spheres of influences
6. The extended single-parent community
7. The opportunity for young people to mature, gain independence, and feel needed and valued as contributing members of the household.

Chapter 3

The Creative Approach to Single Parenting

As single parents, it is easy for us to feel overwhelmed by the many pressures we are under—home and family, our jobs, paying bills, trying to make a good life for ourselves and our children—while still having time for a life of our own and, somehow in the middle of all this, trying to maintain our sanity and ability to cope. We are besieged with advice from family, friends, counselors, the media, well-meaning coworkers, and other acquaintances about what we "should do." Several parenting courses are also available for advice: The three best known are Parent Effectiveness Training (PET), Systematic Training for Effective Parenting (STEP), and the system developed by Rudolf Dreikurs in his book: *Children: The Challenge* (New York: Hawthorne, 1964). Each of these systems has its own advantages, but many of us, overwhelmed and frustrated by our single-parent status, latch onto one system and cling to it desperately as an anchor in an otherwise turbulent world. Although any of these systems can help, it can be risky to rely on any one as the all-inclusive solution for our family problems. The question is, do we need to rely on *one* parenting system to solve all our family problems? Is there an alternative? What have other single parents done?

Many single parents *have succeeded* in building a stable, secure, and supportive family for themselves and their children while allowing time for themselves and each of their children to enjoy a fulfilling life of their own. Although each parent must consider the needs of her or his individual family, many successful single parents have used similar approaches. Sometimes, only one single parent has used a particular method. Sometimes, a single parent has used several approaches. Flexibility is the key to successful single parenting. This approach I call Creative Single Parenting (CSP).

WHAT IS CREATIVE SINGLE PARENTING?

Used here, the term *creative,* refers to a process and an attitude. The creative process is one where *you develop your own parenting approach.* From the variety of available resources, the creative single parent is able to investigate and use those, if any, appropriate for his or her particular family. The single parent then builds an individual system. It can be unique, it can be based on an already existing system, or it can be a combination of several different systems. What is important is that *you* the single parent determine your family needs and find the resources that are appropriate for *your* family.

The creative attitude is one of open-mindedness, flexibility, and recognition and acceptance of your imperfections. Open-mindedness allows you to accept that other people's values or lifestyles may differ significantly from yours, and that is all right. There is no one right way to raise children. Rather, find the way that is right for you, and allow others to do the same. You are willing to listen to what others have to say, and consider how their ideas, experiences, and insights might be helpful to you. Flexibility can free you from being locked into one way of doing things. If you admit you cannot be perfect, you allow yourself to be honest and genuine with your children. This can help you build a close relationship and avoid the all-too-common power struggle between parents and children.

Creative Single Parenting (CSP) is an *approach,* not a rigid system. The following are major characteristics of the CSP approach to single parenting:

1. A single-parent family is not necessarily a bad or a good family. Rather, it *can be* a healthy, secure, and effective growing envi-

ronment for both you and your children. What makes the difference is your attitude and approach.

2. A single-parent family offers a special opportunity for you and your children to develop close relationships and work together to enable your family to function, at the same time making it possible for each of you to satisfy his or her own needs. The keys, according to the single parents who shared their experience with me, are willingness to make mistakes *and admit them,* being open to new ways of doing things, and fundamental respect for our children *as people,* along with a belief that their feelings, opinions, and thoughts deserve equal consideration with our own.

3. As a rule, we the parents are the most experienced members of our respective families. However, if we are to be effective parents and teachers to our children, we need to be aware of our strengths and limitations, and when necessary, seek help. Personal or family counseling, career guidance, budget and time management, social or support groups, and religious or community organizations are just some of the resources available to us. There is nothing wrong with seeking help. Indeed, one of the signs of a resourceful parent is his or her willingness to explore and use all resources appropriate to a given situation.

4. Your primary concern, however, is not parenting theory, but the individual needs, interests, and temperaments of each member of your particular family. You can then decide whether any resources and parenting systems are appropriate *for your family.* You, not "the experts," are in charge. You don't have to follow a particular system completely to be a good parent.

5. You are a person as well as a parent. As a single person, you will be a happier and far more effective parent if you realize that *your* needs and interests as an individual are every bit as important as your parental responsibilities and your children's needs and interests. Allow time to do things that you enjoy without your children. This will relax you and almost certainly help you recharge your energy, so you can be happier and more content, with more time, energy, and support to offer your children.

6. Many people and organizations are misinformed or ignorant concerning the strengths, resources, and positive concerns of single-parent families. As single parents, our attitudes and re-

sponses to this are very important. Being defensive about single parenthood, or counterattacking, tends to reinforce people's negative feelings, both about us and single-parent families in general. If we can try to understand how other people feel, and treat the situation as a special opportunity to correct some erroneous stereotypes, we can *show* how our family works for us and our children. This can help eliminate ignorance and misconceptions, and make it possible for the outside community to appreciate single-parent families and recognize their many contributions to our society.

WHAT CAN CREATIVE SINGLE PARENTING DO FOR YOU?

We have discussed some of the characteristics of CSP. Are there ways, other than those already discussed, that CSP can help you? Indeed, there are four additional benefits you can gain from CSP:

1. By using CSP, you are better able to know and value yourself. Since you are not concerned with what society says you should do, but with family needs, you are free to develop a life which is rewarding for each member of your family. At the same time, you free yourself from society's negative expectations and stereotypes and are better able to enjoy a life appropriate to your needs as a single parent. *You thus gain a freedom from "shoulds" and from the need to conform rigidly to society's standards for two-parent families.*
2. By allowing yourself to be both imperfect and genuine, you can develop a close relationship with your children, a relationship based on caring, mutual respect, and a shared involvement in all aspects of family life.
3. As you recognize and accept as right and proper the need to fulfill your concerns and aspirations as a person, your honesty and self-respect can free your children to develop their own potential without needing to feel guilty about the numerous self-sacrifices that Mom or Dad made.
4. Your confidence and self-respect, along with your new role as teacher-guide—rather than defensive fighter and disciplinarian—can help the nonsingle community gain a more

realistic appreciation of your single-parent family in particular, and single-parent families in general. In this way, at the same time that you are improving the view that others have of your family, you will be contributing to improving the overall image of single-parent families in our society.

HOW TO APPLY CREATIVE SINGLE PARENTING TO YOUR EVERYDAY LIFE

Accepting and Appreciating Your Single-Parent Family

If you have been a single parent for some time, you probably have already come to accept and enjoy many things that go with being a single parent. However, many single parents with whom I talked have found themselves so overwhelmed by the pressures, demands, and problems of being the only full-time parent in their family that they said they could see little or nothing positive about being a single parent.

While I can understand these feelings, I also know that it doesn't have to be this way. Kathy, from Belen, New Mexico, has been single for one year. She has a ten-year-old daughter, a seven-year-old son, and a four-year-old daughter. Kathy commented, "Daily living is more comfortable without my ex-husband. Our daily routine remains constant because of three children in school. But, other than that, we are free to be flexible in what we wish to do."

My concern, in this chapter, is helping you to build your own family life in such a way that both your children and you can grow, have a fulfilling life individually and together, and feel the comfort and security that go with being part of a strong family.

Building a Stable and Secure Family

Getting Started

A real problem of many single parents is that they spend so much time feeling sorry for themselves that they are not able to start taking the necessary steps to build a new life. Indecision and fear are normal feelings after a separation, divorce, or death. However, the most effective thing you can do is start building a new family life more appropriate to your present situation. You are keeping busy, you can involve your children, and it can bring all of you closer together. For example, Joyce, from a small town in Wisconsin, has been a single parent for eight and a half years. She has two daughters. Joyce recalled that when she was first divorced, "I set up a stable home as soon as possible and tried to put myself in my daughters' shoes as much as possible to help them feel they were secure, and that they were good children, regardless of their father's absence.

"There is a lot of open, honest love and communication in our home. We try to explain things and work together to get done what needs doing, so we can do our thing either alone or as a family. Schedules and continuity are important in establishing a foundation that we can all count on and lean on when need be."

When my children came to live with me on a full-time basis several years ago, I found that trust, security, and a team feeling were vital. One way that worked for us was to set a weekly "goal night." Here, each child could discuss his or her feelings, needs, and desires in a supportive family council. There were no time pressures, and all three of us worked together to help the child whose goals and feelings were being discussed. Either child could talk to me at other times; however, we knew that there would always be the special time, at goal night, for us to discuss in more depth. This made our home more secure and comfortable for all of us in that it established a pattern of working together and helping each other. Goal night was also a good example of a family ritual that helped give us a feeling of closeness.

Sometimes, our own parents can help us. (Obviously, this depends on many factors, such as your relationship with your parents, the distance you live from each other, your readiness to ask for help, and their willingness to help without intruding.) Art, a custodial father for two and a half years, has a seven-year-old daughter. He has "the advantage of a great set of parents. They do not meddle, but give support and help, mostly in terms of sitting. I have been able to have a social life without paying for child care. I fully realize that my relationship with my parents is pretty unique and can't work for all single parents who do not have parents accessible. I stress that mine have been supportive without ever trying to interfere in my free choice as an adult."

A traditional belief is that as parents we shouldn't "burden" our children with our feelings or needs. Obviously, treating our kids as adult confidants *can* be unhealthy. However, many people with whom I spoke felt that by sharing many of their feelings and concerns, they were helping their children see their parent as a real human being, not as a demigod. They found that their children were happier and healthier from having the chance to know and understand their parent as a person. Jill, from a small town near Harrisburg, Pennsylvania, has three girls, ages 25, 33, and 17. During her 11 years as a single parent, she has shared many of her feelings and thoughts with her children. She advises, "Don't keep secrets (such as your hopes, goals, dreams, aspirations, or even your sex life) from your children."

When Angela, from Baltimore, Maryland, became single six years ago, only her two youngest children (girls, teenagers at the time), out of five, lived at home. Angela told me, "We shared responsibilities. Each had her own. We all respected each other's privacy, and strong likes and dislikes. We each did the best we could within our capabilities. Both family rituals and traditions, and schedules and continuity were followed." She suggests, "Be true to yourself first; like and respect yourself; then, the children will respect and cooperate with you. Expect good children, praise much, and discipline fairly, and they will respond."

When you begin building a new identity as a single-parent family, consider some of the methods that have worked for other single parents. Feel free to adapt these or other ideas to your own individual and family needs.

1. Put yourself in your children's shoes; show that you love them and think they are good children—regardless of the separation or divorce. This can help them feel comfortable with their single-parent family.
2. Caring, open communication, and learning to work as a family team can help build a feeling of family solidarity, while making it possible for family members to have more free time to enjoy activities individually and as a family.
3. A regular "goal time" can provide a time and setting for each family member to share problems, concerns, and goals and gain the family's help, encouragement, and support. This gives the children valuable training in working with others and assures

each child a regular time to express himself or herself in a safe and supportive setting.

4. It is far more healthy—and vital to your sanity as a single parent—to live one day at a time, rather than try to plan everything for the next week, month, or year.

5. Independence is important to a single parent. Learn to do what you can, but don't be afraid to ask for help should you need it.

6. A job can help provide independence for a woman and offer an alternative to relying on a man for financial and social support.

7. If you are a man without previous experience with cooking or household chores, compare your situation to learning a new job. Sure, it's strange, but books and friends can help. Most important, household management and cooking are skills you *can* learn and do well. Other men have had to learn these skills and are doing fine. You can too!

8. While your children need your time, you also need time for yourself. Instead of feeling guilty in this area, why not compare your need for time alone to your need for a coffee break at your job. After having done something for yourself, you will probably feel more refreshed and better able to deal with your children and your other everyday concerns.

9. If your money is limited, you can find inexpensive or free things to share with your children. Camping, games at home, the public library, hikes, and singing songs together are only a few of the choices you might consider.

10. Your own parents *can* be a resource. However, you will want to consider your individual situation, your relationship with your parents, the distance you live from each other, your readiness to ask for help, and your parents' willingness to help without intruding.

Another way to get help is to join a single-parent organization such as Parents Without Partners, take a single-again course (available at many community colleges), or join a single-parent survival center or single-parent resource group. In these confidential and supportive groups, you can participate in workshops and discussions where you learn that you are not alone. Equally important, you can learn what has worked for other single parents. Perhaps some of their experiences and insights might be useful to you.

Schedules and Continuity

Organization and a sense of purpose are generally important, but they are particularly so to a single parent. When, as single parents, we have suffered pain—such as separation, divorce, or death—it is easy to feel sluggishness, aimlessness, and general frustration. Difficult enough for us as adults, this feeling in the head of a family can also hurt our children. Your attitude affects your children. If you are content and have a sense of stability, your children will sense this and be comforted. If, on the other hand, you are upset, unsettled, turbulent, and have no sense of continuity, your children will sense your agitation and unrest and will feel troubled or upset—often without knowing why.

For this reason, learning how other single parents have dealt with the issue of schedules and continuity, and how it had affected their family was especially important to me. What I learned reinforced my belief that schedules and continuity are a key to family survival—particularly in a family with only one full-time parent. Children need regularity, predictability. They feel safe with a routine they can depend on. Although we as parents do not need this routine as much, it still has stabilizing value.

One person who has developed a way to make time and organization work for her is Ann, a single parent with a five-year-old son, from Falls Church, Virginia. Ann explained: "I am a highly organized person, and my son is learning to be. We simply do certain things on certain days at certain times—unless there is a compelling reason to alter the pattern. I have three major adult activities I pursue twice a month, and we have two major joint activities we pursue almost every week.

"He attends Sunday school, and I participate in church activities. He is involved in Christmas and Easter pageants which are important to him. He is invited to join in several of the Jewish festivals by my closest friends whose seder and Hanukkah celebrations revolve around their small children.

"A single parent with custody who works does not have much *discretionary* time. Apart from the burden of total responsibility and chronic fatigue, this is the most serious problem to resolve; and one's mental health depends on it. Select at least one activity or hobby you will pursue without your child, and one that includes him. Allow at least three nights a week for chores and rest and recuperation."

Hazel, from Erie, Pennsylvania, has two sons, ages 6 and 3. She has been single for three years and strongly agrees with Ann that schedules and continuity are important. Hazel wrote, "I feel that schedules and continuity have played a big role. I am just completely honest with my children. They understand that there is just so much time before I go to work and what has to be done in the house after I get home from work. They help me at times and try to be patient when I say that I am just too tired or not feeling well. Continuity is essential for the kids, as it builds stability."

Linda, from Parma Heights, Ohio, has been divorced for two years. She has already found that for her and her two young daughters, "daily schedules are pretty much structured because of my working and my children going to nursery school. There was not much choice. Now that the girls are getting old enough for small chores, I am beginning to involve them more in daily routine. They really seem to respond to the explanation that I am only one person and they are two people and I can't do everything for three people. For instance, if they are really starving for supper, the more they do to help get it ready—setting the table, getting the salt and pepper—the sooner they eat. Also, if they are waiting for me to take them somewhere following supper or if their room is a mess, the more they help, the sooner we go. Very little badgering or cajoling is needed."

Mark, a custodial father for two and a half years from a city in Nebraska, has found that he and his three sons have developed "family stability through continuity and time together."

Other single parents have had similar experiences. Jennifer, from Columbia, Maryland, has a ten-year-old son. Ever since becoming single one and a half years ago, she and her son have "set aside an hour each evening as our special time together where we talk, read, or play games. Usually it is reading; for example, the Tolkien Trilogy."

Carol Ann, from Arnold, Maryland, has a 15-year-old son and has been single for eight years. Mealtimes have always been special for Carol Ann and her son. She explained, "I have always tried to keep mealtimes pleasant and will not allow arguments or hostilities to go on during meals. I do not bring up unpleasant subjects either. It is one of the few times that we can enjoy each other's company. I have tried to make the most of it." Carol Ann and her son share weeknight dinners together and discuss the day's activities. Weekend breakfasts are always shared. According to Carol Ann, mealtimes provide continuity and a good time for contact.

A good way to start introducing schedules and continuity into your family life is to divide your individual and family activities into three groups.

Group 1 would consist of those activities *that must be done at a specific time and cannot be changed or eliminated.* The two activities that would fall under Group 1, for most of us, are our jobs and our children's schooling. If there are other commitments that you *must* do at a specific time, list them here, also.

Under Group 2 list those activities that must be done but can be based around your needs and schedule. A good example of Group 2 would be household chores.

Under Group 3, include any activity that you enjoy but may choose or not choose to do, as you wish, and that can be based around your individual and family needs. Examples of Group 3 might be your social life and family outings.

Now take a few minutes to make up a rough daily schedule. On your schedule, list the times and activities for Group 1. For example, if you get up at 7:00 A.M. daily, leave for work at 8:00 A.M., work from 8:30 to 4:30 P.M., and return home by 5:30, your time from 7:00 A.M. to 5:30 P.M. would be filled in. Perhaps at 5:30 P.M. you pick up your children, make dinner, and eat together until 6:45 P.M. Then, you help your children with homework until 7:30 P.M. This means that 12½ hours each weekday are already planned. However, you have "discretionary time" (time that you can spend as you choose) from 7:30 P.M. until you go to bed, and on weekends. It is this time which you can use to plan your personalized family schedule.

What are some things you would like to do with your discretionary time? What are some of the things you need to do? Four types of activities are family fun time, time for yourself and your interests, problem-solving time, and time for household chores. You might be able to think of other activities.

At this point, you might consider sitting down with your children and working out a schedule that's comfortable for you all. This accomplishes two things: First, it involves your children in the decision-making process and gives them a greater commitment to ensuring that the schedule is maintained. Second, since your children are in a better position than you to know what they enjoy and value, by planning family schedules together you can work out a routine that meets the needs of all family members.

When planning your schedule, you will want to consider how many evenings to spend with your kids and how to spend your time together (free fun time together, planned activities, homework, or household chores). You will also need to determine how many evenings you want to spend by yourself or with adult friends and what activities or groups you especially enjoy. On weekends, what must you do? What would you like to do? Perhaps, sometimes, you and the kids can each do what he or she enjoys and at the same time be available to do things together if you all feel like it. Often, a weekly clean-up session followed by a family outing can provide the balance between necessity and fun. This can be a regular part of your schedule. Do you want Friday or Saturday nights free for yourself? Include them in the schedule. Do you want to plan a time for family problem solving? Discuss it with your kids, and pick out a time for doing this on a regular basis if this is important to you.

Although a schedule aims to help you provide stability and regularity in your family life, do not be afraid to change it if the need arises. A schedule is a resource to help you, *not* a rigid standard which you must always follow unquestioningly, regardless of your needs.

Schedules and continuity are valuable in that they help give us a feeling of regularity and dependability. This can go a long way in giving our children that special feeling of security that comes from belonging to a stable and loving family (regardless of the number of full-time parents present in the household). If you can also set aside some special time alone with each of your children, this adds to their feeling that they are important to you and that the family is concerned with their individual needs.

Rituals and Traditions: The Special Side of Family Life

When I think back on my own childhood, one special memory I have is that of my family's Thanksgiving reunion and dinner. From the time, 60 years ago, when my great-grandparents first came to the United States, all the relatives on my mother's side of the family have gotten together on Thanksgiving for dinner and conversation. Even though the family has changed—people moving farther away, and therefore keeping in touch during the year more by telephone than by personal visits, our annual dinner and afternoon together reminds me that we are still very much an extended family. It does more than that: It gives me something special to look forward to each year; I see people whom I have not seen for a while and have the chance to find out what's been happening; I have the opportunity to see people grow. Especially valuable to me is that our annual Thanksgiving reunion has made it possible for me to know many of my cousins and form close relationships based on common interests and values, as well as on family ties. Most important is the special feeling I get from knowing I belong to my family, care about, and am cared about by many people. (My mother tells me that, with my children, we are the fifth generation of our family that has participated in our Thanksgiving tradition. Four generations *still* participate.)

Rituals and traditions can indeed make life special to all of us, whether adults or children. In an age where depersonalization, automation, and mechanical efficiency seem increasingly present, rituals and traditions can be a warm reminder of our humanity, reaffirming our membership in a family in which we are an important part. When parents divorce, they and their children lose the security that comes with their identity as part of a two-parent family. At a time like this, the feeling that you are *still* part of your extended family (as I found at my family's Thanksgiving gathering) can help you and your children.

Sometimes a single parent can build new traditions out of necessity. At a single-parent discussion, one participant, Carla, told the group that her daughter has a newspaper route. Carla found that accompanying her daughter on the route had several advantages: "It's a nice time to be together in a busy schedule. My daughter has told me it's nice to feel that 'Mom is willing to put in the time, even though she's working.' It makes a common denominator. If you're understanding about their job and fatigue, they'll reciprocate. Kids are people too."

A favorite tradition in my family is our "Sunday bagel brunch." We go to our local delicatessen and buy bagels, cream cheese, and orange juice. After enjoying our meal, we are ready for the rest of our "family day." This can be a trip, goal time, discussion, swimming, a game, or some other shared experience. After a relaxed and informal supper, we end our family day by listening to some old-time radio programs on our local public radio station. My kids especially enjoy "Cavalcade of America," "Have Gun Will Travel," and "Jack Benny."

Ethel, from eastern Massachusetts, tells, "We still do a lot of the things we did before the separation and divorce, but the important thing is the new traditions we have started: the Advent wreath, walks in the snow, camping, planting flowers in spring, planning trips together."

Rituals and traditions can mean a lot to all of us. If schedules and continuity are the key to survival, then rituals and traditions can be described as the special side of family life. Even if you can't think of any family traditions or rituals, you can consult with your children and develop your own. What is important is that these are comfortable and enjoyable for each of you. You might go outside your immediate family. Your parents or other relatives, your friends, other single parents and their families, and single-parent groups to which you belong are other possible resources.

How It Is Done

Ideas and strategies can be very helpful. However, what is often most beneficial is to be able to ask others in a similar situation, "How did you do it?" In my questionnaire and in my personal contacts, I was interested in finding people with positive insights and experiences that could help other single parents. I was especially fortunate in finding people who were willing to share how they have been able to succeed as single parents.

Betty B., a friend in Baltimore, Maryland, has been single for five years and has two daughters ages 16 and 14. Betty, in a personal interview, shared some of her experiences and insights with me: "One problem of many women is that they view single parenthood as temporary, rather than as a reality, and count their days in PWP until they meet the 'right person.' We need to see ourselves as single, rather than in limbo.

"How did I create the feeling that we are a real family? When I separated from my husband five years ago, I had to find my own identity. It was the first time I saw myself as an individual, rather than just a part of my husband. As I built a new identity, I was not thinking of any future commitment. I was concerned with building my own family in terms of the needs of the three of us.

"The kids are important. They were insecure and afraid of nonacceptance by the community and church as an 'incomplete family.' I started to feel and act like a complete person in my own right—without needing a man's approval—and my girls also came to see the family the same way, as did the church and community.

"Some of the techniques I used were spontaneous weekend trips, breaking away from straight routines, and a major change from my having all the power and authority to our developing house rules. These were decided by all three of us, put in writing, and agreed to by all and followed by all three of us. Some examples of our house rules were what time the kids had to be home, what nights they could go out (we agreed to base this on their grades), which chores each one was responsible for, the special time and other things they needed from me, and their agreement to assume the responsibility for making sure their homework was complete before watching their favorite television shows (which began at 8:00 P.M.).

"Two of our family rituals were to stop after church for doughnuts and, after mutual dates, to pick up a pizza and talk until late."

Fay, single for five and a half years, from Vestal, New York, has a 13-year-old daughter and an 11-year-old son. She follows her ideals of what family life should be: "I try to be interested and knowledgeable about what they are interested in. I support their efforts and am available to see that they *can* participate in school, town, and church activities. I try to keep the lines of communication open with both and spend time with each. We have rituals for special holidays and birthdays; unfortunately, we have been a little lax in observing these since I've been working."

Harriet, from Potomac, Maryland, has three sons (ages 15, 14, and 11) and has been single for one and a half years. She has found that "both family rituals and traditions and daily schedules and continuity have remained fairly constant. We have practiced more religious rituals. This continuity, remaining in the family home, and family therapy as a family unit have been prime factors in easy relationships at home." Harriet suggests that "whatever you feel comfortable doing is OK for you. If you sneak around your children, I believe you only teach them to be sneaky."

Martin, from Belen, New Mexico, is a widower and custodial parent with four children, ranging in age from 18 to 9. He told me, "My children have always shared many common interests with me. We have been very close to each other, and the hardships we've overcome have drawn us even closer. I'm a farmer and my children often go to the fields with me. Their playhouse on these occasions have often been a shade tree at the end of the field; their toys—sticks, rocks, or whatever they found at home. At home, they have nice toys, but their initiative to make do with what they have is very impressive. I make the best of any situation." When I asked what suggestions he had for other single parents, Martin replied, "I would suggest closeness, not the sticky kind, but genuine love and being able to express this love. Touch, kiss, tell them you love them. They need this reassurance."

Barbara B., from Belen, New Mexico, was married twice. She has been a widow for two years from her second marriage. Barbara made the point that she was always the single head of her household, even when married, since her first husband was gone a lot and the second was a long-line driver. She believes that "daily routines and schedules are a *must*. Rituals and traditions are always treasured, regardless of the marital situation." Barbara recommends that you "remember who is the *parent*, who is the child, who is responsible for making a family. Discipline is vital for the child to mature and the parent to survive. Things are as they are—make the best of it."

Carolyn, from Middletown, Connecticut, has six children ranging in age from 4-22. She comments, "We use family rituals and traditions, and schedules and continuity. We do things as a family but have our own activities. We have fun together and we play together. We work hard for what we have. We appreciate the little things and each other."

Art, from Enumclaw, Washington, has already discussed how his parents have been of great help to him and his daughter. Art has had a secure job for 14 years. When he became single, he moved from the country to town. His seven-year-old daughter, of whom he has custody, can now walk to the local library, store, her friends' homes, and school.

Dorsey, from Silver Spring, Maryland, has had custody of his two sons (ages 10 and 8) ever since his separation four years ago. His family is based on equal respect for everyone's feelings. He emphasizes each person's responsibilities. There is a lot of hugging and kissing, which Dorsey believes (as I also do) will teach the boys that men can express warmth, affection, and caring without feeling ashamed or being unmanly.

Alice, from Fort Wayne, Indiana, has been single for six years. However, only her youngest daughter, a girl of eighteen, now lives with her. Alice and her daughter have stuck to the same rituals and traditions as before the divorce: Christmas Eve dinner, Easter at Grandma's, and so on. "She cooks and I do dishes. Each does their own laundry. We do things together such as camping, movies, eating out. We talk about our feelings and where we are at. And sometimes we fight." She recommends, "Don't let your children make you feel guilty about the divorce, not being able to give them everything they want, or play you against your ex. The ideal is working together as a team with everyone feeling important and needed."

For single parents, it is important not only to build an effective family routine but to develop rewarding relationships with our children that are satisfying for all of us. The best description of how these family goals actually work in practice was offered by Carol H., a single parent for eleven years, from Hillsville, Virginia. Carol is very pleased about her relationship with her 16-year-old son and 14-year-old daughter. We can all benefit from the opportunity to share Carol's experience and insights as a single parent:

"How do I succeed on a day-to-day basis? For one thing, I delegate as much responsibility as I can to the kids. It has always been a real hassle getting them to help with household chores. Each is so scared he or she will do more than their share; so, the best way I've found to lessen my work load is to let each care for their own individual needs. For instance, each of us has a hamper in our bedroom and each does his or her own washing. Amazingly, they never object to this! This saves me much time I did spend sorting, folding, and putting away clothes. Also, I bought a microwave oven about six years ago and I'm sure it's paid for itself by now. Like most families today, we are seldom able to eat at the same time; so, everyone can have a hot meal (on a paper plate—no dishes to wash) whenever we come in. Neither of my kids likes to cook (much to my dismay), but they will gladly heat up a plate of already-prepared food in preference to just a sandwich. Better for them and my conscience! I also put a stop to the daily hassle of getting them up and off by buying an alarm clock, two or three years ago, and telling them it was entirely up to them to get to school on time. If they're ready on time, they can ride out with me; if not, they walk to the bus stop. Our mornings are *much* more pleasant, now—I used to be tired before I left the house.

"One other thing I think has helped us is that I've stayed young. We enjoy the same music, the same movies (well, usually), and often borrow each other's clothes, records, and books. They think it's great that people are always saying that I can't possibly be old enough to be their mother. I look in the mirror and see wrinkles and gray hairs and think I look 37 (which I am); but people say I can't be and I guess it's because I think, feel, and act young. I've always lived in jeans and saw no reason to change just because I turned 30. Most of the men I've dated have been younger than I am; and so are most of my female friends. This helps me see where my kids are 'coming from,' as they say.

"Also, I can stretch a dollar further than anyone in the world. I can remake worn-out or out-of-style clothes. I watch for bargains and pay with cash, so we are able to live better than many with high incomes."

Dorris, a widow and single parent for 16 years, from Riverside, California, has a 30-year-old daughter, a 27-year-old son, and a 20-year-old son. Her brief but to-the-point insights and experience almost sum up this whole section of "How It Is Done" with its emphasis and suggestions. Here are Dorris's insights and experience in her own words:

"We not only love but *like* each other. Through the years, we have worked as a team, held family conferences on all problems and decisions, and shared household responsibilities. During their years as minors, daily schedules of household chores were important. Family traditions such as Easter Dinner were stressed, but we were flexible as to date if other commitments interfered." She suggests, "Family conferences on any subject at any time. Listen to children, make them feel a necessary part of the family, but not a burden; share time for social life as well as responsibilities."

Obviously, each successful single parent has his or her individual approach. Some of the keys to their successful single parenting include

1. Flexibility

2. Involving the children in decision making and in setting up family rules
3. Family rituals and traditions
4. Schedules and continuity
5. Making the best of a situation—and asking for help when needed
6. Prayer
7. Showing openly your love for your children
8. Developing a life of your own, as well as one with your children
9. Effective and meaningful discipline (discussed in Chapter 5)
10. Respecting equally the feelings of each family member
11. Behavior modification
12. Not feeling guilty, either about the divorce or being unable to give your children everything they want
13. Not allowing your children to play you against your former mate
14. Involving your children in household tasks and responsibilities
15. Taking the time to know your children and their interests and values
16. Holding family conferences and working as a team
17. Remembering that children need the security of a *parent* in the home and keeping it clear who is the parent and who is the child

Balancing Needs, Interests, and Time

Along with time and organization, a major concern of single parents is balancing needs in two particular areas: (1) balancing our needs with those of our children and (2) balancing the demands of our work and our family.

Balancing Your Needs and Interests with Those of Your Children

This is a problem encountered at some time or other by nearly all single parents (or any parent, for that matter).

Joyce, from a small town in central Wisconsin, generally puts her children's needs first, but she has found that her family is flexible enough to let her meet her own needs sooner or later. Lois E., from

Elizabeth, New Jersey, considers the needs of all but puts her own needs first as long as her children do not suffer and know they are loved.

Barbara G., from Gaithersburg, Maryland, has found that what works for her and her 11-year-old daughter is "partly by becoming interested in similar things. My daughter has learned to knit and read because I like to do these things. I appreciate gymnastics because that is one of her interests. Also, as she gets older, we do have times in the week when we can be at separate places. My work has always given me a separate interest and time away from her. Sometimes she can participate in various aspects of my work."

My own system for balancing needs relies on three things. The first two, mentioned earlier, are *family day* (usually Sunday), when we confer and work out a mutually acceptable plan of activity, and *special time,* the 15 minutes at the start of each day devoted to one of my children, alternately. The third is my method of dealing with disagreements and conflicts. My favorite expression is to tell each child that "you're a very special member of the family and your needs are important to all of us," and act accordingly. We have all enjoyed my son's Cub-Scout meetings, my daughter's ballet classes and Brownie picnics, and my chorus concerts. The most important thing, generally, is to find out who is the most involved. If my son really is concerned and his need does not cause a major problem for me, I usually go along and acknowledge the legitimacy of his concern. ("It's important what you think, since you're an important member of the family.") On the other hand, if something is important to me, I need to assert myself. ("This is important to me. Aren't I an important member of the family?") Our system has worked well in making it possible for each of us to satisfy our needs while maintaining the mutual respect and ability to work as a team, for the benefit of each and all of us, that is so essential for effective family life.

A major source of conflict for most of us who are single parents is our need to go out—without the kids—to socials, on dates, or to adult activities. Our children are frequently jealous or possessive of our time. I know that this was a major problem for me when my children first came to live with me several years ago. We resolved it at one of our family goal nights, where we agreed to compromise: I would generally go out *no more than* two weeknights and two weekend nights per week. I don't go out nearly that often; so, if I occasionally need to go out more than this, my children understand and accept the situation, especially since they participated in the decision making.

Ethel, from Massachusetts, has worked out an effective system with her seven-year-old son. "How have I reconciled my needs with those of my son? I would say mainly by explaining that he has friends and activities that I don't share in and I need some that he doesn't share in. He has friends his age and I need friends my age. We still have time together; we both see to that. He also sees that I'm much happier now than when I didn't take care of my needs as an adult."

Those of you who are from rural or small town areas might be especially interested in how Martin, from Belen, New Mexico, works things out with his children. He has found that "I have spent a lot of time doing 'kid' things with my children. I have learned to enjoy many things adults are not supposed to enjoy. Nature has been an ally in this field. We walk through the woods and field and enjoy each other and nature. You can't imagine how much joy I've found explaining where the cottontail rabbit lives in the mesquite, or what kind of flower that is that's grown and bloomed since we were by here the last time, where the animals go when it rains, and so on."

Hazel, from Erie, Pennsylvania, has found that "It is really difficult to give the kids all the time they would like, but I occasionally try to spend some time playing puzzles and games with them. It seems to me that they need more to know that I will just be available when they need help; otherwise, they are doing their own thing out in the yard or in the basement, whatever. But when a bump or bruise or fight needs soothing, they want me around. Also, I try to schedule my paperwork, sewing, and other leisure activities that I enjoy for after they are asleep. The time between getting home and their going to sleep is for housework and them."

Jayne, from Renton, Washington, has been single for two years. She has two daughters, ages 20 and 14, and an 18-year-old son. Jayne has always enjoyed her children and this shows in her comments and suggestions: "I have always had many interests and my children are used to it. They would not know how to cope with a mother who watched TV all the time. We have discussed my need for adult companionship and the children seem to understand very well. I have my evenings out and my (14-year-old) daughter schedules something to do while I am gone. I worked before divorce, so the kids understand the demands of a job too. It is great having children this old because we can work out schedules and compromises. And it gets better and better.

"My son's major interest is music and it forms a bond between us (and the family). His rock band practiced in my basement for about a year after he moved out. Then the band broke up. But music is still a major interest for myself and all the children, and we all can enjoy any type of music together.

"Another of my major interests has always been children. The kids have always felt free to have their friends over and that continues. One night there was a knock at my door about 11:00 on a Friday night. It was my son. 'Hey, Mom, is it OK if I have some of the guys in to play pool?' 'Sure, son.' In trooped about five teenage boys. I like it. More recently, my older daughter called from college in Ohio. 'Hey, Mom, some of my friends are going to be in Seattle next week and they need a place to stay. I told them they could stay with my mom. Is that all right?' 'Sure, daughter.' So I had three house guests for over a week. I like knowing that my kids know that I truly enjoy them and their friends and that singleness has not changed that at all. My older daughter said, 'Mom, I can go anywhere and do anything and survive any trauma because I know you will be there if I ever need you, my Rock of Gibraltar.' I cried. That is one of the nicest things anyone has ever said to me.

"My suggestions might not be valid for anyone who is not so basically child centered. My kids' well-being takes precedence over my own needs when there is a conflict of interest. This is rare but sometimes happens. Not everyone can do that or wants to. But I figure kids are sort of on loan for 18 years, and they are their own persons after that. In another three and a half years, I can put myself first for the rest of my life, if I choose. I guess if my kids were younger, it wouldn't seem like such an easy choice. I feel for parents of very young children in a single-parent situation."

When your own needs conflict with your children's, consider who has the greater need. What kind of compromise can be worked out? It is all-too-easy to be so concerned with your children's needs that you overlook the importance of your own and your right to satisfy them. If you are able to balance needs, you can all benefit.

Perhaps your children have the greater need in a given situation.

If you are willing to give in, sometimes, you can expect similar consideration from them. Often, you can share your children's interests and encourage them to share yours.

Balancing needs is a universal problem experienced by *all* parents, single or not. As you have seen, it can be done in such a way as to increase family respect and closeness. If you respect your children as individuals, take their needs into account, assert your needs as being of equal importance, and work together with your children to resolve problems and disagreements in a manner comfortable for you all, you will have succeeded—not only in balancing needs but also in improving family communication, solidarity, and closeness.

Dealing with Conflict between Your Work and Your Family

How many of us have felt a conflict between the demands of our job and our family responsibilities? Does it have to be this way for any single parent? Cynthia, from Silver Spring, Maryland, might well speak for many of you who are single mothers when she says, "I've had trouble working in a career which used to be typically male and have even been told that I couldn't move (at one job) because of my 'other responsibilities.' "

There are many ways to deal with this problem. You can accept the problem. Or, you can fight back, as did Carlene, from Rockville, Maryland. Carlene, whose daughter is now 14, has been single for 11 years and is an accounts executive for a major company in the Washington, D.C., area. Here is Carlene's experience in her own words:

"My strategies have been to make my male colleagues feel guilty by identifying problems in terms that could well affect them, while giving the feeling of confidence that I am not completely alone (by having family, friends, or a housekeeper to keep my daughter). For example, my male colleagues asked me, 'Won't you have to take time off if your daughter gets sick?' I responded by asking them, 'What will you do if you get sick or your children or wife get hospitalized?' When they expressed concern that my daughter was all alone, I invited them to call and talk to my friend who was watching my daughter for the day. The main thing is to give the impression that you are confident and resourceful enough to deal with any situation that might arise—

or that you already have anticipated and resolved the situation. Sure, I occasionally encounter hostility and discrimination because of being a woman in a responsible position, but I know how to deal with it. I strike back hard and fast. I'll never forget how one of my customers—a furniture store manager in Norfolk, Virginia—asked me, 'What are you doing, taking a man's job? Why aren't you home?' I replied, 'That's a good question. Are you going to take care of me and my daughter? Are you going to give me furniture when I need it?' After a moment of stunned silence, I added, 'I have to take care of my family the same as you do.' That really shut him up!"

Ted Carlyle, (not his real name) counsels employees at a federal agency in the greater Washington, D.C., area. Many of the employees are or have been single parents. Mr. Carlyle explained how being a single parent had helped many employees achieve greater satisfaction in their lives.

"When there is stress on the job and tension and hostility at home with one's husband or wife, employees tend to be more upset and frustrated generally. Since they have no escape outlet, they frequently turn to alcohol or drugs and vent their frustrations on their children. This also results in hostility, dissatisfaction, low productivity, and other problems on the job. As a result, many employees are sent to other counselors or myself as a last resort.

"A single-parent employee who has made it past the initial stage is usually more content with herself or himself away from the job. The absence of discord with a husband or wife, the increased sense of control over how they spend their time, and the opportunity to build a new life based around their needs as a person and parent seem to have a stabilizing effect on single-parent employees. This appears to enable them to make their peace with the job and to work more constructively with their supervisors in resolving problems, both of a job-related and personal nature."

Some single parents have dealt with combining work and family by owning their own business. Lane has custody of his four-year-old daughter and two-year-old son and publishes a newsletter in the Washington, D.C., area. He told me, "I reduced my hours from 70 to 14 per week. I found the business could survive and has continued to be successful. The payoff, for me, was that I now have far more time to spend with my kids. From having no time with them, I now have gobs and gobs of time. It's great for all of us."

Janet has three sons—one 16 and twins who are 9—and lives in Fort Worth, Texas. When she got divorced, she started her own writing and secretarial service for authors and organizations that want to hire writers (Literary Services Unlimited, in Dallas, Texas). She wanted to be independent and had had business experience before being divorced. She makes less money than if she were working for an employer in a comparable position. The business takes more time than if she had regular hours as an employee. However, Janet believes "the benefits are independence and tremendous job satisfaction. I'm doing what I enjoy and I'm not dependent on an employer. I make enough money to enable us to live decently, if not extravagantly."

Ralph, a noncustodial parent, had a particular difficulty. He and his children both lived in New York City. However, Ralph accepted a better position in Washington, D.C. Ralph told me, "I have not regretted the move. I enjoy myself more and I still have good quality time with my children. As a matter of fact, since we don't see each other routinely and can't take each other for granted, we really enjoy our time together. If you take care of yourself and your own needs, you will be a far better parent and your kids will benefit."

Another possible solution for some of your problems is Flexible Work Hours, or *flextime*. Flextime is an innovation that has been adopted by many private and governmental employers. Under flextime, you can choose your own starting and quitting time with general limits. For example, at my job, I can arrive anytime between 6:30 A.M. and 9:30 A.M. and leave eight and a half hours later. Often you can "flex"—take time off during the day—provided you stay later to make the time up by 6:00 P.M. that day. (Some employers will let you make the time up within a week, rather than require you to make it up the same day.) Everybody gains: Your employer gets a full day's work, and you gain the flexibility useful in combining your job and your personal and family needs. This has helped me a lot. I am in a "child car pool" with another single-parent employee. I generally try to work the 6:30 to 3:00 P.M. shift; so, the other parent takes my children to school. Since my shift ends at 3:00 P.M., I can pick up all of our children when school ends. You might want to see if your employer does offer, or might consider, flextime.

Many of you, especially newly single mothers, may have never held a job. A special resource available to women over 35 without work experience (other than homemaking) is one of the Displaced

Homemakers Centers throughout the United States. (See Chapter 8 for a discussion of this resource.) You might want to check your community for the location of the Displaced Homemaker Center nearest you.

SUMMARY

You have seen here some ways that single parenting has worked. You have seen how other single parents have built effective families which meet the needs of both themselves and their children. Time and organization, effective daily schedules, and continuity can provide the necessary structure for survival and security. Developing meaningful family rituals and traditions can give that little something that makes a family really special to each of its members. You know that you are not alone in having to balance needs and that a working-together, team approach has enabled many single parents to satisfy the needs of each family member while improving communication, mutual respect, and caring between family members. Finally, you have seen that although there can be conflicts between your work and family responsibilities, they are not insurmountable. Asserting yourself while working with your employer to find a mutually acceptable solution (of which flextime is one example) can help both you and your employer. It also helps to be prepared for different situations, so that you do not have to constantly ask favors from your employer. You can then be matter of fact and treat the family-job conflict as an occasional and unusual occurrence. Sometimes, owning your own business can be a way to become independent; however, long hours and, frequently, diminished income are things you might need to take into account. Even if you are a woman who has never worked before, there are resources such as Displaced Homemaker Centers that can help you gain the necessary training and orientation to enter the job market.

Chapter 4

Parent-Child Relationships and the Everyday Concerns of Child Rearing

A concern that we share as single parents is how we can develop close relationships and effective communication within our family. This can better enable us to deal productively with problems and concerns that affect individual family members or the family as a whole. In this chapter, we will discuss problem solving, providing security and nurturing, encouraging our children's responsibility and independence, helping our children develop values, and disciplining.

HONESTY, EMPATHY, AND SELF-WORTH: THREE KEYS TO YOUR FAMILY RELATIONSHIPS

Honesty

I have heard time and again in single-parent discussions, as well as in my correspondence and interviews with single parents, that honesty is important in single parents' relationship with their children. I have also found honesty to be essential within my own family. Children are naturally straightforward and if we are too, we can base our family relationships on the kind of people we really are, rather than on fears and misconceptions. Honesty breeds trust, respect, and dependability.

Jeff, from a medium-size community in California, has custody of his eight-year-old daughter. His biggest problem with her has been her habit of lying. As Jeff puts it, "My solution has been punishment for lying, not the initial offense. It seems to be working."

If we want our children to be honest and trust us, then we must set an example of honesty.

Empathy

Honesty has always been thought important. Not as many people realize that empathy, the ability to put yourself mentally in another person's situation and show them that you understand the way they feel, is equally important. Honesty without empathy often resembles a razor blade without any lather or shaving cream: It does its job effectively but savagely, and leaves a lot of pain behind. However, honesty does not always have to be blunt and painful if we are to genuinely feel empathy. Two ways of showing empathy are remembering when you might have experienced a comparable situation and *active listening*, which consists of reflecting without judging.* For example, if my son has just said that he hates school, a traditional response might be, "If you try harder, you'll do fine. It's always bad in the first month of school." This type of response tells my son that I have already judged what he said, found it invalid, and am telling him what he *should* do. While this "judging" response might sometimes work for young children, your children, as they grow, are going to want to make their own decisions, and they may resent your attempts to meddle and make decisions for them.

The active-listening response, on the contrary, encourages an

*Active listening is a concept originated by Dr. Thomas Gordon. It is discussed far more fully in his book *Parent Effectiveness Training*, © 1970 and 1975 by the author, and available as a New American Library paperback. Active listening is the art of responding to your children's feelings by showing that you understand and accept them—without judging these feelings as either "good" or "bad."

ongoing dialogue between you and your child. For example, in the situation just described, my response was, "It's kind of scary starting a new year without any friends and not being sure what the teacher is like, isn't it?" This showed my son that I understood and accepted his feelings, and it encouraged him to tell me more about what he was feeling. Every person—whether adult or child—needs to feel understood, accepted, taken seriously, and listened to. (How many times as a child did you say to yourself, or your friends, "My parents never listen to me; they just don't understand.")

I have also found it helpful to remember when I might have experienced a situation similar to that which my children are going through. For example, when my daughter is upset, I frequently say, "I remember when I was . . . I was hurt and confused when this type of situation was taking place. Is that anything like how you are feeling now?"

Hazel, from Erie, Pennsylvania, explains how empathy has helped her solve family problems which involve her and her two sons, ages six and three. "Because the kids are so small, most problem solving is left up to me alone. I try to define what the problem is exactly. Then, I try to consider how a small mind like their's might feel about the situation. An alternative way of handling it usually can be found, and then I will present the whole thing to them to see how *they* feel about it. If this fails, I go to see a professional counselor for fresh ideas and advice."

Unlike a judgmental response, empathy encourages communication, openness, and trust, and provides a basis for family solidarity and closeness as the children grow up. It can enable all family members to relate as people, regardless of age.

Self-Worth

There is a familiar saying, If I am not for myself, who is for me? If I am for myself alone, what good am I? This applies very much to single parents. I remember that during the worst period of my marriage, when I had a poor opinion of myself, I was frequently so involved with my own problems, asking for help, reassurance, and advice from anyone who would listen, that I simply did not have the energy or time to help anyone else. After I became single again, when I began to see myself more in terms of my strengths, abilities, and positive characteristics, I began to value and appreciate myself as a person who had something to offer to himself and others. For me, the key was finding interests and activities I enjoyed and was good at doing. As I played the piano, had one of my musical compositions performed by a chorus to which I belonged, started a new club for single adults, found that I *could* raise my children without help from a partner, and began writing this book, I realized that I was a pretty special and worthwhile person. This gave me self-confidence and a feeling that I, indeed, *did* have something special to offer my children. Because I feel good about myself, I am better able to help my children grow and realize their own potential.

Roselle, (a single parent from Birmingham, Alabama) has mentioned the importance of keeping busy and being ambitious for yourself. If you keep busy in activities you enjoy and already are proficient at doing, or try areas you would genuinely like to learn, you will probably be a much happier and fulfilled *total person* whom your children can identify with and respect. When you do things because you enjoy them, not because you think you ought to, your children soon come to realize that you spend time with them and help them *because you want to*, not necessarily because it is your responsibility as a parent. Equally important, as your children, inevitably, grow up and leave home, you will have developed a life of your own that offers satisfaction and meaning. Your children will not need to worry constantly about your being worried or bored. You, too, will find that pursuing interests and activities that help you gain a sense of self-worth will make you more interesting not only to yourself but to others (including your children) as well.

THE SMALL CHART OF SINGLE PARENT PITFALLS

Joanne Small is a psychiatric social worker, in Bethesda, Maryland, who works with single parents individually and in groups. At one time she was also a single parent. I asked Ms. Small to discuss some ways (which she calls "pitfalls") that single parents *mistakenly* blame themselves for problems and changes that are actually normal for children at a particular stage of growth. These are described in the chart that follows:

Stage of Childhood
Infancy

PITFALL
1. Single parents "may believe that it is essential that they personally be available to their infant on a full-time basis. It is necessary only that there be a person with whom the child has regular and continuous contact. This can be a natural parent, a surrogate parent, or a sharing between the surrogate and natural parent."
2. "When the infant becomes seven months old, he or she often experiences separation anxiety, and will scream when you want to go out. Many single parents blame themselves for this; and think that this is the result of the child's having only one full-time parent. This is simply *not* true. This 'seven month anxiety' is a normal and healthy developmental sign in *any* child, regardless of the number of full-time parents in the home, and indicates that the child is gaining a new sense of self. You are not alone; this experience is shared by both single and non-single parents."

Toddlerhood

1. "Many single parents are so concerned with their child's needs that they may neglect themselves. As a single parent, it is important for you to realize that you have needs, and it is OK to develop appropriate ways to meet them."

School Age:
"The Middle Years
of Childhood"

1. Many non-custodial parents may feel rejected when their children prefer to pursue their own activities, or see their friends, rather than visiting their non-custodial parent. "This should not," cau-

PITFALL

tions Joanne Small, "necessarily be viewed as rejection. Rather, it is normal for a child to begin to prefer the companionship of peers rather than parents. One way to improve your involvement with your child is to recognize your child's social needs, and invite him or her to bring a friend or two on some of your outings together."

The Teen Years

1. A child's first loyalty, as a teenager, generally appears to be to her or his friends, not the parents (*particularly the noncustodial parent*). "While it can be disappointing not to see your child as often as you might like," Joanne Small explains, "remember that this would also be true if your children lived with you full time. Your child is moving towards independence and adulthood." One suggestion that Ms. Small offered is to "contract with your child and work out a visitation arrangement that is comfortable for *both of you*—rather than one that is imposed by you."

Young Adulthood/ Adulthood

"At this age, there may be almost a reverse of traditional parent/child roles. The children may feel that their parents are incapable of caring for themselves, and need the children to take care of them. This is actually the result of three pitfalls:

1. "This is a temporary stage for the parent. He or she may feel *temporarily* unable to deal with their problems; however, as they gain the self-assurance, familiarity with appropriate resources, and independence to assume the re-

PITFALL

sponsibility for satisfying their own needs, they can have a rewarding personal life. Sometimes, a single parent of a young adult or adult child feels guilt at establishing a life for himself or herself as a single person. I advise those of you who have a young adult or adult children to express appreciation for your children's efforts to help; but be firm in explaining that you have needs and are competent to handle them."

2. "Many young adults and adult children have a need to nurture. Especially if they do not have children, they may see you as an appropriate person on whom to test their nurturing skills. The desire and ability to provide nurturing is a healthy and positive aspect of a child's growth to adulthood. However, recognize as an adult, yourself, that it is healthier for both of you if you strive for personal independence.

3. "Recognize that you may feel guilty (or be made to feel so) by either yourself or your children. It is important that you recognize guilt and understand that you do *not* have to feel guilty about asserting your own needs, and doing what you can to satisfy them. I must emphasize that it is important for you to assess your own needs and your *right and ability* to meet them."

PROBLEM SOLVING WITHIN YOUR FAMILY

A concern of any parent, single or not, is solving problems—those within the family, and those affecting one or more individual family members. Although there are different ways of solving difficulties and disagreements, there are essentially two approaches. One is the *authoritarian approach*. In this approach, the parent—or other person in charge—makes nearly all decisions alone. The single parents I contacted generally found that the authoritarian approach did not work for two reasons: First, the children saw decisions as impositions by their parents. Since they did not participate in the decision making, the children felt little motivation (except that of fear) to cooperate and carry out the parent's decision. Second, as children mature, they need increasingly to assume responsibility for their own decisions. However, since the authoritarian parent has previously made the decisions alone, the children have no prior experience in decision making and therefore must start from the beginning.

The problem-solving approach that seems to work for most of the single parents whom I contacted is what I would call *participatory decision making*. The specifics vary in each family, but the essential characteristic of participatory decision making is that the children are actively consulted and involved in the decision-making process. This can range anywhere from asking their suggestions and taking these into account to making a truly joint decision that all family members have worked out together.

In short, we involve our children. For example, Janet, from Fort Worth, Texas, lets her three sons (a sixteen year old and twins of nine) make many of their own decisions in areas such as decorations, supper, and groceries to buy. However, she has the final word.

Art, from Enumclaw, Washington, has always allowed his daughter (now seven) to make real decisions, even when she was younger (she was four and a half when Art became single). As Art explains, "I make most decisions but set up choices for her to make. For example, 'Shall we have soup and a sandwich, or bacon and eggs for lunch today?' Or, 'What day would you like to have the roast?' The choices are both acceptable to me, but she gets the power to choose."

Anita, from Greenbelt, Maryland, takes the ideas of her four-year-old and seven-year-old daughters, tries to use them, and rewards the girls for their contributions.

Norene, from Binghamton, New York, has raised her ten-year-old daughter by herself since her daughter's birth. Of necessity, Norene had to solve all problems by herself. Now, she mentions "our" problems to her daughter, elicits her suggestions, and encourages her to solve her own problems, without butting in.

Judy, from Vestal, New York, and Barbara B., from Belen, New

Mexico, have found it helpful to live one day at a time and deal with each problem as it occurs. As Judy, who has been a single parent for six years (with a nine-year-old daughter, and seven-year-old son) puts it, "I live one day at a time. [I] deal with each problem on an individual basis, as it occurs. For some, if I feel my children are experienced, I let them make their own decisions. Otherwise, I decide; although I always listen to their feelings. A sense of humor is most important to us all."

While Barbara B's children are older (daughter, 20; sons, 19 and 16), she remembers how she raised her children: "I would deal with each problem as it occurred and use a common sense approach. If I was unsure for any reason, especially when my children were smaller, I would ask, 'What would you do if you were me?' They'd usually be stricter than I would."

Besides our weekly family conference, or goal night, an approach I have found effective is "contracting" in writing with one or both of my children. I first used this when my son, Nick, then in third grade, was renting two musical instruments (violin and trombone). Because of other commitments, he was doing little or no practicing on either instrument. My requests to please practice were ignored. Finally, in December of that school year I asked Nick to sign a contract in which we agreed that by the end of January, if Nick improved his practice habits, we would keep the instruments; otherwise, we would return them. (I explained that there was nothing wrong with returning them, as we all had to make choices.) We both initialed and dated the contract. At the end of January, at another goal night, there had been virtually no improvement in Nick's practice habits. Nick protested; but when I showed him the contract that we both had signed, he agreed that "I signed it; it's only fair that I return the instruments."

Contracts can also be used as positive incentives in which you agree to something, provided a prior agreement is carried out. It can also be a way of making more "official" a promise you all have agreed on. For example, if you need to save on baby-sitting costs, and your children are mature enough to watch themselves, you might sign a contract that stipulates if they can watch themselves for relatively short periods, when you are close to home, one half of all money saved could go into a "fun fund," which you can all use for a family outing or other special treat; one quarter gets split up as extra allowance among your children; and one quarter goes into your pocket.

Jean, from Portland, Oregon, uses family discussions with her young teenage sons. "We work out our own discipline that the child feels is fair. The parent agrees. We have a set of rules and consequences that are written down (the family makes and agrees on both). We prepare contracts for problem areas, and all family members sign and live by them."

Setting priorities among possible decisions is also important. Annelle, from a small town in Missouri, and her eight-year-old son "talk about the alternatives and the consequences of each alternative, then we decide."

Sometimes, children can help each other. Carolyn, from Middletown, Connecticut, has children ranging from 4 to 24. She has found that, sometimes, her children can help each other. She feels that the closer they are in age, the easier it is to relate.

Dorris, from Riverside, California, recalls that during her first ten years of widowhood, her family developed problem-solving techniques that they still use, even though the children are now grown. As Dorris explains, "We used family conferences around the dining room table, and still do so. We discuss the problem and try to find a solution. Sometimes, we only express opinions. But the conference continues until everyone is satisfied. Some of our conferences have gone on until the wee hours of the morning when I had to go to work the next day; but we never have used that as an excuse to stop the problem solving."

Participatory decision making involves your working together with your children, rather than your making most decisions by yourself. The following suggestions may give you some ideas which can help you use participatory decision making to solve family and individual problems:

1. Whatever the ages of your children, offer them some real choices over which they can have control. (Two examples are meals and family outings.)
2. Consider a regular time each week for family problem solving and establishing individual and family goals.
3. A family council is one way that all family members can share in problem solving and decision making.
4. Encourage your children to make their own decisions and solve

their own problems, whenever possible, with your help (when requested), understanding, and support.

5. Contract with your children to fulfill mutually agreed-on tasks, goals, and other responsibilities. Contracts can also be used as positive incentives and a way of making more official something on which you have all agreed.

6. Help your children consider alternatives—and the consequences of each alternative—before reaching a decision.

7. Base your problem solving on mutual respect, rather than solely on parental power.

8. Above all, try to see your children as less-experienced equals. Admit when you are wrong; and allow yourself to be imperfect, admitting your mistakes. This encourages a far greater degree of trust and respect—while encouraging your children's active participation in problem solving—than if you are seen as the perfect parent.

SPECIFIC PROBLEMS FACED BY SINGLE PARENTS AND THEIR CHILDREN

The problem-solving strategies mentioned can make it possible to deal more effectively, than could be done otherwise, with the many types of problems confronting single parents. Also helpful may be to look at some of the specific problems that have been faced by other single parents and learn how these problems have been overcome. Let's set the stage with a concern expressed by single parents at a Baltimore PWP discussion. One member expressed his concern that children in single-parent families are unwilling to complete tasks, have low tolerance for frustration, and need instant gratification. This is a serious concern, and one that is shared by many people who are not single parents. However, after further discussion, the group raised the point that these problems were not necessarily unique to single parent families; they might also exist in a two-parent family where both parents work full-time.

Another misconception, believed by many professionals and nonprofessionals alike, is that broken homes cause juvenile deliquency and other major problems in children. From my research, and my contacts with both single parents and professionals who work with them, I have found that it is not the one-parent family that is at fault. Rather, such considerations as income, social class, family stability, and the type of community in which we live are far more important contributing factors to children's problems than is being a one-parent or two-parent family. Above all, as single parents we *can and do* help our children: both in how we involve them in problem solving and decision-making and in our ability to work effectively with professionals to overcome problems faced by our children or us.

Let's now examine some specific problems that have been faced by single parents.

Separation and The Fear of Being Left

Love, reassurance, patience and counseling have helped both Ethel and Hazel deal with their childrens' problems in these areas.

Logistics

A weekly check-off list arranged by priority, and a balance of time alone and time with her son are some ways that Ann (Chapter 3) has been able to develop a dependable routine for her family.

Lying

In our discussion of honesty earlier in Chapter 4, you saw that Jeff, from California, handled this problem with his daughter by punishing his daughter for lying—not for the initial offense.

Societal Discrimination

Single parents often play untraditional roles. Julia, a widow from Belen, New Mexico, recalls that "A few years back, one of my daughters was laughed at because she called her mother about a car problem. She had all the confidence in the world that I would take care of the problem. I did; and she had the satisfaction of saying, "See! I told you Mom could fix it."

Some problems are not so easily solved. Lois E., from the Newark,

New Jersey area, has found that most community activities for children seem to assume there will be a full-time mother or chauffeur available to drive the kids places. Since this is not true for single-parent families or families where both parents work, their children *in this type of community* do suffer. This is the fault of the community, not the parent(s).

Harriet, in Potomac, Maryland, has found that her synagogue is not equipped for single-parent families.

Neither Lois nor Harriet has answers for their problems. However, perhaps a few suggestions can be offered here. Lois' area is part of the New York City metropolitan region. Perhaps by consulting PWP chapters in her region Lois can find a nearby community which does offer more support for single parents. (One resource, discussed in Chapter 8, is the Latch Key program, where before- and after-school care is provided in the schools.) Often, a constructive suggestion, and willingness to contribute time and effort to implement the idea, can go far in obtaining the support of school and community leaders, where complaining—no matter how valid—may not.

Harriet's problem, unfortunately, is *not* unusual for single parents, regardless of their religion. In Harriet's situation, several resources are available for single parents in the Washington, D.C., area. Perhaps by contacting Vivian Weiss, Family Activities Director for the Jewish Community Center of Greater Washington (interviewed for this book), Harriet could find out what synagogues in greater Washington, D.C., are concerned with the needs of single-parent families. Perhaps she might want to join one of these synagogues.

School Problems

Unfortunately, discrimination against single-parent families is still present in many parts of the United States. (We will discuss this in more depth in Chapter 8.) For example, Lois E. from a community in the Newark, New Jersey area, has a six-and-one-half-year-old son and a four-year-old daughter. She had difficulty finding adequate day care for her children, before and after school. When she did find a sitter, the local board of education refused to let her children ride the school bus to the sitter's house after school. Lois had no alternative, except to transfer her children to a private school which was willing to make the necessary adjustments.

Jayne, from Renton, Washington, has been single for two years. Her daughters are 20 and 14, and her son is 18. Jayne believes that "schools unconsciously discriminate against children with only one full-time parent. All functions are set up for couples; invitations are only issued to the custodial single parent; class discussions center around two-parent families, all without thinking. My kids shake their heads in disbelief, but they all learn to cope with it after a while."

If we are not careful, it is easy to become paranoid, and blame all school problems on the fact that we are single parents. Frequently, like children in two-parent families, our children may experience academic or other problems in school that have little or no relation to our being single parents. At such times, the most effective solution is to work together with your child, teacher, and other interested people to solve the problem.

Theft and Keeping Your Child's Trust

A good way to end this discussion is with a problem that none of us likes, but some of us have to face: theft by our children. How do you act when you learn that your child has taken something that belongs to someone else? With righteous indignation? Do you pretend it hasn't happened? Is there another way to handle the situation?

That is one reason that I was especially interested in the experience that Betty L. from Lincoln, Nebraska, had with her youngest daughter (age 13). Let's let Betty describe the incident in her own words:

"My youngest daughter got in with some 'new' friends, went to town shopping; and, a couple of days later, came to me crying with a handful of junk jewelry she had 'picked up.' I was glad she had confided in me; I didn't want her singled out for punishment; but I felt she needed some direction. We decided to put the jewelry away; and when she had earned enough through babysitting and her paper route, we got a money order which covered the jewelry and the tax, and sent the same with a letter apologizing for her behavior to the manager of the store. This may not have been legally or morally right, but it was our way of handling it. The time it took her to save money (she had to give up a lot of things she wanted to do to save money) she had to think about what she had done; and yet I didn't force her to get involved with the law. I feel she won't do that again and that she feels I'm fair in all ways I can be, and will come to me with any problems she has in the future. Because she had to pay for the articles, and the store didn't lose any money, I feel it was a lesson she learned. Also, this was just between the two of us; we didn't bring others in the family into it, or anyone else. I'm sure my ex-husband would have spanked her, then forgotten the rest, which would have made her not want to confide in us again."

PROVIDING SECURITY AND NURTURING FOR YOUR CHILDREN

Earlier in Chapter 4, Joanne Small mentioned the need that children of all ages have for nurturing and security within their families. Jennifer, from Columbia, Maryland, commented that her ten-year-old son "gets loving he needs, when he indicates the need for it, in the quality of time we spend together."

Joyce, from central Wisconsin, has two daughters, age 11 and 6. She commented that she is there with love, understanding, and sometimes a scolding and a cross word, when needed. She tries to be as positive and constructive as possible to help them build a good self-image. She is honest too; so, when something is bad, she tells them about it.

When Julia (from Belen, New Mexico) became a widow seven years ago, her daughters were 17 and 15. According to Julia, "Security was a home, love, and financial support when needed. They knew they had to be responsible for themselves when they came of age."

The comments of Betty L., from Lincoln, Nebraska, are brief and to the point. They almost summarize many of the values that we discussed earlier in Chapter 4. Betty explained, "They know I am there like a rock—that's their security. I don't lie or cheat; they know they can depend on me."

Nurturing and security are vital for children of any age. Some of the ways in which you can provide this, as a single parent, are by being available to your children when they need you, allowing for special time with your children—together and individually—and showing your love and concern through your actions, as well as your words.

ENCOURAGING YOUR CHILDREN'S RESPONSIBILITY AND INDEPENDENCE

If providing security is important, so is encouraging children's independence and sense of responsibility. After all, if we as parents have done our job well, our children should be prepared by the time they reach adulthood to assume the responsibility for their own lives. They may also want to nurture their own children. As parents, we provide the foundation by which our children can develop both responsibility and independence.

Probably, many of you have heard how children today are spoiled, lazy, and irresponsible. I was happy to find that this is not necessarily the case in single-parent homes.

Norene, from Binghamton, New York, and Jean, from Portland, Oregon, both use a system of positive reinforcement. Norene comments, "I explain that privileges are related to maturity. More responsibility, more privileges; the more dependable and trustworthy she is, the more freedom she can receive. I encourage my (10-year-old) daughter to make her own choices, and stand behind her." Jean's two sons, ages 14½ and 13, "are given liberties. If they are not abused, and I have no problems with them, more independence is granted."

Hazel, from Erie, Pennsylvania, has worked out a more thorough system for her six- and three-year-old sons. As she tells it, "Little by little, I have asked the boys to help around the house. The older boy makes his own bed, picks up toys and clothes, takes care of garbage, etcetera. The three-year-old even knows how to take care of his own coat, put clothes in the hamper, and so on. Being a mother, it is hard to let my boys run free to be boys; I try to intervene only when I feel they are in danger of bodily harm—like when I see the three-year-old hanging over the edge of the cyclone fence. Many times, the boys do not want to help out around the house. I just ask them if they really want to live in such a mess, and they must help to keep the house clean, so we can all live in a clean place. They still balk at this but I am now seeing a certain sparkle over the idea of being older and having responsibility. Perserverance is the name of the game."

Evelyn, from Rockville, Maryland, has a 14-year-old son and two daughters, ages 12 and 10. She has "made constant use of logical consequences. They know from this that they are responsible for their own behavior and feel secure that they can handle their own problems."

Cindy, from a small town in central Wisconsin, believes in letting her six- and four-year-old children struggle. She teaches indirectly and praises them for their accomplishments.

Jeff, from California, has found that "by necessity my daughter has assumed responsibilities for herself. For example, I let her make sure she gets to school on time. She also does her homework, cleans her room, and puts her things away. She responds better to this freedom than to doing what's told."

Art, from Enumclaw, Washington, expects his seven-year-old daughter to pick up, feed the dog, and clean the table.

Responsibilities, in general, are great to talk about. However, a real part of single-parent family life is the necessity that our children help us with many of the everyday chores, such as cleaning the house or apartment. Nancy, a friend from Columbia, Maryland, explains how she has succeeded in obtaining the cooperation of her ten-year-old son and eight-year-old daughter with household chores: "All our chores are put in a hat. Each child picks one chore from the hat. Saturday is our cleaning day. When we finish one of the chores, everyone has one-half hour of free time. This provides a much-needed break and gives the encouragement we all need to finish up as soon as possible. Each of my children also has three simple chores to do after school. My son empties the dishwasher, brings all dishes into the sink, and empties the garbage. My daughter waters the plants, walks the dog, and straightens the living room. If they don't complete their daily chores, I don't say anything but deduct a certain amount from their weekly allowance of two dollars (which also covers entertainment).

Jayne, from Renton, Washington, has been fortunate. Her two daughters (ages 20 and 14) "have taken the initiative in taking responsibility. I didn't even have to ask. My younger daughter does much of the cooking, all of the ironing, and keeps two rooms of the house clean. She dusts, picks up after herself, and helps with yardwork. She makes her own dental, doctor, and hair appointments, and has made arrangements for repairmen, deliveries, etcetera. She has pushed for independence, and I gradually give her more freedom."

Carol H., from Hillsville, Virginia (with a 16-year-old son and a 14-year-old daughter), notes that others have commented on the children's maturity, especially when they were in elementary school. She adds, "I have always expected them to be mature, and kids tend to live up to our expectations."

The following suggestions for encouraging your children's responsibility and independence are based on the positive experience and insights of single parents (including myself):

1. Relate privileges to responsibilities. The more responsibility your child can handle, the more privileges he or she can be given.
2. Emphasize a working-together, team approach as a means of encouraging your children to help with household chores and other family tasks.
3. Use logical consequences ("everything you do has a result—sometimes good, sometimes bad") as a way of encouraging your children's independence. This will also help them to choose alternatives which have positive effects (for them).
4. Be willing to acknowledge and accept the consequences of your own mistakes—and use them as examples for your children.
5. Plan a regular time for doing household chores, and involve your children in determining who will do each chore.
6. Plan special fun excursions or special treats after the necessary chores have been finished. This gives all of you an incentive to finish the work as efficiently as possible.

VALUES AND THE SINGLE PARENT

As single parents, we are of course concerned with helping our children develop values appropriate for our society. Single parents' values are not noticeably different from those of nonsingle parents. However, what is different is that as single parents we particularly need to take the time to develop a person-to-person, rather than authoritarian, relationship with our children. Norene, in Binghamton, New York, sets an example and discusses problems with her ten-year-old daughter. She tries to make her daughter realize that everyone has the same rights as she does.

Cynthia, from Silver Spring, Maryland, tries to "show love for them [my children] and teach them that being kind to others and tolerance of others are the most important things in life. I try to teach them how to be kind to each other also."

Florence, from Vestal, New York (with a 13-year-old daughter and an 11-year-old son), and Lorraine (from the Washington, D.C., area) both value honesty above all. Florence emphasizes, "I will not tolerate lying, cheating, or stealing. If I see instances of child cruelty, I talk about it. A favorite expression of mine is, 'What would you feel like if . . .?' " Lorraine stresses honesty. Also, Lorraine says, "I try to get my daughter to accept others with their strengths and weaknesses; but, more importantly, to accept herself first."

Thrift and saving for what she wants are important values to Donna, from Baltimore, Maryland, who has an eight-year-old son. In Donna's own words, "Nothing is wasted. Money is carefully spent on something long desired. Explanations are always given for whys and why nots."

Margie, from central Pennsylvania (with a 16-year-old son and daughters who are 19 and 15) respects property, neighbors, and saving to pay for gifts and purchases.

Sharing feelings is important to Joyce, from central Wisconsin. She and her two daughters "talk about what things mean to us and why. I leave the way open for them to form their own values, although I do point out my feelings and the reasons why."

Sometimes, values can change. This has been true for Jeff from California, who has found, "I've been through changes in my own values; so, I'm not as dogmatic as I once was. I try to let my daughter see my values in my own life." Harriet, from Potomac, Maryland, now puts less emphasis on trusting others and more on taking care of oneself, love, caring, and respect.

One of the complaints that many teenagers have is that their parents try to impose values, rather than encourage them to develop their own. For that reason, I felt pleased when Cathy, from North Bend, Oregon, told me that she encourages her teenagers' own values and praises them. She adds, "I try not to impose my own values. I point out the pros and cons, and let them decide."

Although single parents do differ in their individual values, some values are held in common by most, or all, of those whom I contacted. These values include:

1. Respecting the rights of others

2. Selfworth
3. Being kind to others
4. Thrift—saving for what you want
5. Not lying, cheating, or stealing
6. Taking care of oneself
7. Encouraging children to form their own values, and supporting the children in these areas

DISCIPLINE AND THE SINGLE PARENT

Any discussion of raising children must sooner or later address the question of discipline. Discipline is a method of teaching our children desirable and undesirable behavior, not merely a system of punishment (as many people believe). Let me begin by recommending a book that every single parent should read: Dr. Fitzhugh Dodson's book, *How to Discipline with Love* (Signet paperback, 1977 and 1978). Dr. Dodson discusses in detail several ways of helping your children through the use of discipline. In addition, his chapter on the single parent is one of the few in any book which does *not* assume that a single-parent home is unhealthy for a child.

We are concerned here with the positive experiences and insights of single parents. Fortunately, many single parents have developed disciplinary techniques which have worked for them. Phyllis, from Billings, Montana, has found *grounding,* suspending privileges, to be effective for her 15- and 12-year-old daughters. Grounding has also been used effectively on her daughter by Norene, from Binghamton, New York, who explains, "My usual punishment is grounding, or being sent to her room. If it is an area where there is a constant need for discipline, I ask how I can help, and what punishment will help not to do it again?"

Cathy, from North Bend, Oregon, makes her children responsible for themselves. Often, they set their own punishment or face the natural consequences. Cathy commented wryly, "It's not always easy."

Logical consequences are also important to Alice, from Fort Wayne, Indiana. She lets her children (who are teenagers) make decisions and bear the consequences of their actions.

· Harriet, from Potomac, Maryland, has learned to be more firm. Her sons are not shattered when she says no.

Terry, from Bethany, Oklahoma, has "tried to encourage the younger girls to think more about the results of their actions; and, for the most part, less discipline seems needed."

Jeff, from California, found that "at first, discipline was a real problem. Because of the excessive physical violence of my daughter's mother, it was hard for me to discipline her [my daughter] without violence. Now, I send her to her room, away from the TV, or withhold other privileges."

An effective technique for young children, as Anita (from Greenbelt, Maryland) points out, is a *time out*. In a time out, a child spends time alone for misbehaving (usually about ten minutes). This gives the child time to calm down and think while also removing him or her from the area where the problem occurred. This was explained in more detail by Ethel, from eastern Massachusetts: "I spank very little. I find time to think is very effective; so, usually I send my (seven-year-old) son to his room to think about what he has done. Usually, he will come out with an apology and a promise to try to do better. At times, I've taken away the TV, but that is less effective. On one occasion, when he was four and a half, he was not allowed to go to the circus because he had hit a child over the head with a shovel."

Sometimes, kids can settle their own problems. Nell, from El Cerrito, California, tries "first to let the kids settle it themselves (this is mainly concerned with sibling rivalry). If they come to blows, I send them to their rooms. Docking some or all of their allowance I use for more serious matters."

"Being fair in discipline," Hazel, from Erie, Pennsylvania, comments, "is a hard thing at times, as the older boy does things to be bad simply to get my attention. I feel that even if I spent 24 hours a day with him, it would still not be enough for him. Anyway, I try to be fair between the two of them. Discipline usually consists of being confined to their room with no toys, sitting in a chair, missing TV shows they really want to see, or a good spanking for something like the day the six-year-old hit the three-year-old on the head with a hammer. It was small (the spanking), but it hurt."

Sometimes, especially when they are teenagers, children may simply refuse to listen to you. At times such as this, Lois J., from Johnson City, New York, withholds her services as a chauffeur from her children. She has found that the realization that their mother is not going to accept disobedience without retaliation causes her children to cooperate more than they otherwise might. (Chapter 14 in Dodson's book, entitled "How to Use Parental Muscle," explains this technique in more detail.)

Discipline is tough for any parent. The following suggestions have proved effective for other single parents:

1. Use a time out for younger children. This involves sending your child to his or her room, or some other quiet place, to be alone for a certain period of time—usually about ten minutes. This gives the child time to think while also removing him or her from the area where the problem occurred.
2. Let your children determine their own punishment.
3. Grounding—or removal of privileges—can be effective for children of any age.
4. Encourage your children to consider—and accept—the consequences of their actions.
5. Talk things out. Perhaps there's been a misunderstanding or a communications problem.
6. Use discipline that is appropriate for the problem.
7. Finally, remember that discipline is a way of teaching, *not* merely a system of punishment.

SUMMARY

You have seen in this chapter how other single parents have successfully dealt with some of the everyday concerns that you too may have. Their experiences with problem solving, coping with both day-to-day and special problems, and providing their children with nurturing and security while encouraging their responsibility; the values that they consider important; and the ways in which they handle discipline within their families have helped you to realize you are not the only single parent with these concerns.

If you have an opportunity, go to your library or bookstore and read some of the recommended books discussed either in this chapter or in Appendix D. They have helped other single parents and may well offer you additional insights and new strategies.

Chapter 5

Single Parent Plus . . .

You have seen in Chapters 3, and 4 how other single parents have dealt with some of the issues that are common to all of us who are single parents, whether custodial or noncustodial, divorced, widowed, or never married. Many single parents, however, have special needs beyond those common to all single parents.

In most single-parent families, the parents are divorced or separated, the children live with the mother, and the father is the noncustodial parent. However, this is only one type of single-parent family. Widowed single parents, single parents who have never been married, fathers who have custody—and mothers without custody—parents with shared or divided custody arrangements, and gay and lesbian single parents make up some of the different types of families in the single-parent community.

Other single parents have succeeded in these parenting situations. If one or more of these apply to you, this chapter will help you realize that you are not alone and that *your* particular type of single-parent family can offer you and your children a *special* opportunity to know, appreciate, and enjoy each other while making it as a single-parent family.

THE ONLY SURVIVING PARENT: MAKING IT AS A WIDOW OR WIDOWER

As a widow or widower you have lost your partner and your children's other parent through death. Although you don't have the bitterness and hostility of divorce, it can be a sudden, unpleasant shock to realize that you are the *only* parent that your children now have.

One problem is how to tell your children about their dead parent, without being morbid or unduly depressing. Rita, a 28-year-old widow from Lawrence, Kansas, has been a widow for two years. She describes how she tells her two daughters (ages 4½ and 22 months) about their father:

"My older girl has frequently asked about her father. When she was a little younger, I answered her question, 'Where's Daddy?' with 'In heaven with Jesus.' Now that she is four, she does want to know more. I do what I can and what I think that she is able to understand in telling her about his accident while he was at work and how he was electrocuted on the job. We talk about him occasionally, though this does somewhat bring back memories for me—I just try not to dwell on them. My children have the right to know about their father and what he was like. Sometimes, if the girls are doing something their father liked to do—such as reading books or drinking milk—I will mention that their father liked to do that also. In ways, they remind me of their father. Of course, the baby is not yet two years old and has no recollection even of what a father is and I do not know if this will cause a problem later or not. I feel, either way, I will be able to handle the situation as far as their questions are concerned."

Widowers can often have their own special problems. Arthur, from a small town in Pennsylvania, has been a widower for seven years. At the time of his wife's death seven years ago, Arthur's six children ranged in age from 6 to 15. His mother, brother, and sister have been very helpful; his mother, in particular, has been an effective surrogate parent for his children. Arthur's children accepted the fact of their mother's death. However, Arthur explained, "It was very hard to help them understand why she died (of a disease). Also, they felt their remaining parent should not associate with the opposite sex, but after family discussions—both separately and collectively—we all understood the needs of each other."

Many widows had been dependent on their husbands for economic support and family identity. In this situation, getting going again can involve working toward personal and economic self-sufficiency. Julia, from Belen, New Mexico, found that "when I became a widow, I lacked the education needed to hold a job which would pay a decent wage. I enrolled in the university two months after I was widowed. Two and a half years later, I received my degree and was employed." Julia advises other widows to "set goals and strive for them. Like the saying goes, 'can't never do anything.' "

I was particularly impressed by two widows with whom I had the opportunity to talk. Cindy is a younger widow from a small town in central Wisconsin who has a six-year-old daughter and a four-year-old son. She has been a widow for two years. Doris is a mature widow whose children range in age from 15 to 31. She has raised her children alone for over ten years.

In her questionnaire, Cindy commented that "as a widow, I feel our society does not allow us to grieve properly. We can only get out so much grieving; then we are supposed to get on with our lives. I had to move from the area that I lived in because I felt I would go crazy if I stayed. The few times I cried in church and had to get up and go out, the minister made such a big deal out of it in the prayer."

Cindy has found PWP and church and religious organizations to be useful resources. (While many communities have organizations devoted to the needs of widows and widowers, PWP appears to be one of the few that deals with the needs of *widowed single parents*. Many PWP chapters have special widow/widower groups; and PWP discussions relate to the needs of single parents, whether widowed or divorced.) As Cindy described her experience, "Through PWP I have made friends, gotten out, and become involved. It has given my children a chance to be with other children in similar situations." She continues, church "has helped me get my life back together. It has helped my children understand (a little bit, anyway) about their father's death."

Many widowed single parents feel cut off from their married friends. If you are in that situation, you might find Cindy's experience helpful. She explained, "At first, I felt deserted by my married friends from my married period. However, the ones that were good friends did not really desert me. They did not know how to cope with death or our friendship either. My children are still friends with their children and miss them because we moved."

Cindy has found that problems do occur. She discussed one of her major concerns: "I feel that the death of their father has set my children back in maturity, which is causing a problem with my first grader. There is a good possibility that she will have to take first grade over again because of her lack of maturity. I have accepted the fact that this could happen, and I feel holding a child back a year at that age could be an advantage." She also has found that in her town, many people believe single parents are inferior parents.

I was especially impressed when Cindy shared some additional thoughts with me: "My late husband's death was a shock to me and my children. He was killed in an automobile accident, and we probably will never know exactly how the accident happened. I found it very difficult to accept his death, but somehow you don't have any choice. I was very depressed and cried a lot for about one year. Then I decided I had to go on with my life. I started reading material about death and grieving and acceptance, and came out of the depression with a very positive attitude for life. I have made *many* major decisions in a short time, and I am a much stronger person than I probably would have ever been.

"I did have one period of depression which lasted for about three weeks, after I was on the way again. I look back at the depression and hope that I don't go back there again.

"I try to laugh at the problems that come my way. They have to be worked out, but it's much easier to see the humor in every situation.

"I am a religious person and I believe I could not have come out of this in as good a shape as I did without praying for guidance.

"I became involved in PWP last summer; however, I wonder if I could have joined any sooner. I really believe in timing and its relationship to our coping with things.

"I have enjoyed the friendships I have made through PWP. I hope that I will be able to help others because of my experience.

"I feel my children suffered because of my year in limbo (so to speak). I love my children very much, but I need to get out more—which I seem to be doing all of a sudden. I sometimes feel that I am supposed to give the love and attention of both parents, which there is no way that I can do."

I called Cindy and asked her for any suggestions she could offer

for widowed single parents (men and women alike) who have young
children. She had two suggestions to offer:

1. "Talk about the death of the other parent and encourage your
   kids to also, even if it hurts like the dickens. It's better to share
   these feelings openly than to have them burn silently within like
   a slow poison.
2. "Give your children additional responsibilities and encourage
   them to grow and try new things."

Doris was married twice. The first time, she was divorced after
13 years of marriage. After a happy second marriage in which her
youngest son was born (and her second husband adopted her other
four children), her second husband died. Doris has been a widow for
11 years. At the time she became a widow, her two daughters were
grown and her sons were 16, 10, and 4.

In the few months that I have been friends with Doris, I have
come to respect her ingenuity and resourcefulness. I asked her,
"Wasn't it hard for you, raising three sons by yourself?" "Of course it
wasn't easy," replied Doris, "but I had two things going for me. First,
we all accepted as natural both my husband's death and our feelings
about it. We never smothered our feelings or put ourselves down for
having them. Secondly, my boys all enjoy sports; so, I was able to ask
the advice and help of their coaches and use the coaches as surrogate
partners." (Widowers can do the same thing by asking the advice of
Girl Scout or Brownie leaders and other leaders in groups that are for
girls.) Doris has four suggestions for widows and widowers who are
single parents:

1. "Don't be afraid to tell your children, 'I don't know.' Until recently, I was afraid to do this and would tell my children, 'Ask
   me an hour from now.' It's such a relief to be able to just be
   myself—and the children respect my honesty.
2. "Don't be afraid to ask for help from the children's school,
   coaches (or other appropriate leaders), or your friends or family.
3. "Don't feel you have to be perfect. It's far easier to live with
   yourself if you don't set yourself up as an idol. My oldest daughter (32) was shocked to learn I *wasn't* perfect. When she learned

to cope, we could become friends. Before, she had hangups because of the fact that she saw me as perfect and wasn't comfortable with the fact that she wasn't perfect.

4. "Relax and listen to your children. I don't believe in the old cliche, Children should be seen and not heard. I remember visiting a lady who was on an important conference call. When her son interrupted her, she asked, 'Is it important?' When he said yes, she excused herself and took the time to help him. She *didn't* just shut her son up by saying, 'Later, when I have a few minutes!' "

Suggestions for Single-Parent Widows and Widowers

The following are some ideas and suggestions from widows and widowers who are single parents:

1. Be open with your children about their deceased parent. Encourage them to talk about their feelings and feel free to share yours, but beware of burdening your children with more than they can handle.
2. Set goals and strive for them.
3. Keep busy and involved.
4. Do your crying in private. People will want to be around and help you more.
5. Give your children additional responsibilities and encourage them to grow and try new things.
6. Don't be afraid to ask for help. It's not only helpful but important to find and use appropriate resources. This can help make life easier and more satisfying for your children and you.
7. Have *realistic* expectations of your friends; that is, don't expect from others what they are unable to give. For example, although married friends *can be* supportive, they often find it impossible to relate to your widowed status. Support as a widow or widower is far more likely from others in a similar situation. Two places to find other widowed single parents are single-parent groups and organizations for widows and widowers.
8. Don't feel you have to be perfect; and don't be afraid to tell your children, "I don't know." It can help you relax and be yourself,

while reassuring your children that you are a real human being,
rather than a demigod or super parent.

9. Listen to your children; respect them and take them seriously.
   This can help your relationship, not only when they are young
   but also as they grow to adulthood.

10. Above all, honesty, empathy, being willing to ask for help when
    necessary, and working with your children can help all of you
    develop a happy and satisfying family.

MAKING IT AS A NEVER-MARRIED SINGLE PARENT

Raising your own children having never been married has always set
people apart from the mainstream of society. Traditionally, "nice
people" don't talk about this type of situation; and single, unmarried
parents and their children were, at best, pitied and, at worst,
shunned. For this reason, I honestly feared that it would be virtually
impossible to hear about positive experiences and insights of single
parents who had never been married.

However, I was fortunate in hearing from several women who
have been able to make their families work as never-married single
parents. For example, Beatrice found that PWP, her church, and the
Bluebirds (part of Camp Fire Girls) helped her. Norene, from Endicott, New York (with a ten-year-old daughter), went a step further
when she explained that the fear was worse than the reality. As
Norene put it, "I expected to run into problems, but, have had very
few. Most were the first three or four years and were caused by
myself, because I felt so guilty about what I had done. Once I got
myself straightened out, I found people (friends, dates, employers)
accepted me for what I was doing with my life and respected me for
trying so hard to raise my daughter as best as I could. This is especially true of the people I've met through Parents Without Partners."

This approach also worked for Vanessa, from Baltimore, Maryland, who has two daughters, ages ten and seven. Vanessa told me
that she found her situation very scary at first; however, she soon
realized that there were resources that could help her. Her family
helped with baby sitting and money; a living-together arrangement
(LTA) with a man provided a male figure in the home. (Even though

Vanessa and her friend have split up, he is still a friend to the children; and they call on him for advice and help. He also visits them frequently.) Vanessa has always worked and the support of her family has given her the energy and time to enjoy being with her daughters to the benefit of all three.

Vanessa commented, "The two things that have helped me most are my ability to make the best of any situation and my willingness to accept reality and deal with things. If I was to offer one suggestion, it would be don't worry about what *could* happen. Accept the situation as it is, examine your choices, and deal with things the best you can. That's all any of us can do."

After my conversation with Dolores, from a rural community in central Wisconsin, I came away even more convinced that before that the type of family situation is *not* nearly as important as the way in which we handle it. I hope Dolores's story will move you as much as it has me and make you vividly aware of both the challenge *and opportunity* for children and the parent to gain and grow from a never-married single-parent family. Let Dolores share her story with you.

"Both my children have different fathers and both my pregnancies were really traumatic for me. I had six brothers and no sisters and I was never taught about sex and birth control. I was real ignorant. Only after having two children did I come to understand the importance of birth control. I nearly lost my own life when I had my second son. (My boys are now nine and five.) I was on ADC (Aid to Dependent Children) and lived in a mobile home on my parents' property. I let them make all the major decisions about my children and my life and was scared to assert myself or be independent.

"The turning point for me came when I began seeing a counselor. Seeing him made me realize that I didn't like myself and was not giving my kids the physical affection that they needed. My counselor helped me to see myself in a more positive way and gave me the courage to change and take control of my own life.

"I became more social and developed a life of my own; moved away from my parents and became more independent. I went back to school, while working part time and raising two kids. I graduated with honors; however, after a bunch of unsuccessful job interviews, I was nearly ready to give up. My friends encouraged me to try some more. At the very next interview, I got a job at the State Public Defender's Office, which I have held for three weeks. It feels so good to be independent and able to take care of myself and my children. I guess it can all be summed up when my mother recently took me aside and told me quietly, 'We're proud of you.'

"What suggestions can I offer other unmarried parents? There *are* problems: both financial and emotional. However, living alone can be positive. It gives you an opportunity to be alone with your thoughts, a chance for creativity, and a way to tap your own resources. Be open to change and growth. Treat life as an opportunity as well as a challenge. Don't be afraid to reach out for help. My friends have helped and my counselor gave me the support and encouragement I needed to take control of my own life.

"I have made it as an unmarried single parent. You can too, if you believe in yourself; ask for help when you need it and—above all—treat life as a chance to grow and find yourself as a person and single parent."

The following suggestions were made by some of the never-married parents with whom I talked:

1. Set goals—both long term and short term—and work to achieve them.
2. Be positive and think back to what you have already accomplished.
3. Don't waste time feeling sorry for yourself. What good does it do? Rather, accept the situation as it is; examine your choices and deal with things the best you can. That's all any of us can do.
4. Be honest with your children; explain why you never married and why they don't have a father. It is far better for your child to hear it directly from you—with love and understanding—than to hear it from someone else or through the grapevine.
5. Develop a life of your own, as well as one with your child. Single-parent groups, such as Parents Without Partners, offer a way for you to gain the support, friendship, and insights of other single parents, without having to feel ashamed of your never-married status. A support group of never-married single parents is another possibility. See Appendix C, under Black Unmarried Mothers, for one such group.
6. Living alone can be positive. It offers an opportunity for you to be alone with your thoughts, a chance for creativity, and a way to tap your own resources.

7. Be open to change and growth. Treat life as an opportunity as well as a challenge.
8. Don't be afraid to reach out for help. Counseling, single-parent groups, friends, family, and community organizations are usually able and willing to help—provided you take the first step of contacting them.
9. Above all, realize that you are not the only unmarried parent who has raised children alone. By developing your own potential, and applying some of the suggestions *that have worked for other never-married single parents*, you *can* succeed as a never-married single parent.

MODIFYING TRADITIONAL FORMS OF CUSTODY

Traditionally, in divorces where children were involved, the mother kept the children. However, many single parents have found alternative custodial arrangements that work for them and their children. In this section, we will examine some of these alternative forms of custody as they have worked for other single parents.

You Can Do Just Fine: Making It as a Custodial Father

Many fathers are realizing that *they* can raise their children. Mark, from a Nebraska city, has custody of his three sons (ages eight, six, and four). He has found that his having custody has helped maintain stability through continuity and time together. His biggest problem is child care. His six- and eight-year-old sons must stay alone two to three hours before school and after school. However, they do well. Mark feels it is important to "keep your word. Spend time in an area where the kids can get you for the 30-second periods they need you."

Martin, from Belen, New Mexico, thinks many of his children's friends are jealous of how much time his children spend with him and how much they do together.

"I know that I was scared when my (then) seven-year-old son and four-year-old daughter came to live with me full time. However, I believe that our enjoying and appreciating each other as people, our family traditions and rituals, our ability to work together, listen to

each other, and have fun together have made our family really special
to all of us."

Art, from Enumclaw, Washington, has had custody of his
seven-year-old daughter for two and a half years. The mother had left
because she needed to have complete control of her life. Art commented, "I've always been involved in raising my daughter, ever since
her birth. I had an equal share in raising her. What problems do I
have? None, really, that single mothers don't have. It is sometimes
even an advantage in my relations with women—they're refreshed by
having a man who understands motherhood. What suggestions do I
have for fathers considering custody? Don't be afraid to try it! Escape
traditional sex roles if it's what you can be most comfortable with.
Don't worry about what people will say."

While having custody of children is still the exception for
fathers, many men are finding that they are able to provide their
children with love, stability, and guidance—on a full-time basis—so
that both the children and father can benefit.

If you are presently, or consider becoming, a custodial father,
here are a few suggestions that may help you:

1. Pay more attention to what you are gaining (the opportunity to
   help your children grow to adulthood) then to what you are
   losing (the freedom of having no full-time responsibilities other
   than your job).
2. Stick to your word, and show your children that they can depend
   on you.
3. Be real and be yourself—rather than try to be the model parent.
   Your kids will appreciate your genuineness and humanity and
   you will be more comfortable too.
4. Build on your individual strengths, and realize that you have as
   much to offer your children as does their mother.
5. Don't be afraid to ask for help. Single-parent and men's groups
   can give you support, friendship, and ideas from others in a
   positive setting.

   An excellent magazine for single fathers and fathers who
   have remarried is *Single Dad's Lifestyle*. Single copies are $1 each;
   a year's subscription is $12. (For more information, write to
   Single Dad's Lifestyle, Phoenix Rising, P.O. Box 482, Scottsdale,
   Arizona 85258. Attention: Robert A. Hirschfeld, Editor, Telephone: 602/998-0980.)

A very supportive nationwide organization for men who choose to break free of gender-based stereotypes (such as the idea that a man can't be as effective a parent as a woman) is Free Man, which operates through workshops, support groups, a monthly newsletter, and educational and informational activities. (See Chapter 8 for a more complete description of the group.)

6. Develop a life for yourself, as well as one with your children. Single-parent groups' family activities offer you and your children an opportunity to feel part of an extended family.

7. Above all, when considering custodial fatherhood, let your main consideration be, "Is this what I am most comfortable with?" rather than "What will people say?" Remember, other men are succeeding in raising their children on a full-time basis and there is no reason why you can't too.

A Viable Alternative: The Myth and the Reality of Being a Noncustodial Mother

Women have traditionally been expected to be the primary custodial parent, and any alternative is bound to be frightening to many people.

Montcosps has recently started a support group for noncustodial mothers. (This is an option you might want to consider either in your community or your PWP chapter.) I was impressed by the positive experiences and insights of two members of this group: Scotty and Gail.

Scotty has two sons, nine and eight. She found that the pressure of being a full-time parent was too much for her. Her former husband was remarried, made more money, and could provide more security and stability than she could. Scotty told me that "I just needed to find myself and get myself all together so I could have more energy for myself and my kids. I felt a lot of guilt, at first, about giving up my children; but I have found—somewhat to my surprise—that it has been good for all of us. The support of other members of Montcosps' noncustodial mothers group has helped me realize that I'm not the only one in this situation. Most important, I've had to realize my own capabilities and needs. As I've built a new life for myself, I've had more time and energy for my boys. Our time together is really quality time and I'm available when they need me. I think that feeling better about myself and my own life has made it possible for me to be a more effective and caring parent. This would never have been possible if I had remained locked in to my traditional role of full-time mother. My suggestions to those of you who are considering becoming noncustodial mothers would be

1. Realize your own needs and capabilities.
2. Get involved in your work or recreational activities.
3. Talk to others in the same situation.

Gail was one of the founders of Montcosps' support group for noncustodial mothers. She has a 13-year-old daughter and 11-year-old twins (son and daughter). Gail discussed in detail her feelings, experiences, and insights about being a noncustodial mother.

"At the beginning I had two main fears. My former husband was very negative and controlling and I was sure that he would turn the children against me by intimidation and his behavior and attitude toward me. (I think that only the potential of my initiating a custody fight has stopped him.)

I was also concerned that I would lose contact with my kids and not be a part of their lives. I knew that I would miss the continuity of knowing them on a day-to-day basis, participating in PTA programs, and doing things such as playing games with my children.

I found, however, that my fears were far worse than my expectations. I have found four major ways of coping that have helped both my children and myself

1. I would pick up on *what they were interested in* when I saw them. For example, if my son was interested in soccer, we'd go to a game or watch it on television. My daughter is interested in disco (my 13-year-old, that is), so we go to discos together. The main thing has been to learn what they are interested in and share their interests with them.
2. I call them often. I emphathize with them and give them support when they need it. I show that I care and encourage them to share their feelings with me.
3. I try to communicate with my former husband.
4. When they visit me, I encourage them to bring their friends.

"Being a non-custodial parent has taught me a lot," continues Gail. "We now have more respect and consideration between us. We notice and appreciate little things about each other that are easy to overlook in a day-to-day, pressure-laden living situation. We are more able to communicate and share feelings than we were before. I am able to be more of a friend than a disciplinarian. We participate a lot in group activities."

Two special benefits that Gail has noticed are

1. We can just sit and enjoy each other. I no longer feel the same pressure to entertain my children constantly.
2. Our communication is increasingly more honest and open. I feel particularly good about this, since I believe this will enable me to more effectively know and help my children as they continue their growth through adolescence to adulthood.

Gail can offer four suggestions to those of you who either consider being or presently are noncustodial mothers

1. A support group for both mothers and children can not only help you but can help your children realize that they are not oddballs for not living with their mother.
2. Share on your children's level. Share positive feelings as well as negative ones. Be sensitive enough to follow through on *their* interests.
3. Give your children a major role in planning your activities together.
4. Try to see your noncustodial role as a period of growth for yourself. Know yourself. As you gain more self-confidence and become smarter, you can gain more respect as a human being: from your children, other adults, and—most importantly— yourself.

Being a noncustodial mother can be an opportunity for you to know and find yourself and gain the energy and control of your own life to develop a quality relationship that can be positive for both you and your children. Like any option, it is important to consider your own and your children's needs, base your decision on what is best for all of you (rather than on the fact that being a noncustodial mother is *not* traditional and many people will probably not understand your choice), and find support groups and resources to make your new way of life work for you all. Consider the following suggestions that Gail and Scotty offer—both from their personal experience and from other members of Montcosps' noncustodial mothers' group:

1. Realize and accept your own needs and capabilities.
2. Consider how being a noncustodial parent can *help* your children and you. Possibilities include developing your own potential, which will help you become happier and more fulfilled and free you to enjoy, appreciate, and help your children when you see them. You can have more quality time with your children and have the energy and desire to really be with them. Also, you will help your children become individuals, ungoverned by gender stereotypes.
3. Get involved in your work or other activities.
4. Join a support group of other noncustodial mothers. If possible, involve the children. This can offer help and encouragement for you and help the kids feel that they are not the only ones who do not live with their mother.
5. Share on your children's level. Be interested and supportive of their interests. Be available when they need you. Give them a major role in planning your activities together.
6. Use your noncustodial situation as an opportunity for personal growth. Know yourself and build your self-confidence. This will help you gain more respect—both from yourself and others.

Joint Custody and Coparenting: Sharing the Joys, Responsibilities, and Involvement

Many single parents are rejecting the idea of one parent having sole custody of the children. They see this as owning the child and have chosen a joint or shared-custody arrangement in which the parents take equal responsibility in being the full-time single parent. While this requires work on the part of both parents, joint custody or *coparenting*, as it is often called, can offer substantial benefits for children and for parents. (An excellent book on this subject, written by a woman who has successfully chosen a coparenting arrangement and interviewed other single parents who have succeeded as coparents, is Miriam Galper's book, *Coparenting: A Source Book for the Separated or Divorced Family* (Running Press, 1978). If you can't find it in your bookstore, you can order directly from the publisher. For price and order information, write to Running Press, 38 South Nineteenth St., Philadelphia, Pa. 19103.)

My personal concept of joint custody differs slightly from that just described. I believe that the key ingredient of joint custody is a commitment to consult, work together, share the involvement and responsibility, and share the decision making insofar as possible. This is more important than the amount of time a child spends with each parent. For this reason, I prefer the term *coparenting*.

Harvey B., from Baltimore, Maryland, has a daughter who was a teenager at the time of the divorce. She was sent away to school and alternated vacations between her father and mother. Thanksgiving was spent with one, Christmas with the other. This gave her a sense of having two homes and eliminated much, or all, of the rivalry that is frequent among divorced parents who are vying for their child's love and attention.

My former wife and I also agreed on a joint-custody arrangement. Joint custody encourages us to work together and share in major decision-making; one parent is *not* left to feel resentment, hostility, or bitterness, or a sense of exclusion from the children's lives. Several single parents have succeeded as coparents by sharing or switching living arrangements. Leo and his former wife live in the same neighborhood in a suburb of Baltimore, Maryland. His children alternate weeks: One week they live with him; the next, with their mother. The children also visit back and forth. This gives them the feeling of having two homes.

Harold, from Wheaton, Maryland, has six children. He and his ex-wife have adopted a different approach. The children stay in their own home and the parents take turns living for six months at a time in the house with the children. The rest of the time, the parent who is not with the children has his or her own apartment.

Jill and her former husband live in a small town in Pennsylvania. They have an informal coparenting arrangement for their youngest daughter (who is now 17). Jill told me that she is happy that the coparenting arrangement seems to work (especially since they were unable to work together in the case of their two older daughters, now

25 and 23). Let Jill describe how her coparenting arrangement works.

"Since we reconciled the support payments, my youngest daughter simply comes and goes between our homes. When she's with me, he pays; when she's with him, I pay. My former husband and I have accepted each other even though our values are different, and we do get together socially with his wife and my special friend.

"I would recommend that parents share custody time and expenses 50–50, even if it means that the child moves and goes to a different school each year. The kids would have two sets of friends and they would learn to live in two environments. They could switch every six months, but I think every year would be better. Of course, they could visit the other parent during the year, if distance wasn't a factor. This would give each parent time with the child, as well as 'free' time! As a teacher, I don't think switching schools would hurt them."

Saralee, from Baltimore, Maryland, has two daughters, ages 18 and 16, and a 10-year-old son. She has an exceptional coparenting arrangement with her former husband. While they both have remarried, Saralee recalls how coparenting worked both when they were single parents and now as remarried parents—each with a new spouse:

"Technically, I suppose, I have always had custody because the children always lived with me. However, my former husband and I have always respected each other and been able to work together as friends and coparents for the children's benefit. Once a month, at least, from the beginning, I would keep him informed as to the children's feelings and activities. For example, this summer my 18-year-old daughter was ambivalent between independence and dependence. For this reason, she did not want to go on vacation with her father. When I gave her father my 'emotional weather forecast' for our daughter, he was able to see that our daughter's decision related more to her normal growth and changing feelings than to a rejection of him.

"The children's father and I have always consulted together as to what was best for the children. For example, our oldest daughter was recently accepted at Yale. The question arose as to who should take her to Yale. His job made it easier for him to take her. However, I felt it was important for me, as her mother, to take her. While I would certainly have done what was agreed on, by the two of us, my former husband has a high regard for me. He said, 'It feels right for you, as her mother, to take her.' If we were both still single, we might well have both taken her.

"We also let the 'power of the event' take priority over our individual convenience. For example, at our younger daughter's sixteenth birthday party, the following people attended—and *all* had a good time celebrating our daughter's happy occasion—my husband and myself, my former husband and his wife, my parents and those of my former husband, and the three children.

"Flexibility is vital. My son spends most weekends with his father, while my daughters tend to spend many of their weekends home.

"I have three suggestions for other coparents or those considering coparenting:

1. "Keep the other parent informed as to the child's feelings and goings on—almost like an 'emotional weather forecast.' This can help the parent whom the child is visiting be more knowledgeable about the child and better able to help the child, while developing a mutually rewarding relationship.
2. Flexibility and free and open communication between the parents is essential. When my younger daughter got sick at camp, we consulted and were all set together to go pick up our daughter.
3. Allow the power of an event (for example, a birthday) to supersede the normal relationship between the parents. Allow the other parent and his or her family to share in joyous occasions. This helps your child feel that she [or he] truly has a special family that cares enough for her [or him] to be able to temporarily put aside their differences."

Joint custody is potentially the most difficult custodial arrangement; however, the rewards can be substantial—both to the children and the parents. The following suggestions may help you in deciding whether joint custody is the answer for you and in making joint custody work on a long-term basis:

1. Both parents are important to the children and neither one should be deprived of a close relationship with them.

2. It is important for both parents to trust and respect each other *as parents* and be willing to work together and communicate *directly*—with little or no bitterness.
3. Flexibility and the ability to consider the children's needs, not merely the parents' wants, are vital.
4. A family mediator can be a real aid, both in helping arrange for joint custody and in getting it to work with a minimum of friction.
5. Don't put your children in the middle. Work together with the other parent to ensure a cooperative, supportive relationship between the parents, rather than one based on conflict.
6. Joint custody can be invaluable to your children by showing them that although the marriage has ended, they still have two involved parents who care about them and can work together for their welfare.

Divided Custody: Intensive and Selective Parenting

Another option of many single parents is that of *divided*—or split—*custody*, in which *each* parent has one or more of the children living with him or her. (For example, the sons might live with the father and the daughters with the mother.)

Dick, from a community in central Wisconsin, has found that one major benefit of divided custody is that it saves court costs and battles and transfers the energy that might be used in court fights into helping the children. Another benefit is the love and understanding between parent and child. When I asked Dick during a telephone interview for more specific ideas and suggestions, Dick replied, "I think the major advantage is that you and the children living with you really have a lot more time together than might otherwise be possible. Get the kids used to it and get yourself together. The two keys to success, I believe, are flexibility and the ability to work together with the other parent. (While my son lives with me and my daughter lives with her mom, my children still see each other—almost like an extended family.) For example, when my parents visited from the West Coast, my former wife agreed to let our daughter stay with me for two weeks. When my wife wanted to go camping for a week, *of course* I let

my son go with her. We respect each other and are able and willing to
put the children first."

Divided custody *can* really work for everyone involved. The best
single example of this was given by Jayne, from Renton, Washington
whose 18-year-old son lives with his father, while her two daughters
(ages 20 and 14) live with her. Let Jayne share her experience, insights and suggestions for making divided custody a beneficial and
positive experience for parents and children alike:

"The children were ages 18, 16, and almost 13 at the time of the
divorce. Their father and I decided that the only arrangement that
would be *fair* to the kids would be to allow them to choose which
parent they wanted to live with. We wanted, more than anything, for
them to be as happy as possible under the circumstances. It was the
hardest thing I have ever done in my life. Naturally, I wanted all of
them with me and I was scared to death to let my daughters live with
their father. Fortunately, it worked out well. My son chose to live with
his father because he felt his father needed him more than I did; his
father could afford the car insurance, etcetera, for a teenage boy
more than I could; he felt more comfortable discussing sex with his
father than with me.

"It hurt, but I could understand and accept his reasons. He is a
beautiful kid and his father did need him. The girls chose to live with
me, which has also worked out well.

"The benefits are that the kids are reasonably happy with the
arrangement and have adjusted well to the changes in their lives. I
also haven't had to worry about casting a teenage boy in the role of
man-of-the-house. The girls have had the female guidance and understanding that they need at this stage of their lives. Plus, both parents have had someone to live with all the time, so that neither was
entirely alone at any time. Plus, it kept their father involved in parenting so that he did not feel left out of it or like a visitor."

Jayne continues, "Some of the problems: I don't get to see my
son as much as I would like, and I don't get to know all his friends.
Since he works, goes to school, and is very active in musical groups, it
is very hard to catch him at home. His father says he doesn't see much
of him either. My ex-husband complains of not seeing much of our
older daughter, so it is a two-way street. Otherwise, problems are few.

"What suggestions have I for other single parents considering
divided custody?

1. "Don't live too far apart.
2. "Don't allow yourself to feel jealous of a step-parent spending time with your child.
3. "Do look at the benefits to the children.
4. "Make sure that *all* of your children know how much you love them.
5. "Keep communications open."

Divided custody is an untraditional approach to child rearing. Here, especially, it is essential to consider the needs of each child and the needs and capabilities of each parent. At its best, divided custody can combine custody of one or more children with joint custody. However, *you* will need to determine whether divided custody is right for you and, if so, what arrangement is best for your children, yourself, and the other parent. If by divided custody you mean that each parent will have sole custody of one or more children and the children living with you will have little or no opportunity to see the other children or the other parent, then there is no need for you to read further in this section. You can read Chapters 3 and 4 for ideas that can help any single parent.

If, however, you see divided custody as an opportunity to help your children by combining the positive aspects of sole custody and joint custody, you might consider the following recommendations:

1. Be flexible.
2. Respect and work with the other parent and be willing to put the children first.
3. Try not to live too far apart from the other parent.
4. Don't allow yourself to feel jealous of a step-parent spending time with your children.
5. Do look at the benefits to the children.
6. Make sure that *all* your children know how much you love them.
7. Keep communications open.

BREAKING THE MYTH: THE GAY AND LESBIAN SINGLE PARENT

A particularly difficult negative image to overcome is that of the gay or lesbian single parent—who is all too often seen as so preoccupied with personal sexual needs that he or she has little time, energy, or

desire to be an effective parent. Although I have no first-hand knowledge of being a gay or lesbian single parent, my conversations with
several gay parents have convinced me that this negative stereotype is
not necessarily true. Like any other type of single parenting, *it's what you
put into it that makes the difference.* Gay and lesbian single parents have
the same concerns as other single parents—with the exception of their
sexual orientation. I was fortunate in getting one detailed response
from a gay single parent from the Washington, D.C., area.

Alan, a gay single parent, shares a house with another gay father
with whom he has an intimate relationship. He has joint custody of his
12-year-old daughter and 10-year-old son. His children have lived
with him for two out of the four years that he has been separated
from his wife. Because of the way Alan has apparently been able to
maintain a stable family, while considering his own needs as a gay
person, I would like to share his comments with you, virtually in their
entirety.

"Sharing the house with another gay father has been very supportive. We help each other on baby sitting, work around the house,
talk after work, and so on. It has also been very emotionally supporting to have an ongoing intimate relationship and someone to go
places with and share with.

"My children have enjoyed the family situation and seem to
have adjusted very well. They like my friend very much and treat him
as one of the family. When doing things with the kids, it has helped
having two adults they can relate to. They are not so concerned over
spending time with me alone.

"While continuity has suffered because of the moving and shift-
ing, the children have adjusted to the new daily schedules and made
new friends. They must feel that they are secure in our love and that
the situation they are in is stable.

"I would offer the following advice to other men or women
considering a situation similar to mine:

1. "Take time to explain your relationship with others, so that your
   children know that you feel they are still the key relationship.
2. "Seek cooperative living arrangements with compatible friends.

"How have I reconciled my needs and interests with those of my
children? It is a balance sheet that constantly has to be rebalanced.
There are times that your needs must come first; at other times, theirs

come first. Just so that within every week there is a balance, then I think they understand and are willing to accommodate to that.

"I think explaining promiscuity is a problem. They also take great care to see that my gayness does not get communicated to their friends at school. I have cooperated with them in seeing that gay situations are not present when their friends are here.

"Our approach to problem solving is for all of us to state our opinions and discuss the problem, until we reach a decision that everyone is willing to live with.

"I handle discipline by insisting on some things and negotiate others. Some things, like TV watching, tend to slip away. Single parenting puts you at a disadvantage when supervising two kids with minds of their own.

"Security comes from a stable, cooperative environment and your love and concern. If anything, they have to take more responsibility and independence in single-parent situations.

"I keep the values I want to see followed up front and visible; otherwise, I encourage them to develop their own values.

"Why do we have joint custody and how has it worked? My wife insisted we both take responsibility and I felt I did not want to be cut off from the kids.

"The benefits are

1. We both get rest and relaxation when the kids are with the other parent.
2. We both have full, intensive interaction with the kids.
3. The kids get different viewpoints of life and values. They learn to be flexible and adjust to new living arrangements.

"The main problem is that my living situation is determined by availability of schools. I would prefer living farther into the city than I now live. My time and energy for gay concerns is limited when the children are here."

Alan continues, "Our shared-housing situation is very supportive for all of us. My son is on the YMCA soccer team.

"The children's mother and I basically respect each other and rely on the shared-custody situation to give ourselves a break from parenting. I would suggest to other single parents that a big motivation for working together with the children's other parent is to be a little selfish. Think of the time you will have to do things if you don't have the kids all the time. Share them instead.

"I keep my negative feelings about the children's mother to myself. It is no business of the kids, and they have to adjust to both of us.

"My parents and brother live in town and are supportive. We visit.

"Where my single friends are concerned, I have to plot my time with concern for the kids. If I can combine the two, it usually works out. My friend has become part of the family. Sporadic dates are far more difficult, especially if they sleep over.

"I still keep in touch with my married friends and they still visit once in a while.

"I would suggest that if you are a noncustodial parent, involve your children as much as possible in the things you like to do. Let them meet your friends. Make them feel that whenever they are with you, they fit right in."

A. Billy S. Jones is a social psychologist and the founder of Parents Who Are Gay (P-WAG), a support group for gay and lesbian parents in the Washington, D.C.–Baltimore, Maryland, area. According to the group's brochure, "P-WAG is for the man or woman who is a parent and who is gay or bisexual, for exchanging information about one's role as a parent and support of one another in his/her lifestyle and for discussions of oneself in relationship with children in an atmosphere of honesty and openness." P-WAG has offered a course in parent-effectiveness training for gay parents. Some of the other types of programs offered by P-WAG include a general meeting once a month with a "rap" session on a discussion topic or perhaps with a guest speaker; and at least one other "rap"/social event each month which includes the children.

Lacking personal experience with the needs and concerns of gay and lesbian single parents (except those common to all single parents), I would be presumptuous to offer suggestions. At my request, Billy Jones has kindly agreed to write for this chapter an article dealing with gay and lesbian single parents. I believe that Dr. Jones' article, while helpful to gay and lesbian single parents, can be valuable for those of us who are not homosexual. We can gain a realistic view of the needs and concerns of gay or lesbian single parents; and we can see that gay and lesbian single parents love their children, want to help them, and share many of the needs and concerns of other single parents. Thus, Dr. Jones' article is an ideal way to conclude our discussion of the gay and lesbian single parent.

LESBIAN MOTHERS
AND GAY FATHERS

"Being gay, to me, means that I see other members of my own sex as possible loved ones and that I am capable of being attracted sexually, emotionally, and spiritually to another man.

"Through my rejection of the prescribed masculine role and my acceptance of myself as a potential lover of another man, I believe that I am moral. This does not mean that I reject women, hate women, or will never sexually interact with women. It does mean that I am saying loud and clear to my children and other significant persons in my life that my current sexual orientation, preference and choice, is to relate to a designated man.

"Thinking of lesbians and gays as parents is beyond the realm of reality for many people who think only of parenthood as a result of a heterosexual union or who buy into the myths that gay men and lesbian women hate the opposite gender. The reality of bisexuality is often denied by gays and nongays.

"Many lesbians and gays do not make a sexual choice or become aware of a sexual preference for the same gender until after they have had some sexual experiences with the opposite gender.

"If we acknowledge that our psychosexual development is an ongoing process starting at birth and ending at death, we can understand, in part, the transition from a heterosexual union which brings about children to a single parent as a lesbian mother or gay father.

"Many lesbians and gays become parents by choice. Alternative approaches to parenthood such as foster parenting, adoptive parenting, extended families, and artificial insemination are often examined. Sometimes contractual arrangements are worked out between a lesbian woman and a gay man, or between a lesbian or gay person and a supportive nongay person. The death or sickness of a family member, close friend, or neighbor sometimes results in a lesbian or gay person assuming the responsibilities of a single parent.

"Shean became a father unexpectedly when he agreed to take custody of a child who was wandering about with his natural drug-addict father. Whereabouts of the mother is still unknown. Concerned about the child's immediate need for food, shelter and cloth-ing, Shean gave the addict father $25 and agreed to keep the child for a day. A week later the natural father showed up at Shean's home and begged him to keep the child. That was two years ago. With little resistance from the courts or social service agencies in San Francisco, Shean is now the legal father of a seven-year-old boy and continues to live as an "out of the closet" gay person. Now in his late 20s, Shean reflects that he had never thought of himself or any gay man as a parent.

"Unfortunately, society sees all lesbian mothers and gay fathers as 'single' parents. Wherein there are no legally recognized same gen-der marriages (although holy unions/blessings between same gender couples are performed, and Internal Revenue Service openly dis-criminates against lesbian and gay couples) there are many same gen-der families who do not consider themselves 'single.' If a family is defined as people who love and take care of each other while living together, then lesbian and gay 'couples' should be recognized and granted the same legal rights as heterosexual couples.

"The decision to share one's lesbian or gay identity with one's children should not be made until the lesbian or gay parent is com-fortable with his or her own sexual identity. Without self-acceptance, communication with children on sexual or intimate issues will be dif-ficult, superficial or impossible. Most parents are so uptight and unin-formed about human sexuality that children's innocent inquiries about hugging, kissing, nudity, penises, vaginas, or breasts still bring about responses referring to 'the birds and the bees' or 'when you are older.' (Just think of the parents' reaction to questions about anal or oral intercourse, masturbation or lesbian and gay relationships.)

"While many lesbian and gay parents feel that they cannot be 'openly' gay, I have chosen to be public about my sexual orientation, to be a gay activist, and to speak out on issues regarding gay and lesbian parents because I don't want the generations which follow me to have to experience the oppression, degradation, ignorance, and hostility of our current society. I want to be as positive a role model for those to come and for those who are as Martin Luther King was for Blacks, as Ghandi was for India, as Jesus was for Christians. My activism as a gay father is not a rejection of heterosexual parenting, but an example of alternative parenting—just as Gloria Steinem's ad-vocacy for women's rights is not a rejection of men's rights. My openness and modeling is also a way of furthering my personal growth. Becoming a 'single' parent has been a difficult decision that has involved many family chats, has brought many tears, and has aroused many fears. But I cannot continue the middle of the road stance connoted either by the status of bisexuality or as a gay married man; I cannot stay locked into presumed responsibilities to my children and use those presumed responsibilities to divert my energy and retard my personal growth. By being open and honest, I enable my children to relate to me as I really am, rather than as a dishonest traditional male role model. This has helped me to be a much better father than I otherwise might be.

"Many lesbian and gay parents recognize the importance of 'coming out' to their children when they examine the risks of their children learning from sources who are insensitive and ignorant about the issues of homosexuality. Some of these issues are ill-informed peers, pornographic literature, comedians' jokes, homophobic adults, or prejudiced media coverage.

"Other lesbian and gay parents refrain from 'coming out' to their children because they are not sure

A. How coming out might affect their children's sexual identity;
B. How their children might feel about them after learning of their parent's lesbian or gay identity;
C. Whom their children might tell—neighbors, family, peers, and
D. What kind of psychological impact "coming out" might have on their children.

"Alan Bell and Martin Weinberg of the Kinsey Institute for Sex Research reported in their recent study published in *Homosexualities—A Study of Diversity among Men and Women* that those homosexual men and women whose children knew about their sexual orientation tended to report that their relationship with their children was not noticeably affected by the children's knowledge or suspicion of their homosexuality. It is my observation that with more community lesbian- and gay-parent support systems (such as Parents Who Are Gay in the Baltimore-Washington area and Gay Fathers in San Francisco), changes in custody and visitation rights, removal of archaic sodomy laws, and changes in religious and cultural attitudes, lesbian and gay parents are more likely to go out of their way to share with their children what their sexual orientation is. With the coming about of women's rights, gay rights, and less rigid gender roles for men and women, even nongay parents are less uptight about their children being around and in the custody of lesbians and gays.

"Living arrangements for lesbian and gay couples reflect a variety of lifestyles which would baffle the best of sociologists. Wherein it is becoming more acceptable for unmarried male-female couples to live together openly and to share their status honestly with their children from previous relationships, such is often not the case with lesbian and gay couples—especially if one or both happen to be a parent.

"Courts often restrict custody and visitation rights of parents who have revealed their lesbian or gay identity. It is not uncommon that a lesbian or gay parent can see their children only in the presence of an 'appropriate' adult or courts may order that a 'lover' or same-gender friend or roommate cannot live in the same household with parent and child. While visitation rights are seldom denied (although they are more restricted than for nongay parents), custody is seldom granted to the parent revealed or thought to be lesbian or gay.

"The combination of heterophobia (fear of nongay family, friends, neighbors, coworkers), lack of self acceptance, homophobic authority persons (such as judges) and archaic laws regarding sexual issues and till-death-do-us-part marriages create deceptive living arrangements which often creates tension between parent, lover, and child(ren). Some lesbian and gay couples who do decide to live together will identify each other as roommate, member of the family (cousin, sister, brother, parent), or just friend. Often separate bedrooms are maintained 'for the sake of the children' and a great deal of restraint is imposed not to touch or use endearments 'in front of the children.'

"Some lesbian and gay couples maintain separate households while others set up separate bedrooms which are used only when the children visit. Many lesbians and gays in heterosexual marriages will remain in these marriages long after awareness of their homosexuality 'for the sake of the kids,' thereby modeling only a heterosexual lifestyle and option to their children. Married gay men and lesbians often treat their homosexual identity as a separate entity: as a secret to be shared only with another intimate friend, as a taboo subject not to be discussed with their spouses or their siblings. As highlighted by the 100 members of GAMMA (Gay Married Men's Association) in Baltimore and Washington, many married men who do come out to their spouses find it far more difficult to come out to their children.

"Many lesbian mothers and gay fathers are concerned about how parents' sexual orientation affects their children's sexual identity. This concern is reinforced by popular notions of appropriate gender behavior and what affects it, same-sex role models being considered critical to the development of properly feminine or masculine identity. Most parents are not aware of or have not accepted the conclusions of sex researchers such as Dr. John Money and Dr. Richard Green, that the essentials of gender identity are established very early in childhood (starting with parental programing and finalized at least by age five) by a process that is too complex for an explanation here. What parents do influence is their children's *attitudes* toward sexual issues and sexual orientation, parents influence their children's comfort and acceptance of people—black or white people; Jewish or Catholic people; crippled or retarded people; young or old people; rich or poor people; gay or nongay people. If parents lack self acceptance of their sexual orientation, of their lovers, or of certain sexual or intimate behavior practices, children will perceive that there is something negative about homosexuality, something sinful about same-gender lovers or something dirty about certain sexual/intimate acts. Children's orientation to sexuality itself is strongly affected by parental attitudes and behavior.

"In addition to reorienting themselves, lesbian and gay parents also find themselves teaching values and concepts not sanctioned by family, neighbors, or schools. By just honestly being themselves and feeling comfortable with themselves, their lovers and their children, lesbian and gay parents teach their children that it is OK to kiss and hug someone of the same sex; that it is OK to compliment men as well as women, that it is OK to hold and touch both men and women; that dads can cook, wash, and change diapers in addition to fixing cars and repairing the lawn mower; that moms can paint walls, repair roofs, and balance a checkbook as well as sew rips and iron jeans. While activists of the men's movement, women's movement, and lesbian and gay movement are making the demands and protesting the roles women and men have been locked into, single parents—especially lesbian mothers and gay fathers—are quietly but assertively undoing the stifling roles of masculinity and feminity, of mothers and fathers, of brothers and sisters.

"Of course the attitudes of others also influence the sexual attitudes of children—teachers, playmates, family, neighbors, baby sitters, media, et al. But parents generally have the greater amount of interaction with their children and have a greater amount of trust. If there is secrecy and tension around the topic of sexuality in the home, children may grow up believing that sex is something to be frightened of, something immoral and illegal, something sinful, something to keep hidden. In reality, our society does say for the most part that homosexual acts and relationships are immoral, sinful, illegal, dirty, sick, and should be kept hidden. But history has shown that the law of the land and the opinion of the majority is not always what it should be. Every ethnic group in America has experienced oppression and been denied both civil and human rights because they were in the minority and because the majority felt threatened by that which was not a part of their culture or make-up. Lesbians and gays are a minority population (10 percent to 20 percent) which has been denied basic human and civil rights, not because of their behavior, but because they dare to be different and dare to be honest about their feelings. Lesbian mothers and gay fathers are in the best position to teach their children (and thereby the future generations) that homosexuality is not something to be frightened of and to keep hidden. Neither homosexuality nor heterosexuality is contagious; fear, shame, guilt, and deception are contagious. Children are especially sensitive to the feelings and underlying communication of their parents.

"Therapists, activists, and child specialists generally agree that the children's age and personality should be considered when disclosing one's sexual identity. Preschool children are likely to be concerned with changes in their parent's behavior or in their routine parent-child interaction which directly affects the attention they are used to receiving. After a child starts school, there is usually a new interest in comparing the family situation with those of classmates. This is a period when children notice that Mary has a mom and dad, that Johnny has just a mommy, that Susan has grandparents, and that they have two mothers or two fathers. The interest is likely to be in how similar or how different the situation is to that of other children, rather than in the sexual arrangement of their parents. This is an excellent stage of development for the parent to discuss the many differences there are among people and how they live (multi-racial relationships, multi-cultural relationships, family traditions and roots, varying religious beliefs, socio-economic differences, political ideologies, and the positive realities of lesbian and gay relationships). A matter-of-fact attitude toward *all* variants of sexual preference is important; make clear distinctions between the *children's sexual development* and the *parent's sexual preference*. Adolescence is a time when peer approval is of great importance; therefore, parents of teenagers should prepare themselves to deal with some initial rejection of their sexual orientation, relationship, and lifestyle.

"Gay fathers are often concerned about the absence of a female adult in their household if the child is a daughter; lesbian mothers tend to concern themselves about whether or not they should give special attention to their male children. The same concerns exist for nongay single parents. But surveys and opinion polls show that the issue of homosexuality bothers people more than divorce, so the expressions of concern are usually stronger and are taken more seriously by a parent who is lesbian or gay in addition to being divorced. Courts tend to be leary also about awarding custody of female children to lesbian mothers and male children to gay fathers. It is important for lesbian and gay parents not to buy into the socio-psychological theories, the fears and ignorances, or the bigotries and prejudices which reflect overinvestment in sex-role stereotypes and an underinformed protest against homosexuality. It is very rare that children are exposed to a person of one gender only. In most instances, children need only explore their neighborhood, encounter friends at school, or attend community activities to be exposed to adults as well as children of both genders who are not all homosexually oriented and tend to utilize the community support system (Scouting, YM/YWCA, Big Brothers and Big Sisters) for positive role models in much the same manner as other single parents. There is no evidence that the sexual orientation of a parent makes any difference in terms of the child's sexual orientation, interpersonal relationships with peers or adults, female or male mannerisms, or other behavior personality traits deemed important by society's child specialists.

"Realizing that the court system, historically, has been unreceptive to changing lifestyles, advice often given to lesbian mothers and gay fathers anticipating a custody fight is to stay out of court, if possible. If custody is a top priority for lesbian and gay parents, some 'bargains' can be arranged. For example, one may settle for less property rights or grant extensive visitation rights. With the coming about of the women's and men's movements, changing laws granting civil rights to lesbians and gays, and improved attitudes toward homosexuality, custody and visitation rights to lesbian and gay parents are improving. An excellent pamphlet has been published by The National Lawyers Guild (558 Capp Street, San Francisco, California 94110) for one dollar, entitled *A Gay Parent's Legal Guide to Child Custody*. For a clear understanding of the court process, preventive measures, legal terms, court procedures, and dealing with an attorney, this pamphlet is a must. In selecting an attorney, lesbian and gay parents should consult with one who is not only competent and experienced in child custody and visitation rights, but also one who is sympathetic and supportive of lesbian-gay issues. Some legal references are

1. National Lawyers Guild, 558 Capp Street, San Francisco, California 94110, Telephone: 415/285-5066. (They also have offices in Washington, D.C., and Massachusetts. The San Francisco office can give more details.)
2. National Organization for Women, 425 13th Street, N.W., Suite 100, Washington, D.C. 20004.
3. Iowa Civil Liberties Union, 102 East Grand, Suite G-100, Des Moines, Iowa 50309. Telephone: 515/243-3576.

"Child-rearing practices vary among single lesbian and gay parents in much the same manner as they vary among single, nongay or married nongay parents. It takes a while to trust another person to help raise 'your' children, and the transition to 'our' children can be a slow and touchy process. Depending upon personalities, cultures, and one's own upbringing, a great deal of effort has to go into becoming compatible and consistant coparents in the areas of discipline, values, manners, intimacy, etcetera. Often there tends to be inevitable resentment by the biological parent of the disciplining nonbiological parent. It is not uncommon for children to use dissension between the parents to obtain their objectives. As with any parent, lesbian and gay parents will find themselves being criticized for being overconcerned, too strict, too permissive, too rigid, too loose, overprotective, underprotective. And, of course, one's status as a lesbian or gay parent will often cause one to worry about what effect one's lifestyle will have on one's children. Stop worrying! As a single parent, or a lesbian or gay parent, one's children will turn out no worse and no better than they would in a traditional family."

SUMMARY

We have explored together some of the varieties of the single-parent experience. Widowers and widows, never-married single parents, and gay and lesbian single parents each have their own special concerns—as well as those common to all single parents; however, you have seen how each situation *has* worked successfully. If you are in one, you might want to consider some of the suggestions and whether they can be of help to you. If you are not in one of these situations, perhaps this chapter has given you a better understanding of single parents who are.

An exciting part of single parenting today is the different custodial alternatives available. While the traditional arrangement of the mother having custody and the father being a noncustodial parent is still true for most single parents, it is not the only available alternative. Fathers having custody and mothers being noncustodial parents, joint custody or coparenting, and divided custody are three alternatives that have worked for other single parents. Whatever custodial arrangement you select, here are some suggestions that other single parents have found helpful:

1. Base your decision as to what type of custody you select around the needs, temperaments, and interests of both you and the other parent. Consider what can best help your children and you.
2. Treat the other parent with the same respect and consideration—as a parent—that you would like for yourself.
3. Keep the other parent informed as to the children's experiences and feelings—almost like an "emotional weather forecast."
4. Be flexible, and work together—insofar as possible—for the best interests of your children.

Chapter 6

You Don't Have
to Do It All Alone:
Resources to Help
You and Your Child

A frightening thing about being a single parent is that all the parental responsibility is placed solely on your shoulders. You no longer have the comfort and support of a husband or wife. Fortunately, there is a wide range of resources that can help you make your life easier, both as a person and as single parent. The only requirement, in most cases, is that you take the first step of contacting one of these groups. The initiative must be yours.

To help you take that first step, in this chapter I will deal with a variety of resources which can make your life easier. Although, obviously, every resource in the United States cannot be included here, I do discuss a variety of resources—most of which have offices throughout the United States—and offer some ideas based on my experience and conversations with both single parents and representatives of community agencies and various resource groups. If any one situation does not apply to you, please go on to the next. (Complete addresses and other information for these and other resources may be found in Appendix C.)

This chapter will perhaps give you the understanding and courage to better deal with the needs of yourself and your children. If there is one message to emphasize here, it is that you don't have to do it all alone.

FIRST THINGS FIRST: FINALIZING YOUR SEPARATION OR DIVORCE THROUGH FAMILY MEDIATION

Unfortunately, separation and divorce, at least in the United States, have tended to be based on hostility, tension, and arguments and negotiations between lawyers. The result is, all too often, bitterness and a feeling that one has been taken advantage of by the other party. This helps neither parent; and it particularly hurts the children—who want to feel free to love each parent, without being disloyal to either.

In recent years, there has been progress in this area. No-fault divorce—where *neither* partner has to be found guilty of wrong doing—and joint custody, or coparenting (discussed in Chapter 5), are two major improvements. A big step in resolving a divorce so that both parents and their children benefit, without the necessity of a bitter and drawn-out court fight, is *family mediation*. I asked Dr. Mark Lohman, one of the best-known family mediators in the United States, to discuss how family mediation can help single parents and their children.

"Family mediation," Dr. Lohman explained, "represents a voluntary alternative to the legal adversary system for separating spouses who want to work out a fair and equitable settlement, arising out of their marital relationship.

"The mediator meets with both partners, both individually and jointly, and has access to both spouses and the children. This helps all parties to arrive at a mutually comfortable solution.

"Family mediation offers the following advantages:

1. "It saves money and is less expensive than legal fights.
2. "It offers more creativity in finding solutions that meet the needs of all parties concerned.
3. "It stresses cooperative, rather than destructive, behavior.
4. "It is far more humane and sensitive to the needs of the children than is the traditional legal adversary system."

Dr. Lohman offered the following suggestions for finding a qualified family mediator:

1. "He or she should have experience in settling disputes.
2. "He or she should have at least a Master's Degree, or comparable experience which has demonstrated an understanding of the emotional dimensions of family life.
3. "The mediator should have a reputation in the community and be known for being fair.
4. "The mediator should have no ideological crusades or biases.
5. "The mediator's knowledge should include
   A. "A knowledge of domestic law.
   B. "Familiarity with tax aspects of separation agreements.
   C. "Practical knowledge about household and family budgets."

Dr. Lohman has offered to provide more information about family mediation, generally, and suggestions for locating qualified family mediators in your own area. If you contact him, you might want to request copies of some of the articles he has written about family mediation.

Dr. Lohman's address is

Dr. Mark R. Lohman
P.O. Box 103
Great Falls, Virginia 22066
703/759-9610

EMERGENCY SURVIVAL HELP

Department of Social Services

A problem common to many single parents, particularly those who are newly separated or divorced, is that of simply surviving. If you are poor and need emergency help, you might want to contact your county or city department of social services. They can offer a wide range of services—through programs such as Aid To Dependent Children (ADC), Homemaker Services, free day care, medical assistance, and food stamps. There are many other ways that your local department of social services can help you. Take a few minutes to give them a call.

Not all programs provided by your local social services department are limited to people who are eligible for welfare. If you meet certain income guidelines, you may be eligible for food stamps. If you are eligible, you pay a reduced amount, based on your income and the number of people in your family, and receive a month's supply (you must reapply each month) that you can use to buy food at grocery stores and supermarkets.

Working parents can frequently receive financial assistance to help pay for day care. This aid is also administered by your local social services department.

Legal Resources

If you have a very low income, you might qualify for Legal Aid. Legal Aid provides many legal services at no charge. To find out, contact your local Legal Aid office.

If your income is too high for Legal Aid, you might save money by consulting a legal clinic. Legal clinics, usually listed in the telephone yellow pages under lawyers, use trained legal assistants to handle many of the time-consuming routine aspects of your case (paperwork and basic research, for example). For this reason, and because legal clinics handle a larger volume of cases than do many private lawyers or law firms, they often charge lower fees than individual lawyers. Legal clinics frequently offer a less-expensive means to handle divorce and separation agreements. For those of you who are concerned about assembly-line approaches associated with clinics consider that at a legal clinic you are assigned your own lawyer. Because the repetitive and routine aspects of your case are handled by legal assistants, your lawyer is able to concentrate on the unique and distinctive aspects of your case.

If you call a legal clinic, remember that, usually, the first visit is free. At that time, you consult with a lawyer. Advice may be all you need, but you can discuss fees and other concerns at that time.

Most local bar associations have a lawyer-referral service, where you pay a minimal fee (usually $10 or $15) for an initial consultation. If you want to retain the lawyer to handle your case, the two of you work out the details at, or after, the first meeting. Like the initial consultation at a legal clinic, a lawyer-referral service offers an inexpensive way of obtaining legal advice.

PWP chapters, and other single-parent organizations, frequently maintain their own lists of lawyers who have helped PWP members. You might want to check with your local PWP chapter.

Medical Resources

Many communities have free or low cost clinics where you and your children can receive routine check-ups, immunizations, and other basic services. For more information, contact your local health department.

One alternative to traditional health care is a health maintenance organization (HMO). An HMO includes many or most health services which are usually located in a central medical facility. In a typical HMO, there will be internists, gynecologists, obstetricians, urologists, pediatricians, surgeons, other medical specialists, and frequently psychologists and/or psychiatrists. In a typical HMO, usually available through your employer, you pay a monthly (or bi-weekly) fee similar to an insurance premium. Then, you pay little or nothing for doctors' visits at the HMO. Frequently, prescriptions are available at reduced rates. A particularly valuable aspect of HMOs is that they include diagnostic, or preventive, visits, and are not just limited to the treatment of illnesses.

Nearly every state in the United States has at least one HMO. You might want to investigate whether your community has an HMO and determine whether this is a realistic solution to your family's health needs.

Day Care

If you have preschool-age children and need to work, day care is almost a necessity. There are essentially two types of day care.

Family day care is when an individual keeps children in her home. An advantage is the personal and home atmosphere, and the fact that, typically, there are relatively few children in a family day-care center. As a result, frequently, each child gets more individual attention than he or she would in a community day-care center. Two possible problems are the higher financial cost—for such care, it is often more difficult to obtain financial assistance from local social service agencies than for community day care—and the obvious fact that if the person providing the day care is sick, or wants or needs a vacation, the day care will probably not be available.

A useful guide to family day-care centers is *Family Day Care* by Alice H. Collins and Eunice L. Watson (Boston: Beacon Press, 1976).

Community-based day-care centers usually have their own buildings, equipment, and staff. They range from nonprofit centers to those operated for profit. The atmosphere is more like a play school than a family; nonetheless, a community-based day-care center is often a good place for children to obtain their first social experience. My daughter, Alia, made many friends at a local day-care center. The experience she gained in relating to other children her own age, learning to balance needs, to socialize and share, and her continually growing self-confidence—and realization that she can do well outside the family setting—have all contributed to Alia's growth.

Community-based day-care centers can usually provide a wide range of activities (from games and walks to trips), and their larger staff provides a greater likelihood than do family day-care centers that they will be open on a regular basis.

Some community-based day-care centers offer a *sliding-scale* tuition fee, which means that your tuition fee is based on your income and number of dependents. This might be something you want to ask about when considering a day-care center for your child or children.

If you have a low or moderate income, you might qualify for financial assistance for day care from your local department of social services. A federally funded program makes it possible for working parents (as well as those on welfare) to receive financial aid to help pay for day care. Eligibility and the amount of assistance are, like the sliding scale fee, based upon your income and the number of your dependents. Often, you have a choice of day centers (usually community based) to which you can send your children. For more information, contact your local social services department.

An excellent book is *The Day Care Book* by Grace Mitchell (Stein and Day, 1979). The author operated a day-care center for many years and has lots of good advice about choosing a day-care center, preparing children for day care and overcoming your guilt at leaving your children at a day-care center.

Before-School and After-School Care

If you work full time, your day-care problems don't end when your children start school. Your youngsters still have to be taken care of before and after school, when you are at work. Unfortunately, many communities still consider the only real family one that includes a mother who is home during the day. For this reason, before-school or after-school care is often unavailable.

I have learned about three successful before-school and after-school programs, which I hope will give you some useful ideas in determining what type of program best suits your needs, and in convincing your community of the need for such a program.

Columbia Association's Before-School and After-School Program

Columbia, Maryland, is a planned community, designed to offer alternatives for working parents. The Columbia Association, a community recreation and parks association, developed the innovative Before/After School Program, which has been in existence for over ten years.

The program is held in elementary schools in Columbia and is available to children from the first through fifth grades. The before-school program is from 7:00 to 9:00 A.M.; the after-school program is from 3:30 to 6:00 P.M. The entire program includes games, trips, quiet time, and other opportunities for group and individual activities. When school closes early, the after-school program begins earlier. Families who meet Federal Housing Administration (FHA) income guidelines for rent subsidies pay one-half the price for before- and after-school care.

A major advantage of the Columbia program is that it is held in the same school that a child normally attends.

During school vacations, and other days (except bad weather) that school is not in session, the Columbia Association offers an extensive Schools Closed Program from 7:00 A.M. to 6:00 P.M.

For more information about the Before/After School Program, and the Schools Closed Program, you may write to

Before/After School Program
Program Coordinator
Columbia Association
5829 Banneker Rd.
Columbia, Maryland 21044

You may also call 301/997-7039.

Reston Children's Center Family Satellite Program

The Reston Children's Center, Reston, Virginia, offers two before-school and after-school programs. One program is similar to Columbia Association's Before/After School Program, except that it is held in one location, the Center's building. Unfortunately, transportation is only available to and from one elementary school.

The Reston Children's Center Family Satellite Program is a unique approach to before- and after-school care for children ages 5 through 12.

The family satellite program differs from a center-based program in that care is offered by providers in the community. Providers are individuals in the community who provide child care in their own homes on a regular basis. The provider/child ratio is no larger than 1:5. The family satellite program offers children the flexibility of attending their neighborhood school, and being cared for in homes in their own neighborhood. This allows children greater opportunity to participate in extracurricular and community activities, greater proximity to their friends and siblings, and greater individual attention than they could get at a center-based or school-based program. The program is available throughout the school year and during school vacations, teacher workdays, conference days, and snow days. Parents have flexibility in the hours they are available for full-time employment.

Providers are trained and supervised by the Reston Children's Center. This combines the flexibility of a provider-based satellite program with the resources and services of a major community-based day care center. This day care center/provider relationship is the basis for the family satellite program.

For more information about the Family Satellite Program, write to

Reston Children's Center
12100 Sunset Hills Road
Reston, Virginia 22090
703/437-9478 or 703/437-5828

Latch Key

The Single Parent (the magazine of Parents Without Partners, Inc.), in its May 1979 issue, discussed a program, called Latch Key, that has worked in Minneapolis and other communities. (Many YMCAs in New Jersey offer the Latch Key program. For more information, if you live in New Jersey, contact your local YMCA.) With the permission of Barbara Chase, editor of *The Single Parent,* I am reprinting this article—entitled "Too Young To Go Home Alone" by S. Holly Stocking—in its entirety.[1]

Betsy Foster remembers it as a kind of nightmare.

When she took a regular part-time job after her divorce in 1972, she had an "incredible" time finding daycare for her two sons.

It was a particular problem finding care for her older boy. As a first-grader, he was too old for most preschool programs and family care situations. And in her mind, at least, he was still too young to go home alone after school.

As she recalls it, she "scrambled around" for months. At one point, she did find a family care home that would take both boys, only to discover the woman who ran the home was "almost cruel" to her children, and the home unclean and unsafe. The house had bugs, broken banisters, and uncovered heat registers on the floor. And when Betsy realized the mistake she had made in her desperation, she pulled her sons out immediately.

"It's the most awful experience to have to depend on some-

---

[1]*The Single Parent,* XXII, no. 4 (May 1979), pp. 7–9, 41.

body dug up from a pothole or from under a rock and hope that they are competent," she says, looking back on the situation. "Having to worry about hand-to-mouth daycare was the most untenable thing about the divorce for me."

It wasn't until a year or two later that Betsy and a couple of neighbors in similar situations learned of "Latch Key," a program which parents could organize to provide before-school and after-school care for school-aged youngsters. "One of us heard of the possibility that the shool district would allow (such a program) in our school—and the idea was just pounced on."

The group met with the principal of the neighborhood elementary school. He was supportive of the idea. They then contacted the school district. Personnel in the district's Community Education Department were actively encouraging members of the community to use the public schools for activities other than traditional schooling. If the parents would develop the Latch Key program themselves, Community Education personnel and local child care groups would help them apply for state and federal start-up money. They would also help them figure out the state licensing requirements, funding and fee structures, and the myriad of other sticky details that make such programs run.

It was enough. A corps of about eight parents met in the evenings to plan the program. The principal found them a room in the basement of the school—a damp and ugly storage room whose ceiling was criss-crossed with water pipes. And the parents set about fixing it up. One father built a platform which was gated on three sides and stuffed with pillows to form a "loft." Others helped paint the concrete walls with huge, whimiscal monsters from Maurice Sendak's children's book, *Where the Wild Things Are.* A number of the parents brought in plants which were hung from the ceiling pipes. The school donated shelving, cupboards, workbenches, tables, chairs, desks, games, and books.

The parents formed task forces—one to figure out the licensing requirements for the state, one to determine fees and seek additional financial support for the program, another to recruit staff, and still another to develop good public relations with school personnel and members of the community. And months later, the program opened with children from fifteen single-parent and working-parent families.

That was a little more than three years ago. Today the program, which many consider one of the city's best, boasts some thirty children, mostly from single-parent families. And, according to Randee Schaefer, city-wide coordinator for the Latch Key program, kids and parents alike love it.

For the parents, the program fits nicely with typical nine-to-five work schedules. It begins at 7:30 a.m. and runs until 6:00 p.m. Children from first through fourth grades (first through sixth grades at other schools) can elect to attend either the before-school program (7:30 to 9:00 a.m.), the after-school program (3:00 to 6:00 p.m.), or both. Kindergarteners, who are on half-day programs in the Minneapolis Public Schools, attend for more than half the day. In addition, the program is open during school holidays, teacher workshops, spring and summer vacations—times which can create enormous headaches for the average working parent.

The program is less expensive than most family care situations—about 80¢ an hour at this particular school (and less in Latch Key programs which are subsidized more heavily with local, state, and federal monies). A state subsidy picks up the tab for parents who cannot afford these prices.

Activities are especially geared to school-aged youngsters—with "large muscle" activities such as gymnastics and floor hockey; "small muscle" activities such as puzzles and Legos; arts and crafts such as painting and macramé; creative dramatics; and field trips to the zoo, swimming pools, museums, and other local places of interest.

And unlike the directors of most after-school activities, Latch Key leaders keep tabs on each individual child. As Latch Key Coordinator Schaefer explained it: "In a regular after-school recreation program, if the kids don't show up for floor hockey, no one cares. With Latch Key, however, if Johnny Smith doesn't show up, we get on the phone to the mother and check . . . Parents feel much more secure knowing someone is keeping track of their kids at all times."

As for the children in the Latch Key program, most seem to thrive on the organized recreation it provides. There is not the stigma to being a "latch key kid" that often exists when the term is assigned to kids who go home to empty houses, keys tied around their necks on strings or lanyards. In fact, it's almost a "status thing" with some children, according to parents. In many of the city's sixteen programs, there are waiting lists of youngsters who want to participate in the program's activities but who have one parent at home and so can enroll only if there are extra spaces available.

Latch Key programs are not unique to Minneapolis. Although there are no official estimates on the number of such programs, federal sources in Washington say the idea seems to be spreading. Programs that provide off-hours care in the public schools for school-age children (while not necessarily called "Latch Key") have cropped up in a variety of states in recent years, including Alabama, Arizona, California, Colorado, and Michigan. And when a Latch Key program in the Detroit suburb of Birmingham was given a couple of inches of publicity in *McCall's* magazine last year, the Birmingham School District was inundated with requests for information.

Observers say Latch Key is "an idea whose time has come." As enrollments decline in many school systems, increasing numbers of schools have empty rooms that can be used for such programs. As the divorce rate rises and the number of working mothers goes up, the need for child care increases. Because pre-schools, daycare centers, and family care homes stand to make more money by providing care to youngsters who need all-day programs, few are licensed to care for school-aged youngsters. As a result, the need for day-care for school-aged children is particularly acute. By one recent estimate, more than one million school-aged children have no formal care at all between the hours of school closing and the parent's return from work.

But probably the greatest single impetus to the development of school-based programs for latch key kids is the community education movement—a movement to make neighborhood schools centers for community-based and organized programs. Begun during the Depression, the movement has been gaining momentum since 1974 when Congress passed the Community Act to foster development of community education programs. To date, some 1500 school systems and some 5,000 individual schools have embraced the community education concept.

Minneapolis Latch Key Coordinator Schaefer believes the adoption of the community education philosophy in a school district is "very important" for a school-based Latch Key program to get off the ground. The organizers of programs in other cities agreed; some go so far as to say it's "essential."

Says Schaefer: "Many people say (taking care of children during non-school hours) is not the school's responsibility, that we have our hands full filling other needs . . . schools should be open from 9 to 3 and that's it." If a school district has already adopted the community education concept, she adds, it is "much easier to convince the necessary people."

Even when a district adopts the concept, however, getting a Latch Key program started is not easy. A basic tenet of the community education philosophy is parent involvement. School systems provide the building. They offer administrative support and may provide some personnel, insurance and supplies. But, with the exception of these things, the program is organized and run entirely by parents. For many working parents, particularly single parents, it can be difficult to find the time that is necessary.

When the program at Betsy Foster's school started, for instance, parents found themselves committed to many night meetings—with other parents, with the principal, and with officials from the school district. They had to fix up the room, decipher the state regulations, help the District's Community Education staff hire a coordinator to run the program, and set the fees. Then, on a monthly basis, the parent advisory board met to oversee the operation.

Betsy Foster, for one, shudders to remember all the bureaucratic "red tape" she and the others had to go through.

"Dealing with the state bureaucracy was really a hassle. You know, you stand in line for hours and then get to the window and they tell you that you're in the wrong line? It was an awful lot of work!"

The parents at her school also ran into some minor teacher resistance—individuals who didn't think schools should be used for daycare purposes.

But, all in all, she and others like her figure the end result is worth the effort. "It just saved my life," she recalls now. "I can't tell you what it felt like having a responsible, stimulating program available."

Of course, Latch Key does not solve all the problems of working parents. Some parents, for example, need daycare for their school-aged children only a few days a week, and most Latch Key programs take part-time children only if they have extra space. Understandably, programs depend on full-time enrollment for financial support. The Minneapolis Latch Key programs also do not provide care for sick children. Parents must find their own solutions when children come down with colds or the flu.

Latch Key does provide some needed answers, however—particularly for parents who feel their children would glue themselves to the "boob tube" or get into mischief or serious trouble if left untended.

As for Minneapolis' Betsy Foster her older son ironically was never able to take advantage of the program. By the time the program started, he had entered fourth grade and taken up piano lessons and sports. On the days he was not involved in such activities, Betsy says he would "curl up with a book . . . He is just one of those children who knows better than to fool around with matches."

For her younger son, though, Latch Key was (and is) a "lifesaver. It's a personality difference," Betsy says. "My younger son is just not as responsible."

In her view, Latch Key is much more than just another daycare program. In a very real sense, because she helped organize the program, Latch Key is hers. And for that reason, probably more than any others, it has worked.   □

You Can Start a Latch Key Program in Your Community . . .

It's not easy to organize a Latch Key program in the public schools. However, according to Randee Schaefer, Latch Key Coordinator for the Minneapolis Public Schools, you can minimize many of the problems if you follow a few simple steps:

- First, find out if your school district has adopted the community education concept. According to the concept, schools exist to be used by entire communities and to serve community needs at all times and not just during school hours. It can be much easier to develop a Latch Key program if your school district has embraced the community education philosophy.

If it has not, contact the Federal Clearinghouse for Community Education in Rockville, MD (800) 638-6698. (In Maryland—770-3000.) The Clearinghouse will provide you with everything you will need to know to lobby for community education in your school system.

- Write for information about Latch Key programs from other communities that offer them. For information about the Minneapolis Latch Key program, write: Randee Schaefer, City-wide Latch Key Coordinator, Florence Lehmann Educational Center, 1006 West Lake Street, Minneapolis, MN 55408. For information about Latch Key programs in Birmingham, MI, write: Shirley J. Bryant, Community Education Specialist, Birmingham School District, 746 Purdy Street, Birmingham, MI 48009.

- Find four or five individuals in your neighborhood who need before- and after-school care for their school-aged youngsters. Enlist them as full-fledged partners in your efforts.

- Make an appointment with the principal of your neighborhood school. Backing from the principal is essential. Go armed with information (Latch Key can work; it has worked in other places; we need it; if you provide us with in-kind services and a room, we'll do the rest). Ask if he or she is willing to promote the program with his or her staff and to endorse a survey of parents concerning their interest in such a program.

- If the principal is supportive, seek additional support from individual teachers and other key school personnel, from the PTA, and from other parent and teacher organizations. Also seek support from the local school board if it is needed and from local community groups—the Park Board, for example, or advocacy groups for child care. It may be possible to coordinate activities or services with some organizations.

- At the same time, conduct a survey to assess parents' interest. Explain what a Latch Key program can do for them. Emphasize that the program, while offered in school facilities, will be organized by parents and supported primarily by them. Get names, addresses, and phone numbers. Determine the number of children needing Latch Key, the hours, and vacation periods when Latch Key is needed.

- If response is good (50 replies out of 300, for example), call the parents and arrange a meeting. Be sure the principal and other key school staff are there. If people seem willing to develop a program, set up parent task forces to deal with state licensing requirements, staffing, programming, public relations, and financing. Remember the needs of each community will vary. One of the goals of Latch Key programs organized under the community education concept is to fit programs to needs. When programs are organized by parents and community groups—instead of by school or government officials—such fits are more likely to occur.

PAYING THE BILLS ON A REDUCED INCOME

Patricia Nurse, MEd., is an education consultant and home economist with expertise in housing and family management. Ms. Nurse mentioned three resources (their addresses are given in Appendix C) she believes can help single parents:

1. Consumer Credit Counseling Service (CCCS) provides financial counseling. (CCCS operates in all states except Delaware, Arkansas, Mississippi, and Alaska.)
2. Family Service Association of America (FSAA) agencies offer individual and family counseling, workshops, and other education programs. (These agencies provide service in Delaware, Arkansas and Mississippi.)
3. Extension Home Economics (usually listed under County Government, or with the Land Grant University in that state) offers workshops, educational programs, and other advice in areas such as food shopping and nutrition.

Money and Divorced Parents

I asked Ms. Nurse if she had any ideas or suggestions that might help single parents. Ms. Nurse offered the following:

"Money is a highly emotional topic and many couples, either going through a painful divorce or trying to rebuild their lives, are unable to discuss finances in a rational manner.

"Most couples ignore the financial aspect of their divorce and fail to realize that there is, usually, no way they can continue the style of living they presently have *and* establish a new residence for the other partner—given the same income.

"Divorce is a double-edged sword in terms of money. As financial counselors, we see women who for the most part not only have the responsibility of the children but are usually earning less than the man. They have a very difficult time trying to continue to work, care for the children, manage the repairs on the house, and wait for child-support payments that may be not only late but inadequate.

"On the other hand, we see newly-divorced fathers who are having a hard time financially trying to pay child support, possibly short-term alimony, and establish a new home that is adequate in terms of accommodating the children for visits.

"Fathers often have an awkward time during the children's visit, since the surroundings are unfamiliar and may be viewed as some sort of a holiday. Fathers frequently fall into the trap of entertaining the children on the weekends—a very costly and often less-than-satisfying visit.

"Money is the final bond that remains from the marriage relationship. It becomes, at times, the link between the two couples if they cannot communicate as parents or friends.

"Money, for the divorced couple with children, can be

> *Positive*—a time to discuss the way to maximize their resources in order to best meet the needs of the children and adapt to their new lives as single parents.
>
> *Negative*—a time to continue stress and resentment toward each other by refusing to adjust to lower life styles based on reduced income and continuing to blame each other for financial problems.
>
> *Manipulative*—a rejected woman can try to turn the children against their father by blaming all their troubles on his 'unwillingness to support his family.' She can use her anger to prevent his visitation from being carried out smoothly by requesting additional money in front of the children, or by forbidding the children to accept any gifts from their father.
>
> A rejected man may try to maintain control by using the child-support payments to force his own wishes or by withholding the payments to 'get back.'

Money can also be used by either partner as their only topic of discussion—excuses to phone or to continue arguments because they have not been able to establish a working relationship as parents, formerly married, who may or may not wish to remain friends.

Destructive—Children caught in the middle of two parents and money will be quick to play both ends against the middle. Also, they may label the parents and see the care-giver parent as stingy and mean and the visitation parent as nice and fun.

"The care-giver parent is viewed as the disciplinarian while the visitation parent becomes the entertainer—a truly false set of values that can have a destructive effect on the single parent–child relationship for both.

"Also, single parents should realize that they will have to discuss money as long as there are children involved, since circumstances will change and decisions will have to be made that are financial and involve both parents. The couple who develop communications skills as single parents will have the advantage, and I would urge all single parents to seek counseling to help ease the transition and to prevent further stress which will only make their job of single parent even more difficult."

Ms. Nurse recommends *The Family and Today's Money World* by Frances Feldman. The book is available (write for price) from

Family Service Association of America
44 East 23rd St.
New York, New York 10010

Budgeting Assistance

A typical Consumer Credit Counseling Service (CCCS) agency has trained counselors who will provide free budget counseling and help you set up a realistic family budget. CCCS will also arrange with your creditors to have them accept reduced monthly payments through its monthly payment plan. Under this program, you give CCCS all your credit cards (which they cut up and return to the creditors), promise not to incur any new debts without receiving CCCS's permission, and pay a small monthly service charge (the Baltimore, Maryland, CCCS charges two dollars) to cover bookkeeping expenses. In return, CCCS can usually persuade creditors to agree to reduced payments over a longer period of time than you could arrange yourself, so you can pay them and still meet your living expenses. You make your reduced payments directly to CCCS.

It is amazing how in one to three years (generally), your debts can be paid off. The peace of mind that comes with having resolved your debts and building a new life for yourself can be tremendous.

For more information about consumer credit counseling in your area, you can contact

National Foundation for Consumer Credit
1819 H St., N.W.
Washington, D.C. 20006
202/223-2040

Bankruptcy

Suppose you have too many debts and inadequate income to be accepted into a CCCS program. What can you do if you cannot keep up your payments? What happens if your creditors will not accept the CCCS payments? One answer might be personal bankruptcy. While bankruptcy is *not usually* the best solution for financial problems (you are not being fair to your creditors who have trusted you, and it is usually very difficult to ever regain credit), it does eliminate most or all of your debts and makes it possible for you to get a new start in life.

Since bankruptcy laws vary from state to state I would strongly recommend that you consult a lawyer or legal clinic if you are considering bankruptcy.

I MUST WORK, BUT WHAT CAN I DO?

One problem faced by many single parents, especially women who have been full-time homemakers throughout their married lives, is that they now have to work to support themselves but are unsure of what skills they have, or what jobs they can get. Also, many men and women who do have jobs may be dissatisfied and want to find more satisfying or financially rewarding jobs or careers.

Displaced Homemakers

The Displaced Homemakers Network offers women (and men, if they meet the qualifications) who are at least 35 years old and full-time homemakers who have suffered a loss of income due to separation, divorce, disability, or the death of a spouse, help in training for jobs and finding appropriate careers to enable them to support themselves and their children.

I was fortunate in having an opportunity to talk with Joyce Shemer Keating, director of training for the Displaced Homemakers Center, in Baltimore, Maryland. Ms. Keating explained how the Baltimore Center's program operates:

"After determining a woman's eligibility, she receives counseling. At that time, a plan of action is determined. The woman may need more counseling, legal assistance, food stamps, family counseling, or housing. (The Women's Legal Center, in Baltimore, can offer legal assistance, if necessary.)

"There is a common myth that a job solves all problems. We have found that before beginning to train for a job, a woman needs to progress from an emotionally overwrought state to a more stable emotional situation. At that time, we enroll her in our Career Path.

"The Career Path is a one-month series of workshops that is divided into three sections:

1. *"Self-Evaluation*—Here, a woman learns that she is not alone in her situation. Others, too, have experienced the same problems.
2. *"Coping Skills*—Here, she learns how to manage stress; assertiveness; time management; and how to set priorities.
3. *"Job Preparation*—Here, we teach skill identification, job-market realities, nontraditional careers, career investigation, and interviewing for jobs.

"During a woman's participation in the Career Path group, a group cohesiveness develops. From this, she gains strength and a feeling of self-assurance. A participant also has higher self-esteem. The Career Path helps her translate and identify her home skills into job terms.

"At the end of the Career Path Program, a participant receives feedback from all our staff. Then, she returns to her counselor and, together, they determine whether she is ready for training.

128

"We have two requirements for training: emotional stability and a sense of direction.

"We also have four criteria for job readiness:

1. "An ability to keep appointments on time, and be on time, generally.
2. "Being able to arrange your life so you can work a certain amount of hours when needed. (This might involve you and another participant splitting a full-time job.)
3. "An ability to set realistic career goals and plan realistic steps to achieve them.
4. "Knowing and having confidence in yourself.

"Training consists of sending a participant to school, on-the-job training, or providing a Center internship. (An internship is a six-month job in a supportive setting.) Here, a woman can get used to working and having some money coming in.

"An example of self-employment training was a woman who did independent home cleaning by contract. After a four-week class, she continued to have regular meetings with her counselor. We loaned her a vacuum cleaner until she could afford her own. After eight months in business, she had earned over $25,000 in gross income.

"We have found that, generally, three to six months are needed before a participant's self-confidence and attitude improve to a major extent. (On-the-job training is financed by Center stipends.) For example, one woman got a job as an intake assistant in the Victim Witness Assistant Program of the County Department of Juvenile Services. Her first evaluation, one month after starting, showed [that she had] little self-confidence. However, by the time of her second evaluation, several months later, she had developed a new program, suggested changes, and made other major contributions. In short, she was like a whole new person.

"Untraditional careers are another possibility. For example, one woman had fixed things at home. She had taken apart her lawn mower, and wanted to work with electrical systems. With a traditional employer, there was too much pressure. Now, she is enrolled in an electricity course.

"The major problems of our participants are age—the average age is 48 [people can join if they are as young as 35]—and a lack of self-esteem.

"One suggestion I can offer potential clients is to volunteer regularly and treat your volunteer job as a 'paid' job. If you work at the same volunteer job on a regular basis, you can gain skill, confidence, and self-esteem."

Displaced Homemakers has developed a national network. For information about the Displaced Homemakers center nearest you, contact the national headquarters.

Displaced Homemakers Network
755 8th St. N.W.
Washington, D.C. 20001
202/347-0522

Other Career-Counseling Services

Community colleges frequently offer free career counseling to adults. They also have practical career-based programs, which are usually inexpensive and relevant to available jobs and employers in your area.

Colleges frequently offer extensive career-counseling services for adults. Frequently, they can help adults better understand their interests and find an appropriate career-based or academic program.

Alternative career-counseling services can help you to develop your own life and career goals, and give you support and advice in finding the right type of job for you. Unfortunately, I don't know of any national organizations which maintain a list of these centers. You might check with women's groups, colleges, and libraries in your area.

LEARNING PRACTICAL SKILLS

When you become a single parent, you and you alone have the responsibility for your home, your car, and those other essential aspects of day-to-day life. Community colleges, "open" or alternative universities, or learning centers frequently provide courses in such areas as automobile maintenance, cooking, home repairs, and the like. If such courses are not offered, you might want to express your interest to one of these schools. This might well encourage them to offer this type of practical skills program.

Your local state university may well have an extension division which offers community-based programs. For example, the University of Maryland's Home Extension Division offers advice in planning balanced and nutritious diets within income limits. Your local department of social services or family service agency may be able to offer advice and help in household and time management.

Your local YMCA or YWCA may be another place which can help you to acquire the practical skills you need. Frequently, your local single-parent group (PWP, for example) can start a co-op or exchange program. In this type of program, you contribute a skill or resource; in exchange, you receive help from someone else who contributes a skill or resource you need.

I recently had an opportunity to talk with Marie Mayor, the vocational education equity specialist for the Maryland State Department of Education. According to Ms. Mayor, every state in the United States has at least one vocational education equity specialist whose job it is to ensure that public schools make available to men and women (students and adults) a full range of courses—on a nonsexist basis—to prepare them for the dual role of career person-homemaker. According to Ms. Mayor, adult men should have no hesitation in investigating home economics courses in public schools or community colleges. Likewise, women should not hesitate to check the availability of career-based programs. If these programs are not currently being offered, they generally can be—provided you can find ten people who want to enroll. For more information—both about how your schools can help you develop homemaker or career skills, and the name and address of *your* state's vocational education equity specialist, who can give you more specific information about programs in your area—you may contact

Ms. Marie Mayor
Vocational Education Equity Specialist
Division of Vocational-Technical Education
Maryland State Department of Education
200 West Baltimore Street
Baltimore, Maryland 21201
301/659-2566

GOING BACK TO SCHOOL

Frequently, you will want—or need—to return to high school or college. The reasons can vary. You may just want to get a college degree; possibly, you need specialized training for a career. You may merely want to take courses for enrichment or enjoyment. Whatever your reason, institutions of higher learning are increasingly attempting to meet the needs of adults (particularly since the declining birth rate is causing a decline in the number of younger students).

Community colleges are generally inexpensive and offer career counseling, and career-based programs in areas such as nursing, computer programming and accounting. Most community college career programs are closely related to your local economy. For this reason, there is usually a good chance of your finding a job when you complete the program.

Colleges and universities offer a variety of programs, both career and academic. If you are considering a new career, one thought might be to contact the individual institution's placement service to ask what fields seem to be in demand by employers. You might also indicate your own interests and ask the placement staff's advice. Thus, you can gain a more accurate idea of what career is best for you. You can then contact the college of your choice for admissions and degree requirements.

Colleges and universities are increasingly realizing that adults usually have great difficulty attending classes full time. For this reason, many institutions are offering alternative ways of obtaining a degree.

In the Washington, D.C.–Baltimore, Maryland, area, for example, there are at least two institutions that offer special degree programs for adults. The University of Maryland has one entire college—University College—devoted to serving the needs of adults. Under one program, students do most of their work at home, on an independent-study basis, and attend classes full time for a few weeks each semester.

Another innovation in higher education is *experiential learning*. Under this program, a student's experiences outside the classroom (home, work, hobby, or other appropriate experience) are translated into college-level credits. This means for achieving such credits is through a portfolio. Here, a student documents and tries to justify his or her life experiences as equivalent to college-level credits. If the faculty agrees, it recommends how many credits a student should receive.

A list of colleges and universities throughout the United States that offer experiential learning is available from the Center for the

Assessment of Experiential Learning (CAEL). CAEL's publication, *Opportunities for Prior Learning*, 1979, is available for a charge from

CAEL
American City Building, Suite 212
Columbia, Maryland 21044

You can also learn about institutions in your own area that offer experiential learning by calling CAEL's toll-free number (except in Maryland): 800/638-7813.

Another option offered by University College, and several other colleges throughout the United States, is the British open-university approach, developed in the 1960s and adapted for United States needs.

According to David Ruth, at University College, the Open University is characterized by

1. Six to nine credits per course
2. Courses which are interdisciplinary in scope
3. A program designed for highly motivated adults who are taught by tutors in a more personal student-oriented framework than is possible in traditional education
4. Optional classroom attendance
5. Printed lectures which are available as a substitute for in-person attendance
6. Contact with one's tutor through optional weekly seminars or the telephone
7. Flexibility of time and hard work as the key ingredients

The institutions in the United States and Canada that currently offer the Open University include

University of Maryland: University College
Southern Illinois University at Edwardsville
Empire State University, New York
Minnesota Metropolitan University
Athabasca University in Canada.

A consortium of New York City colleges and universities uses a program developed by WNET-TV.

For more information about the Open University and where it is offered, you may call Open University's New York City office: 212/935-8956, or write to them at

Open University
110 East 59th Street
New York, New York 10022

For information about the various programs for adults offered by University College, contact

University of Maryland
University College
Adelphi Road and University Blvd.
College Park, Maryland 20742

Notre Dame College (Baltimore, Maryland) offers a weekend college, which allows students to attend classes every third weekend. In this way, college courses can be integrated with students' individual life styles, rather than interfering with job and family responsibilities. For more information, write to

College of Notre Dame of Maryland
Weekend College Director
4701 North Charles St.
Baltimore, Maryland 21210

Notre Dame college also offers an extensive continuing education program for women who want to take courses for either credit or enrichment. For more information, write to

College of Notre Dame of Maryland
Director, Continuing Education Program
4701 North Charles St.
Baltimore, Maryland 21210

A useful guide, available at most public and academic libraries, is *A Guide To Alternative Colleges and Universities* by Wayne Blaze, Bill Hertzberg, Roy Krantz, and Al Lehrke (Boston: Beacon Press, 1974). The book lists campus-based B.A. programs, two year A.A. (Associate in Arts) programs, external degree programs (where students spend little or no time on campus), special programs, and free universities. Tuition costs do not have to be a major problem. There are basic education grants, provided by the federal government to help students of any age attend college. Many states also provide financial aid. There are also special loan programs to assist students. For more information about these and other financial aid programs, contact the college of your choice, and ask for the financial aid department.

FINDING YOURSELF

Obviously, you have to adjust to your life as a single parent. Your attitude and adjustment will probably determine whether single parenting becomes a positive experience or a burden. Fortunately, there are counseling resources to help you get through the traumatic stages and begin to discover your own potential as a person and single parent.

Peer-based Counseling

Hotlines and walk-in counseling centers are two examples of peer-based counseling services. These are staffed—often 24 hours a day—by trained nonprofessional volunteers. These centers are places where you can talk about anything that concerns you. The nice thing is that you are talking with a "real person" (as opposed to a professional) who may well have some of the same experiences you have. The peer counselor can be understanding and supportive, rather than judgmental. This can help you realize that your situation is not as frightening as you thought. Peer-based counseling centers usually provide extensive information and referral; for this reason, they are a good source of learning about community resources and finding long-term professional counseling.

For myself, I have found the advantages of peer-based counseling centers to be the following:

1. They are available when I need them—usually 24 hours a day.
2. I can be anonymous, if I choose.
3. They are "safe places" to help me work out my problems and prevent me from burdening my friends with more than they can handle.
4. I receive empathy, support, and encouragement, not criticism and judgment.

5. I am talking to other real people, many of whom have experienced what I am going through.
6. If I need help, I can quickly obtain information and referral service.

Single Again Courses

Many community colleges (and some colleges, and community organizations) offer special "single again" courses. These courses, generally 6-8 weeks, offer the newly single person an orientation to single life. Some of the topics discussed include divorce; alimony and child support (usually discussed by a lawyer); building a new life; dating, relationships and sex; and being a single parent. Check to see if your local community college, or other community organization, offers a "single again" course. If not, possibly a singles' resource center (such as SOLO, in Portland, Oregon) may offer this type of program.

Individual Counseling

A professional psychologist, social worker, or psychiatrist can be a big help in working out your personal problems and helping you build a new life for yourself. Your county or city mental health department can give you the names of clinics, community mental health clinics, and individuals in private practice. A peer-based counseling center and your local single-parent organization are other sources of information about counseling resources.

The Family Service Association of America (FSAA) is the national association of, and accrediting body for, family counseling agencies throughout the United States. Family Service Association of America agencies offer individual and family counseling for adults and children. Frequently, these agencies offer support groups and other special services for single parents and their children. Fees are usually adjusted based on your income, number of dependents, and expenses. For more information, and to learn which FSAA agency serves your area, contact

Family Service Association of America
44 East 23rd Street
New York, New York 10010
212/674-6100

Therapy Groups and Other Support Groups

Therapy groups can be either a substitute for or a supplement to individual counseling. In a therapy group, there are one or two professional therapists who are facilitators and ensure that no participant is hurt or injured by the group. At its best, a therapy group offers a setting in which a participant can discuss his or her feelings and receive other group members' support, encouragement, and suggestions.

Single-parent support groups, women's or men's groups, and consciousness groups are other examples of support groups that have helped other single parents.

The Beginning Experience

The Beginning Experience is an attempt to help separated, widowed, or divorced people who are past the initial stage make a new beginning in life. This weekend experience—similar to Marriage Encounter—is designed by and for Catholics but is open to members of all faiths. For more information about the Beginning Experience, see Appendix C (under Single and Single Again Resources).

YOU AND SINGLE-PARENT ORGANIZATIONS

With the help of single-parent (and singles') organizations, you can make a new life for yourself as a single parent and as a single person.

Parents Without Partners (PWP)

The largest, and best-known, single-parent organization in the United States and Canada is Parents Without Partners (PWP). Starting as an idea in 1957, PWP has expanded into an international self-help organization for single parents and their children. There are over 170,000 members in the United States and Canada, as well as an affiliated—but autonomous—PWP group in Australia.

PWP's information center, located at the organization's headquarters in Washington, D.C., includes an extensive collection of books and pamphlets relating to the needs and concerns of single parents and their children. PWP headquarters is responsible for administering the membership records, coordinating regional, zone, and national conferences, and other nitty-gritty organizational activities. PWP also acts as an advocate for single parents before Congress, and elsewhere in matters affecting single-parent families. The organization also has published several excellent lists of recommended books and other resources for divorced and separated people, widows and widowers, fathers, and other groups. For a list of these and other useful materials, write to

Information Center
Parents Without Partners, Inc.
7910 Woodmont Ave.
Washington, D.C. 20014
202/654-8850

Virginia Martin, PWP's executive director, told me that when she first started working for PWP several years ago, she was shocked to learn that there was no information center, where books and other materials relating to single parents were collected and housed. Aside from being the publishers of *The Single Parent* magazine, PWP was essentially a confederation of local PWP chapters, with little or no national coordination. In the past several years, however, PWP has developed an information center, greatly expanded its educational and information activities, required PWP chapters to devote more time to educational and family activities (rather than emphasize social functions), served as an advocate for single-parent families, and increasingly gotten involved in coalitions and other groups concerned with families.

Connie Manfreda, PWP's international president from 1979-1980, told me that "PWP represents all single parents—whether or not they are members of PWP." Ms. Manfreda is proud of PWP's educational and family activities, both local and national, and believes that PWP should be a true community—nationwide, worldwide—of single-parent families. (As a matter of fact, she suggests that anyone who is interested should write to PWP's information center in Washington, D.C., for the address of other single-parent organizations throughout the world.)

It is the local chapters of PWP that are of most interest and help to single parents. The weekly dances and other social activities are well known. Equally—and possibly more—valuable are the discussions, family activities (trips and holiday gatherings, for example), parenting courses, workshops, and local publicity about the positive characteristics and needs of single parents and their children.

Joyce Wilcox, president of PWP's midstate chapter, in Baraboo, Wisconsin, told me that in her small town, PWP offers its members a real sense of community. "We care about each member," Joyce told me. "We keep in touch with each member by phone, showing that we care about her or his welfare. The family activities offer a real sense of comraderie, while the discussions provide much needed support and encouragement."

In my own PWP chapter (Chapter 1, Baltimore, Maryland), I have enjoyed the discussions. It is a great feeling to know that I can be myself, share my feelings—and learn about those of other single parents—and realize that I am part of a single-parent community, not an isolated single parent with insurmountable problems. Also, the social activities offer an opportunity to see old friends and meet new ones.

When I think of family activities, I will never forget the first time my children attended a Washington, D.C., PWP family activity. This was an afternoon outing in Lake Needwood Regional Park, shortly after my children had come to live with me. I was excited yet scared. I felt isolated from both the single community—with its primary emphasis on activities for adults—and the nuclear family society, with its stress on two full-time parents. It felt good to "come home" to "my" community of single parents. The children and adults relaxed, and there was an informality and a ready acceptance of each other that made the afternoon remarkably pleasant. After that experience, I realized that I need never again feel isolated. I knew, then, that I could—and would—succeed in making it as a single parent.

PWP family activities can be tremendously supportive for non-custodial parents, also. An outing such as this one to Lake Needwood Regional Park offers them a way to enjoy being with their children, while sharing an activity as part of a single-parent community. The children can make new friends, and the parents can benefit from the company of other adults.

I have seldom been as proud of being part of PWP as I was when, in September 1979, Nancy McGrath—a teacher, and the program and education coordinator for Baltimore's PWP chapter—invited me to participate on a single-parent panel for a class she was teaching, on "Single-Parent Families," to a group of junior high school teachers from Baltimore County. As my two fellow panelists and I discussed the ways in which our single-parent families were a *positive* influence on our children and ourselves—as individuals and as a family—and as we pointed out some of our problems with the schools, while offering some suggestions for resolving them, I realized that we were examples of successful single parents. As recently as two weeks ago, Ms. McGrath told me that we had really opened people's eyes. She explained, "Most of these teachers just see the crisis and trauma stages of single-parent families. You three gave them a chance to see how a single-parent family can—and does—work on a long-term, successful basis."

PWP membership is open to any single parent who has one or more living children and is single through separation, divorce, death, or never being married. (Some chapters require that at least one child be under 18, or under 21.) Each prospective member must have his or her single-parent status verified by a minister, doctor, or person who knows the applicant personally. Child custody is not a requirement for membership. Once a PWP member, you can participate in *any* PWP chapter.

For more information about PWP, and information about PWP chapters in your local area, contact

> Parents Without Partners, Inc.
> 7910 Woodmont Ave.
> Washington, D.C. 20014
> 202/654-8850

Montcosps: An Example of a Local Single-Parent Group

Sometimes, your local PWP chapter may not meet your needs. This was the case for many single parents in the Washington, D.C., area in 1969. Chapter 60, (the largest chapter in PWP) had nearly 4,000 members. As a result, many younger single parents with school-age and preschool-age children were "turned off" by Chapter 60's bureaucracy, what they saw as its rigidity, and the seemingly overwhelming majority of mature single parents whose children had already grown up and left home. As a result, the Montgomery County Single Parents (Montcosps) was born.

The club has about 350 members. Its motto is Caring. Montcosps sees itself as an extended family of single parents. Its size provides plenty of opportunity to meet new people. At the same time, because Montcosps is a relatively small group, there is a good chance to get to know people well.

What does such a group mean to its members? A member since 1976, I think of what Montcosps has meant to me: The special holiday gatherings are a real antidote to feeling isolated as a single parent. The dialogues (discussions) have a depth, warmth, and sense of caring and sharing that is unusual—even among single-parent organizations. I find the socials are a great way for me to renew old friendships. (As a matter of fact, another member and I have frequently played piano and harmonica duets, spontaneously, in the relaxed atmosphere of a Montcosps social.) Finally, Montcosps has a special virtue: flexibility. The club's smallness, independence from PWP and other organizations, and responsiveness to its members' needs allow for a lot of flexibility. When I mentioned writing this book, for instance, the club gave me its wholehearted support. Special dialogues were even arranged to help me obtain useful ideas. Other members' suggestions have led to athletic teams, special trips, and other programs.

Montcosps is to be lauded for two reasons. First, it is a stimulating and rewarding group for single parents of school-age and preschool-age children (to join Montcosps, you must have at least one child under 18 years of age. Also, only one of the parents may join. If you join, your former spouse cannot, and vice-versa). Second, it is a good example of what can be done when existing single-parent groups do not meet your needs. (Another option is to consider starting a new PWP chapter.)

For more information about Montcosps, you may contact

Montcosps
c/o John Holl
8807 Arliss Street
Silver Spring, Maryland 20901
301/587-6973

Single Parents on Campus and Community (SPOC)

Sometimes, what you need, as a single parent, is not a lot of social activities, but just support and help in succeeding as a single parent. In recent years, many adults have been returning to colleges and universities to pursue their education. Many of these are single parents. Also, many faculty, staff, and community residents are single parents. In response to the special needs of these groups of single parents, Joan Hess Russell, in June 1978, started an innovative resource group on the University of Colorado campus, in Boulder, Colorado: Single Parents on Campus (SPOC). Ms. Russell supplied the following information about SPOC—which I have received permission to reprint from the group's brochure:

"SPOC was organized at the University of Colorado, June, 1978, as a student group. It is a non-social support network for single parents, their children, and others interested in the area of single parenting. The main goal of SPOC is to help single parents accept their present role as a positive and rewarding experience. The SPOC programs are designed to help single parents deal with their multifaceted role by providing ideas and support to assist in keeping problems at a minimum. SPOC offers a variety of support services for single parents and others concerned with single-parent issues. These include

1. A drop-in center, operating from 9:00 to 5:00 P.M. Monday through Friday. The center is the base for all activities of the organization and provides a place for single parents to receive assistance with issues of a personal or academic nature, gain access to educational resources and referral information, and just drop by and chat.
2. SPOC coordinates a big-brother, big-sister-type program, where student volunteers spend time with a child from a single-parent family.
3. Emergency Locator Service provides a means of locating a single parent on campus, in the event of an emergency involving his or her child.
4. Students of Single Parents (SOSP) is a group of university-age

students from single-parent homes who meet regularly to discuss their feelings about growing up in a single-parent home. In addition to providing for each other, SOSP members meet regularly with SPOC members to serve as a resource and sounding board. Sharing between university-age students and single parents has proven to be rewarding for all involved.

5. Rap Sessions and Panel Discussions: Rap Sessions are held weekly to provide a forum for single parents to share and discuss ideas that are important in their lives. Support, solidarity, and a feeling of togetherness is generated throughout these interactions. Panel discussions are planned regularly on topics relating to single parenting.

6. SPOC works closely with university housing officials, and serves as an advocate for single parents in university-related issues.

7. SPOC is now doing research on single-parent issues, in coordination with the university's psychology and sociology departments.

"SPOC is a Colorado non-profit, tax-exempt corporation."[1]
If you would like more information about SPOC, you may write

to

Joan Russell
Single Parents on Campus and Community
University Memorial Center
University of Colorado
Boulder, Colorado 80309

Other Resources

Many communities have their own single-parent resource groups or resource centers, which have no official connection with PWP. Typically these groups offer support and assistance, with few, if any, social programs. See Appendix C (Under Single-Parent Organizations) for a list of these groups.

[1]Single Parents on Campus: *Brochure*. Boulder, Colorado, 1979.

YOU AND THE SINGLES'
COMMUNITY

In addition to your needs as a single parent, you have needs as a single adult. Most communities have at least one club for single people. Generally, there are a variety of organizations from which to choose. Libraries and peer-counseling centers are two places where you can obtain information about available singles' organizations in your area. Churches and synagogues, YMCAs and YWCAs, and Jewish community centers frequently have their own singles' groups. The Unitarian Church offers singles' discussions (usually on Friday nights) that are similar to the single-parent discussions sponsored by PWP. Also, a number of cities have singles' magazines which list both singles' organizations and special events.

Singles Enjoying the Arts (SETA):
An Example of Starting Your Own
Singles Group

Sometimes, you may find that existing singles' groups are not right for you. Possibly, they do not offer activities you enjoy. Perhaps the people are not your type. What can you do in this situation?

One answer is to consider starting a new organization. It takes work, but it can be satisfying to meet not only your own needs but those of kindred spirits. I had this experience in November 1977 when—while driving home from work—I asked Eva Stunkel, "Why don't any of the singles groups in our area offer cultural activities? I would much rather go to museums, good films, and concerts than go all the time to dances and parties." Eva replied, "You and I have these interests, but what do we have in common with other single people, generally, except that we are all single?" It was then that the two of us decided the solution was to start a new organization: Singles Enjoying the Arts (SETA).

We were fortunate in obtaining the cooperation of local newspapers, radio stations, and a cultural magazine in our area (*Forecast*); and, at our first meeting, in March 1977, we had nearly 50 people. At that meeting, a steering committee was organized. We made mistakes—such as focusing on interest groups, rather than on a variety of activities in each local area (SETA serves both Washington, D.C., and Baltimore, Maryland.) Finally, we found area coordinators

144

for both communities. These coordinators have developed activities in their area, informed the public about SETA, handled inquiries and memberships, and printed a monthly newsletter. Our activities have included folk dancing, music listening, visiting museums, wine tasting and gourmet dining, and attending concerts, theaters, and films. SETA members have also assisted in fund-raising drives for local public radio and television stations.

What I especially enjoy about SETA is the opportunity of making friends in a noncompetitive, relaxed atmosphere and of sharing my interests with kindred spirits. I appreciate the friendships I have made with other singles—of all ages—without necessarily thinking of each person as a potential dating partner. It is also gratifying to have helped fulfill a need of the singles' community in the Washington-Baltimore area. (As of the end of 1979, SETA had approximately 600 members.)

To reflect your needs and interests, you can start your own singles' group. Consider who might be interested in your group and what you have to offer that cannot be obtained elsewhere. Publicity is essential. Many newspapers will provide free listings for community organizations, and radio stations will sometimes offer free public service announcements. Bulletin boards at employment centers, colleges, and in your community are another resource. If your area has cable television, frequently a community access television station is available. Perhaps you can arrange for air-time to discuss your organization. You might also contact other organizations (single and otherwise) to gain the benefit of their advice and experience.

To receive more information about SETA, you can write to

SETA
917 Elm Rd.
Baltimore, Maryland 21227
or

SETA, Inc.
P.O. Box 9367
Washington, D.C. 20005

Singles' organizations are a resource that can help you in your new life. Remember, no matter what your interest (social activities, skiing, sailing, the arts), there is probably a singles' club you can enjoy. If there isn't, consider starting your own.

RELIGION AND THE SINGLE PARENT

According to Ann Parks, information coordinator and specialist for PWP International, an increasing number of churches are trying to identify and meet the needs of single-parent families. Ms. Parks recommends that you contact your local church or synagogue to inquire about their programs for single-parent families. If none exists, perhaps you can help start one.

Recall that Unitarian churches frequently offer discussion groups for single people.

The Catholic Church sponsors many groups for separated and divorced Catholics. For more information, contact

North American Conference of Divorced and Separated Catholics
5 Park Street
Boston, Massachusetts 02108
617/742-4461

The Jewish Community Center of Greater Washington offers a single-parent-family supper one weeknight each month. The children help prepare the meals—which are frequently related to individual Jewish holidays. Vivian Weiss, the JCC's supervisor of adult social programs, also mentioned that single-parent families are always welcome at the monthly Sunday family programs. For more information about the center's programs for single-parent families, you may contact

Vivian Weiss, Supervisor of Adult Social Programs
Jewish Community Center of Greater Washington
6125 Montrose Road
Rockville, Maryland 20852
301/881-0100

PARENTING RESOURCES, OR WHERE TO GET HELP AND SUPPORT TO IMPROVE YOUR PARENTING SKILLS

There are three major parenting education groups throughout the United States.

146

American Society of Adlerian Psychology
159 Dearborn Street
Chicago, Illinois 60601

This group sponsors parent-education centers throughout the United States and has excellent educational materials. The method is based on the teaching of Rudolf Dreikurs.

Effectiveness Training Associates
110 S. Euclid Ave.
Pasadena, California 91101

This organization teaches the Parent Effectiveness Training (PET) method of Dr. Thomas Gordon and has parent groups in most cities.

American Guidance Services, Inc.
Circle Pines, Minnesota 55014

This publishing company developed the Systematic Training in Effective Parenting (STEP) method that is used by many PWP chapters. According to Nancy McGrath, program and education director (1978-1980) for PWP Chapter 1, Baltimore, Maryland, STEP is especially helpful for single parents because it requires that only one parent participate in the program.

OTHER PARENT-RESOURCE GROUPS

Do You Lose Your Cool with Your Kids?

Any parent has times of frustration and anger with his or her children. Being a parent, as we all know, is never easy. If we cannot deal with our frustrations, it is easy for them to build up and result in our inflicting bodily or psychic injury on our children.

Fortunately, there is a national organization to help parents (single and married) deal with the anger, frustration and other feelings that could, if ignored, cause them to lose control and hurt their children. This group is Parents Anonymous (PA).

Parents Anonymous, which charges no dues, is a support group for parents. According to one of PA's coordinators for Howard

County, Maryland, the focus is on weekly meetings which are nurturing and supportive, and seek to help parents deal with their frustrations. Many chapters provide free baby sitting during meetings. Also, PA has a 24-hour hotline for parents needing immediate help and support.

The group has statewide headquarters and individual chapters in every state in the Union. For more information about PA, and to learn about PA chapters in your area, you can contact

Parents Anonymous
National Office
22330 Hawthorne Boulevard, Suite 208
Torrance, California 90505
1/800-421-0353 (Toll-free, except in California)
1/800-352-0386 (Toll-free in California)

Where Can You Turn if Your Child Is Gay or Lesbian?

Many parents (including single parents) find that their children are gay or lesbian in their sexual preference. (*Gay* is the popular term used to describe men and women who are sexually attracted to members of their own sex. While gay women usually refer to themselves as *lesbian* women, in this section I will be using the term *gay* to refer to both gay men and lesbian women, as the major resource group for parents of gay and lesbian children is called Parents of Gays.)

Parents of Gays, according to the organization's founder, Betty Fairchild, is a self-help and educational group for parents to share the feelings and experiences they have when they first discover their child is gay. Ms. Fairchild explained that the group promotes a positive attitude toward homosexuality by providing accurate information through the use of good reading material and outside speakers. The opportunity to meet a variety of gay women and men, as well as share activities, also provides positive support for group members. See Appendix D (under Gay and Lesbian Children and Their Parents) for books recommended by Parents of Gays.

Parents of Gays have chapters in most states in the United States, five cities in Canada, and England. For more information about Parents of Gays, and the location of a chapter in or near your local area, contact

National Federation of Parents and Friends of Gays
P.O. Box 24528
Los Angeles, California 90024
213/472-8952

GETTING COMMUNITY ASSISTANCE AS A SINGLE PARENT: DO YOU WANT TO ADOPT?

David, from Silver Spring, Maryland, adopted a Sioux Indian boy eight years ago. The boy is now 15, and David told me that it has been a really positive experience for the two of them.

David offered the following suggestions for single people who want to adopt:

1. "You need to want it a great deal, since you will probably have difficulty persuading adoption agencies to let you adopt.
2. "You need either a sufficiently high income to afford a housekeeper or a flexible work schedule that makes it possible for you to be home when your child is not in school.
3. "While children are no longer stigmatized by being from a single-parent home, you need to be prepared for hostility and misunderstanding from other adults."

See Appendix C, under Adoptions by Single Parents or Single People, for three agencies which help single parents to adopt children.

GETTING SUPPORT WHILE MAKING NEW FRIENDS: WOMEN'S GROUPS AND MEN'S GROUPS

By joining women's or men's groups, single parents can get to know other members of their own sex as friends, not competitors.

Women's support groups have been in existence ever since the women's liberation movement began, over ten years ago. These groups offer women support, help in selecting a career, a chance to share feelings and problems with other women, an opportunity to make new friends, and—possibly most important—an opportunity to see other women as friends and allies, rather than as competitors for men. (One area that women's groups ought to deal with is defining the fears, concerns, and misunderstandings that interfere with friendships between married and single women.) Usually, both single and married women belong to such groups.

A good way to find out about women's groups in your area is to contact your local chapter of the National Organization for Women (NOW). While NOW itself is primarily political in its emphasis, NOW members frequently have an extensive knowledge of other women's groups and resources in their communities. If you know what you want, NOW can help you find an appropriate women's group.

Men's groups have only recently begun to offer to men the same type of resources that have long been offered by women's groups. A national men's organization (of which I am proud to be a member) is Free Men. As Free Men explains in its brochure, Free Men is "founded on the premise that society assigns men, as well as women, limiting roles in which they are expected to perform, regardless of their individual abilities, interests, and physical or emotional constitutions.

"Free Men seeks to promote awareness in men and women of how these gender-based roles limit men legally, socially, psychologically, emotionally, and sexually—and to provide support and assistance for men who choose to break free of gender-based limitations."

Free Men offers a variety of workshops and support groups, publishes a monthly newsletter, and has a growing national membership.

For more information about Free Men, you can write to

Free Men
P.O. Box 920
Columbia, Maryland 21044

HELPING YOUR CHILDREN AS
A SINGLE PARENT

Teachers and Other Adults
Involved with Your Children, and
How to Work with Them

Nancy McGrath is a teacher, a single parent, and the former program and education director for the Baltimore, Maryland chapter (Chapter 1) of PWP. She has also led special classes, for Baltimore County teachers, about single-parent families. For this reason, Ms. McGrath is an ideal person to discuss—from both points of view—some of the problems between single parents and teachers and offer constructive ideas for overcoming these and other problems. At my request, Ms. McGrath agreed to share some of her thoughts.

"Teachers frequently do not understand what the parents are going through, or realize that there is a light at the end of the tunnel. By understanding the different stages and the working through as applied to separation, divorce, widowhood, the teacher can better help the child see his or her single-parent family as an opportunity for growth and learning, rather than as a barrier to it.

"Parents often fail to realize that by sharing their experience— what they are going through—with the teacher, they can enable the teacher to better help and understand their child."

Ms. McGrath continued, "Intellectually, I know that it would be healthier for my own children if I did this, but emotionally, it was difficult to admit weakness. When I left, my children and I packed our things, moved out, and tried to rent a house. The day that we moved was very difficult for the children. I sent them to school, so their normal routine would not be disturbed. After school, I asked my children how the day had been. My youngest daughter, Laurie, said 'The worst thing happened to me.' (Laurie usually is calm and easy tempered; however, today, she was almost in tears.) 'One of my teachers said in front of the whole class, "You're in such a bad mood. You're acting as if this was the worst day of your life." ' At this point, Laurie broke down and cried. At that point, I wished I had told the teacher, so she could have realized that it probably *was* one of the worst days of Laurie's life. In this way, the teacher could have understood, and helped Laurie. I promised myself that I *would* call Laurie's teacher, and the other teachers and administrators, the next morning. I did; and, you know, each teacher commented that they had wondered whether something was wrong, because my children had been acting differently lately. This experience has helped me as a single parent, teacher, and school counselor. As a single parent, I've been through the problem. As a teacher and counselor, I think other single parents need to realize that their children spend six to eight hours a day in school. For this reason, if you, as a single parent, can let the school know what is going on at home, the school can provide special support and understanding for your children.

"Noncustodial parents often lose touch with their children's schools. They frequently don't receive school notices or report cards. Be assertive—if you are a noncustodial single parent—to see progress and report cards."

Ms. McGrath offers the following advice for encouraging a more realistic appreciation of how single-parent families can *help* their children:

"Be square with the teachers, describe the positive things that you're doing, and stress that you are a family. Let the teacher know about your activities, friends, and the positive side of your personal and family life. Society seems to feel that there is something unnatural about being happy though unmarried. People in general are finding that they do not necessarily need to remarry to be happy.

"Frequently, I have found, both as an educator and education and program director in my local PWP chapter, that single parents are sometimes better parents than parents in the two-parent family. There can be more concentration on the needs of each family member, rather than emphasis on the traditional hierarchy—between parents and children—and the competition between parents that is often true in the two-parent family."

For teachers and school administrators, Ms. McGrath suggests, "It is important to know that there are all types of family life styles. It would be beneficial for children to have a knowledge of all of them, especially the positive aspects of each type of family. This can help a child to feel that he or she is a valuable part of their family, regardless of the composition of the particular family. Another benefit is that it can improve understanding and communication in children."

For single parents, she recommends,

1. "Keep the lines of communication open between the school and yourself.
2. "Encourage your children to be open with teachers and peers about their single-parent situation. That way, they can get the support and understanding that they need."

These same principles can be used when dealing with other adults (scout leaders or coaches, for instance). If you show respect and appreciation for the ability and hard work, you can usually find help, understanding, and cooperation.

Other Resources For Your Children

You probably know most of your community's resources. Scouts, athletic teams, interest groups, and other organizations immediately come to mind.

Jim Doherty, former assistant cubmaster for my son's Cub Scout pack, in Columbia, Maryland, had the following comments:

"I believe that the Scouts offer some real advantages for boys from single-parent homes.

"The Scouts are a milieu for forming friendships with youngsters from different backgrounds, and offer a way to see how two-parent families live (as well as vice-versa).

"The Scouts help a young person to gain a moral background and sense of values.

"A boy can find an alternative male model. Here, he is evaluated as an individual.

"The Boy Scouts help boys develop new skills and independence; while the Explorers provide an opportunity to explore career alternatives.

"When I was a scoutmaster, in Westchester County, New York, my pack had one boy from a single-parent home. I arranged for him to have an "adult big brother" within the pack. I knew, as did the other men in charge of the pack, that the boy's mother could not afford the cost of Boy Scout camp. To make camp possible, and save the mother's pride, we arranged for the boy to perform odd jobs (mowing lawns, for instance). This made it possible for him to earn the money to attend camp."

Another resource is the Big Brother/Big Sister program. In this program, an adult of the same sex as the child spends time with the youngster, takes him or her on outings or other special treats, and provides a role model with whom the child can identify. For information about big brother or big sister programs in your area, contact

Big Brother/Big Sister
117 South 17th Street, Suite 1200
Philadelphia, Pa. 19103
215/567-2748

PWP offers a variety of resources for the children of its members. The International Youth Council (IYC) offers teenage children of single parents their own organization. (The parents of IYC members do not have to belong to PWP as long as at least one of the parents is single.) IYC offers discussions, a variety of support programs, and social activities. Buddies offers children ages six to eight their own activities; while Pals does the same for children ages nine to eleven. PWP also has begun a reduced-price summer camp program for the children of its members.

For more information about these and other resources for young people from single-parent homes, write to

Parents Without Partners, Inc.
International Headquarters
7910 Woodmont Ave.
Washington, D.C. 20014
301/654-8850

CONCLUSION

Provided that you make the initial effort, the wide variety of resources discussed in this chapter can provide the support, encouragement, and practical assistance you need. Even though, as a single parent, you can no longer rely on the help of a spouse, you still don't have to do it alone.

Chapter 7

You, Your Relationships, and Your Children

As a single parent, your relationships with other people are, of course, an important part of your life. The people you date, your long-term relationships (whether or not you and your partner live together), and perhaps a person whom you might want to consider marrying probably cross your mind. However, there are also your single friends of both sexes. (Your relationships with nonsingle people will be discussed in Chapter 8.) Your extended family, and possibly that of your former mate, are also important people to you as well as to your children. Finally, there is the inevitable, though frequently upsetting, relationship with your children's other parent, a relationship which—though you may want it to end completely when you separate or divorce—must usually be maintained in some form or other for the sake of the children.

Your friendships, dating relationships, and extended family can add immeasurably to the quality of your children's lives. At the same time, you can't completely neglect your own needs for adult companionship because of your children. (In Chapter 3, we have already discussed balancing your own needs with those of your children.) Your attitude can make a tremendous difference in how your children view your dating and other friendships: whether they see these

155

as relationships that take you away from them, or whether they accept the relationships as fulfilling your need, thus making you a happier person and better parent.

In some ways, for many of you this may be the most important chapter of this book. Many of you—possibly most—have already progressed into the second or third stage of single parenthood and are in the process of building a rewarding life for yourself. As you saw in Chapter 1, the second stage of single parenthood is when we usually have begun to build a new life for ourselves, and reach out for new friendships and romantic relationships that are appropriate to our single parent status. In the third stage, we have usually found out what we enjoy doing, and do it without feeling self-conscious. We have built a stable life for ourselves and our children, and have traveled the full cycle from the trauma and frustration of Stage 1 to achieving a life, as a single parent, that meets the needs of both ourselves and our children. At this point, you realize that your life consists of far more than just you, your children, their teachers, and your job. You probably want to date, develop friendships and romantic involvements, possibly start a long-term relationship which could lead to an LTA (living-together arrangement), or a remarriage. Perhaps you want to be close to your extended family but not have them butt in to your life when you don't need them. How can you manage a relationship with your former mate that benefits your children but does not exasperate or frustrate you all the time? How do you answer your children's questions about their noncustodial parent? How important should your children be to your relationships? Should you encourage your dates to sleep over? Will this damage the children's morals and hurt them as they develop into adulthood? If you are considering remarriage, or a long-term relationship outside of marriage, what must you consider? Are there problems that plague remarried parents? How can you deal with the children's feelings and needs, while considering your own? Is remarriage—or an LTA—the logical final progression from the initial difficulties of single parenthood to developing a full life as a single person and parent? Or, is this only one of a number of possible options that can lead to happiness and fulfillment?

If only there were a book that could answer all these questions! Unfortunately, I don't believe any one person has the answers to all these questions. However, I have been fortunate in having the opportunity—through discussions, interviews, responses to my questionnaire (Appendix B), and personal experience—to learn how other single parents have dealt with these *concerns*. Perhaps sharing their feelings, experiences, and insights, will help you develop your own answers.

YOU AND YOUR FORMER MATE

Relating with your former mate is one area of difficulty that is, or has been, shared by nearly all single parents (with the exception of widows and widowers, and possibly those single parents who have never been married). It is difficult enough to come to terms with your own feelings about him or her but how can you be honest in dealing with your children's questions and feelings?

The Positive Approach

Some of us are fortunate in being able to maintain a positive attitude. For example, Judy, from Vestal, New York (with a nine-year-old daughter and seven-year-old son), and her former husband have always maintained mutual respect and caring as people. Judy told me that she and her former husband *never* made critical remarks to the children about each other. Both love the children and are proud of them. Judy tries hard to be objective about her former husband with the children. She explained, "I want them to realize he is their father, that he loves and respects them as we should him. This was more difficult during the early emotional days of the separation, but we have developed (my former husband and I) a very good friendship. I, also, am friends with his current wife and her children."

Barbara, from Belen, New Mexico, said that neither she nor her former spouse talks about the other. They discuss any major problem, and visitation is very flexible. She recommends, "Don't pass negative opinions on to the children. What's between the parents is just that— between them. Let the children make up their own minds—they will."

Sometimes, the other parent may act the way he or she does, *not* because they don't care about their child, but because of their personality. For example, Alice, from Fort Wayne, Indiana says, "We have remained friends, and he helps out when asked something specifically. Otherwise, he acts like we don't exist. He never calls or sees the kids. They must contact him. But, that's his personality. He loves them, but he has no initiative."

Alice (from Fort Wayne, Indiana) also mentioned another point, one that seems to be shared by nearly all the single parents (custodial and noncustodial alike) who seemed most successful in working with their former mates for the benefit of their children: *The relationship you have with your former mate is different from the one that your child has with him or her.* Your relationship is dissolved; however, your former mate will always be the children's parent. Alice put it this way: "I never run their father down. I've tried to explain the way I feel about him has nothing to do with their feelings for him. He is still their father. That is an entirely different situation. I look at him from a different set of values and experiences than their views of him."

Jennifer, from Columbia, Maryland, has been able to apply Alice's principle, even though she and her former husband live over 1,000 miles from each other (he lives in Florida). She commented, "I have told my son how I feel about his father, and that it is OK by me if he loves him but don't expect me to love him. My son's father and I disagree on many points, and my son should know that adults have differing views on many subjects. It works, in that my son knows both adult points of view; and he acts one way living with me, and another way when visiting his father."

This approach is well summed up by Gail, a single parent from Baltimore, Maryland, who has two sons, ages six and four. Gail explained, "My feelings toward my former husband are just that: my feelings. I don't down their father to them. That kind of talk scars. If they ask questions about their father, I never answer them negatively. Other than that, it is never discussed."

Another suggestion that has worked for many single parents is to be completely honest with their children, to give "straight" answers to their questions. Frank, from northern Virginia, answered his (now 17-year-old) daughter, when she asked why he and her mother were no longer married, "Because we no longer love each other."

Some Difficulties

One problem that continually confronts single parents is the children's relationship with the noncustodial parent. Should it be encouraged, discouraged, or ignored? Evelyn, from Rockville, Maryland (with a 14-year-old-son, and 12- and 10-year-old daughters), for example, found that "at first, I tried to actively maintain my former husband's relationship with the children, but I finally gave it up as not my responsibility."

Cathy, from North Bend, Oregon, has found that her answer is to let her children handle their own relationship with their father. Harriet, from Potomac, Maryland, also lets her three sons (ages 15, 14, and 11) handle their own relationship with their father, with no interference from her. She reports that the arrangement is working well.

If you want not to criticize the other parent in front of the children, should you then avoid any mention of his or her failings? Liz, from Baltimore, Maryland, believes that "the children should not bear the brunt of my hostility. If something their father says or does directly affects them, they should know of his shortcomings. Neither parent should be a saint."

Unfortunately, a large number of single parents find it difficult or impossible to work together with the other parent for the benefit of their children. This is true for Anita, from Greenbelt, Maryland, who said, "I keep my hostility to myself unless the situation is extreme, and then I'd be a liar to not be honest. The kids can handle honesty better than deception. . . . He has talked against me to the children. But my fighting back by talking against him cheapens me."

A vivid example of handling your child's relationships with a former spouse whom you cannot tolerate came from Carol Ann, in Arnold, Maryland, whose son is now 15. Carol Ann explained as follows: "I cannot stand my former spouse. Fortunately for me, he resides in Arizona. I encourage my son to keep in touch with his father, and have no objections to his visiting his father, provided his father pays for his transportation. I explained to my son that his relationship with his father was different from my relationship with an ex-spouse. Luckily, he understands this. I might add that my son chooses to live with me, and does not enjoy his father in Arizona. He has visited his father twice since the move (approximately five years ago). My son did not see his father for six years after our marriage dissolved. I initiated the contact, because it was my initial desire not to see the man. My son was suffering all the while, hanging on to a dim memory of his father. He had visions of a knight in shining armor. When he finally met his father again, at the age of nine, he was shocked and disappointed. He was able to form his own opinion and began rejecting him."

Nell, from El Cerrito, California, responded to my question of how she handles negative feelings about her former spouse by saying, "I try not to bring up the subject. My (nine-year-old) daughter, however, has noticed her father's drinking, and commented on it. When it comes up this way, I agree with her that heavy drinking is bad. Sometimes, at bedtime, my (six-year-old) son cries for his daddy and wishes his daddy lived with him (after three years!). Then, I point out to him that when his father lived with us, he wasn't home very often. So, in other words, if they bring it up, then I comment on it in as unhostile a way as I can. I do try to tell them their daddy loves them, and not turn them against him."

Gladys, from a Maryland suburb of Washington, has been single for seven and half years. Her sons are 23 and 18, and her daughter is 15. Gladys thinks that "the resentments are best not discussed with the children. In times of great stress, due largely to his lack of financial support, they heard my resentments. I feel this was harmful. They felt a need to defend him. [My] being quiet when they criticized him freed the children to ventilate their feelings."

Never-married mothers have a special problem: that of explaining to their children the reason why the children, in effect, have no father who cares about them or shows an interest in them, even on a part-time basis. Norene, from Endicott, New York, has a ten-year-old daughter. Her daughter's father has not seen them since his daughter was two years old, and Norene has never gotten any kind of support from him. She believes that "as my daughter gets older, she will realize who was there all the time, who supported her, comforted her, played with her. She doesn't need me to point it out. I have told her the truth, except that he left because he didn't care; how can you tell someone their father doesn't love them? (They'll see it themselves eventually.) I simply told her that it was better for him to go away; and that, some day, she'll understand."

Thelma, from Binghamton, New York, has a similar situation. Her daughter is now 26 years old and has not seen her father since shortly after she was born. Thelma believes that "negative opinions should not be passed on to the children, but do not present a false picture by making your former spouse seem better than he is or was. Answer questions briefly and honestly, without emotions. If you cannot answer questions or talk about your former spouse, let someone who is not emotionally involved do it for you."

Hazel, from Erie, Pennsylvania, has been able to separate her own feelings about her former spouse (who left three years ago) from the way she deals with the feelings and questions of her two sons (ages six and three). Hazel said that her former husband couldn't care less about their existence. She added, "I feel that as little as possible should be said about him, except that he could no longer cope—that it was not because the kids did something to make him go. We are all rather happy just taking care of everyday things and being together. I feel that I have almost completely forgiven him, but feel it is much better that he stays away. His degenerated way of life would only hamper all the work I have done to help develop the kids so far." When asked by her older son why Daddy went away and did not come home, Hazel replied, "I did not down the father's image. I explained that Daddy still loved his boy, but just got scared and could not stay longer. I explained that he should not worry because even though Mommy got scared at times, she would not leave. Because of this, he has emerged feeling good about himself and openly says that Daddy just went away, and Mommy, brother, and him are just fine together."

A Few Aids

One principle that I personally have found helpful in my relations with my former wife is Expect Each Person to Behave in a Manner Consistent with His or Her Own Nature. An important part of this, for me at least, is not to expect from my former wife what she is unable to give, and to accept and appreciate what she can give. By accepting this reality—without criticizing or condemning her—and letting her know that whatever is comfortable for her is generally fine with me, I encourage her to continue to develop a close relationship with the children that meets her needs.

As explained in Chapter 5, one way in which you can help your children gain the most benefit from their relationship with their other parent is by offering the noncustodial parent an "emotional weather forecast" or map of your children, especially right before he or she visits. As Saralee, from Baltimore, Maryland, has found, this can help the noncustodial parent deal with the children as they really are feeling.

Time and emotional distance can be a big help in overcoming bitterness and hostility toward your former mate. It can also help both of you to learn to cooperate *as parents* for the benefit of your children. Ethel, from a small town in eastern Massachusetts, has had a positive experience in this regard. I asked her, "Have you and your former spouse been able to work *together* for your children's benefit? If so, how have you achieved this? Have you any suggestions for others?" Ethel replied:

"This is a very slow process, but the improvement is remarkable— but not earth shattering. Visitation is sometimes rearranged to allow each of us the opportunity to have our son for special activities. We are able to talk again; we didn't for two years. Part of the improvement has been through mediation; the rest I'd attribute to time. Try not to be nasty toward your ex-spouse. Time will help, and there are places to get help if needed.

"Children don't have to hear our negative opinions to know there are some. I've explained that we don't love each other anymore, and there are some times we don't like things that our former spouse does. I tell him truthfully that I'm glad we can talk to each other again. I try to talk up his [my son's] father's good points. He sees a lot of the bad ones; so, I try not to ever mention them unless my son should bring them up. Then, I explain that none of us is perfect. My son is very mature for a 7-year-old; sometimes, he is more like 20. I have to remember he is 7, and handle such situations in a way that protects all our rights as much as possible. Even at 7, my son respects that. More time is needed, but it's working."

Suggestions and Ideas

To sum up, here are some of the methods that have helped single parents deal with both the other parent and their children's feelings about the other parent. These suggestions will perhaps help you to develop your own method, and possibly gain from the experience of other single parents.

1. Recognize that your relationship with your former mate is quite different from the children's relationship with him or her. Your relationship is ended, but the children's relationship with their parent is a permanent one.
2. While you need to develop your own life, it can be beneficial to

your children if you and your former mate can cooperate *as parents* for their benefit. Some ways you can achieve this are

—By appreciating and accepting what the noncustodial parent is able to give, and by not wasting time and energy expecting, demanding, or hoping for what the noncustodial parent is incapable of giving.

—By giving the noncustodial parent an "emotional weather map" of your children's feelings and experiences, thus enabling him or her to more effectively help the children, without feeling unduly hurt or rejected for things that may have nothing to do with him or her.

—By encouraging, not pressuring, the noncustodial parent to be as involved as is comfortable for him or her.

—By developing a cooperative relationship with your former mate which can help your children and give you more free time.

3. Time, emotional distance, and mediation are three ways which can help you overcome your hostility and bitterness, and learn to work together with the children's other parent.

4. Nonjudgmental communication (identifying *your* feelings and needs, rather than absolute qualities, such as "bad" or "inconsiderate") and flexibility can help the two of you to work together as parents.

5. Be honest—but not needlessly bitter—about the other parent in answering your children's questions.

6. It is a waste of time and energy—and, frequently harmful to your children—for you to continually criticize or blame their noncustodial parent in front of them. One way of handling this is by answering their questions honestly, discussing your feelings calmly, and stressing that their relationship with him or her is quite different than your own.

7. Encourage (and support) your children to develop their own relationship with their noncustodial parent; don't get involved.

YOU AND YOUR EXTENDED FAMILY

Most single parents with whom I spoke felt that their parents and other relatives have been supportive and helpful. For example, Gail, from Baltimore, Maryland, has found that her family is supportive but not intrusive. Her brothers take her sons out to sports events. Julia, from Belen, New Mexico, commented that both she and her children are now better acquainted, and have developed a closer relationship, with her father. Sue, from Chenango Forks, New York, is very close to her parents. Her children feel loved, secure, and "no different" than children from a two-parent family. Art (from Enumclaw, Washington) has parents who have been very supportive, even to the extent of baby sitting his six-year-old daughter on a regular basis.

Joyce, from a small town in central Wisconsin, told me that her parents respect her for her independence and success in raising her daughter alone.

Unfortunately, not all single parents have supportive and understanding parents. Harriet's parents (she's from Potomac, Maryland) treated her like a little girl, until they understood that she would be OK again. Nell, from El Cerrito, California, showed a realistic perspective in her comments: "My parents think I am a failure. But, my relationship with them has always been dependent on whether I lived my life the way they thought I should. My sister has been very supportive."

Carol H. is from Hillsville, Virginia (a rural town in the Bible Belt of Virginia). Carol explained her experience with her parents: "My parents are very traditional, and mine was the first divorce in our family. They saw it as a disgrace, and me as a failure. They saw me as fragile and needing support. They wanted me to rent a mobile home on their property, so they could take care of me and my children. However, I have a stubborn streak in me. It was hard enough living with them for eight months. I rented a home 15 miles away from them, and raised the kids myself. When they saw that I was raising the kids successfully, helping them (my parents) when they needed help, and holding down a full-time job, my parents' respect for me increased substantially. I now have a good relationship with my parents.

"My suggestion to other single parents would be, if it is at all possible financially, don't live with your parents. It reduces your independence; and, in your parents' home, they—not you—make the rules."

Hazel, from Erie, Pennsylvania, has found that her relationship with her parents has improved significantly since when she first became separated. She explained, "I was an only child, no brothers or sisters. At first, my parents found the whole thing scary and shocking—my being deserted with two tiny kids, so that my ex could run off with someone else and leave me with all the bills. After the first year, my parents found that it was the best thing that could have happened. Myself and the children are now much happier, and my parents feel this is the most important thing—not the old relationship."

The following are a few suggestions that may help you develop close relationships with your parents, while maintaining your independence and self-respect:

1. Build a new life for yourself as soon as possible. Your parents will respect you for your independence and resourcefulness.
2. Explain to and show your parents that you are happier now than when you were married (if this is the case). Show how the children are better off since the end of tension between you and your former mate.
3. There is nothing wrong with asking for help and support. However, this is very different from expecting your parents to completely take care of you.
4. If your parents still have trouble accepting your single-parent status, consider (as did Nell) whether that may be their problem; stop blaming yourself for their feelings.

YOU AND YOUR FORMER MATE'S EXTENDED FAMILY

Dealing with your former husband's or wife's extended family can be a particularly tricky area for single parents. I believe that, if at all possible, your former mate's parents should have primary contact with the children through their son or daughter, rather than you. However, there is no reason why—if you feel comfortable—the grandparents cannot contact you to work out arrangements for seeing their grandchildren. The key is how you feel.

The main contact, however, should be between the grandparents and the grandchildren. Nell's approach seems to be realistic. She commented, "I have very little contact with my former spouse's parents now. I send them Mother's and Father's Day cards for Grandma and Grandpa, signed by the children; and they appreciate this."

Sometimes, your former in-laws can be very understanding and supportive of you. When this happens, it can be a real bonus. Barbara, from Belen, New Mexico, is close to her former in-laws. She is happy, because it gives her children more people to relate to.

A final caution: Try to deal with your in-laws as concerned individuals, not as stereotyped in-laws who "of course" will be against you. If they do reject you, at least you've tried.

RELATIONSHIPS WITH OTHER SINGLE PEOPLE

The Value of Friendships

As a single parent, you have an opportunity for friendships based solely on your own needs and those of your potential friend. You don't have to gain the approval of a husband or wife to enter into new friendships. I know that a real bonus of being single for me has been the friendships I have developed with other single men and women. I think especially of my nonromantic friendships with women— something that would have been hard to imagine when I was married. Other single parents have also experienced this feeling of being free to develop new friendships that transcend sexual boundaries.

Many single parents have found special rewards in the friendships they have developed with members of their own sex. Annelle, from a small town in Missouri, has found that other women are supportive, and help her both emotionally and with actual child care.

When I thought about some of the reasons why our friendships with other single men and women are so special—and important—to us, and discussed this with other single parents, I made the following observations:

1. Singles' and single-parent discussions have made me and others with whom I have talked aware that men and women share many of the same concerns and needs. The openness and confidentiality of these discussions encourage a single parent to react to other participants as individuals—rather than sexual stereotypes.
2. Single-parent organizations promote a sense of community and

caring which frequently carries over into one's personal relationships. The realization that there is far more to being a single parent than raising your children and romantic relationships can be truly liberating. Once you reach this stage, it can be tremendously rewarding to develop friendships with members of both your own sex and the opposite sex, based on common values, interests, and concerns.

3. As part of a couple, your emphasis is on your primary relationship. This frequently limits the time and energy you have for pursuing other friendships. As a single parent, you don't have this same type of primary relationship. This can free you to pursue new friendships with others to a greater extent than is often possible in a marriage.

4. Our friends offer us, as single parents, a special sense of community, which is particularly important when you don't have one primary relationship (such as in a marriage). Even if you are in a primary relationship, however, your single friends can keep you from feeling trapped, or "locked in," by it.

Your single friends can also help your children feel a special sense of belonging. Cynthia, from Silver Spring, Maryland, has found that "my single friends have, for the most part, been good for my children. They give them attention they otherwise wouldn't have, and the children learn a lot from interacting with adults."

Barbara B., from Belen, New Mexico, commented, "Very close friends are called aunt or uncle and form a part of our family—several have been for almost all of my children's lives."

Here are some ideas that may help you to develop new friendships with other single people.

1. Put yourself in discussions and other situations where you will have an opportunity to learn how other single parents and single people feel about issues and concerns important to you.

2. Try to see members of the opposite sex as individuals, rather than always as potential romantic partners.

3. Focus on your interests and concerns; put yourself in situations where you can meet others who share them.

4. Remember that family activities of single-parent organizations are a good way to meet other single parents.

5. Consider the common interests and concerns you share with other members of your own sex—rather than the possible competition they might offer.
6. Be true to yourself, and choose friends who add to your positive view of yourself, rather than friends who are *always* criticizing you—for your own good, of course.
7. Finally, remember that friends offer your children an opportunity to enrich their lives by knowing a variety of adults.

Dating and Other Relationships: How These Relate to You and Your Children

Dating and long-term relationships satisfy our need as single adults for closeness and intimacy. Many single parents get remarried. Those who don't frequently enter a living-together arrangement (LTA), or choose a living-separately arrangement (LSA), where each partner maintains his or her own home while spending much time together. Some issues of particular concern to single parents include

1. Should I bring my dates home? Will his or her sleeping over be bad for my children?
2. Is a single parent an unhealthy role model for children— because of the tendency toward multiple nondurable relationships?
3. What type of relationship (dating, LTA, LSA, or remarriage) is best for me and my children?
4. Is something wrong with me if I am not able or choose not to enter into a long-term relationship? Will my children suffer?

A key principle that seems to work for single parents is, Be true to yourself and your feelings and beliefs. Thus, if you believe that your dating should be separate from your home life, act on your belief. If an LTA appears immoral or sinful, don't get involved in one. If, on the other hand, an important quality to you is your date's interest in children, you might want to arrange opportunities to have your date meet your children. Perhaps you feel that an LTA could be the greatest thing in the world for you and your children. If that is how you feel, if and when you meet the right person, an LTA might be right for you.

Often, it is helpful to discuss your feelings *and theirs* with your children. You may be surprised at what you learn. Sometimes, what you thought would be terrible for the children may not bother them at all.

One of the most frightening questions to any single parent is, What would happen if my children saw me making love with a member of the opposite sex? Hazel, from Erie, Pennsylvania, had this very experience. (She has two sons, ages six and three, and has been single for three years.) Let Hazel describe her experience in her own words:

"Once, my older boy walked in and a man and I were in bed together. We were covered, but the man was above me. Embarrassing situation that it was, I kept my cool. The boy asked what was happening. I explained that just like he enjoys me holding him and giving him love, sometimes Mommy needed someone to hold her and make her feel loved. He closed the door and went back to playing without another thought about it."

Timing can be important to a relationship. Art, from Enumclaw, Washington, got involved with a woman shortly after becoming single. She had a daughter and he had a daughter. For this reason, they thought they would marry. However, it was far too soon after his divorce, and before she had established a career—which was necessary for her self-esteem. When they separated, his daughter felt the pain and loss.

Sometimes, your children can cause problems. Nell, from El Cerrito, California, has found that most men that she dates like the children occasionally but would not want the children as a regular part of their lives. Carol H., from Hillsville, Virginia, has taken the initiative in dealing with this problem. She explained, "Some men who are not parents (and even some who are) seem to bothered that I sometimes can't go with them because my daughter is riding a horse in a parade or performing in a play; or my son is playing saxophone or playing ball. The ones who are not understanding don't last long with me."

Jeff, from a California town, said, "I have seen friends rush into new relationships too quickly. I suggest that one learn to be single. First, get over the fear of being alone, before starting anew."

Combining your family life and your dating can be demanding. Barbara B. commented that when her children were small, she met her dates outside the house. Art separates his dates into never-married and single parents. He has found that his never married dates are curious about his children but are wary, lest he be trying to thrust the role of momma on them. With these women, he does only adult activities; while he does family activities with women who are parents.

Some single parents have found that their dating is a positive influence on their children. Cynthia, from Silver Spring, Maryland, said, "My dates have always been good to my children. Also, since my three children are all male, other males to identify with are good. Some of my dates have already taken an interest in the boys, and have often taught them useful things. Also, they've helped me, which indirectly helps the children." Jennifer, from Columbia, Maryland, has found that "the quality of our family life is very good, regardless of who enters from the outside. When there is a breakup, my relationship with my son is strengthened through an honest explanation of what occurred."

Two major questions discussed at a Montcosps dialogue concerning relationships were, Are the many short-term relationships of a single parent a positive role model for children? and How do we handle our children's jealousy of our dates?

In response to the second question, one woman found directness to be a solution. When her five-year-old daughter was being nasty to her dates, the mother finally said, "Look, it's not your fault that your father and I are not together any more. I know you want your father and me to be together again; but it's not going to happen, and nothing you can do will change that." The daughter accepted this explanation and became nicer to her mother's dates.

The first question involved more discussion. However, the group responded to that question by wondering whether dating relationships of a single parent were any worse, for children, than being trapped in a parent's hostile marriage or long-term relationship. In addition, club members observed that the opportunity to see a parent as an individual with needs, feelings, and emotions can give the child a positive role model—one of honesty, genuineness, and the courage to look for a relationship that meets one's needs, rather than give up or settle for what is first available.

Two other concerns were discussed during this dialogue: (1) how should a relationship be handled with your children, and (2) what happens to your children when a relationship ends?

In response to handling a relationship with your children, there were two suggestions. One woman felt that since her date's primary relationship is with her, he should be friendly but distant from her children. The general consensus, however, was that you encourage your date to be himself or herself and not try to replace the other parent. He or she can still be a friend.

There were two comments regarding how to handle the end of a relationship with your children. Libby discourages all contact with her former "friend's" daughter—despite the fact that the daughter (now in college) wanted to keep in touch and ask Libby's advice. Libby explained that it hurt to keep in touch, and it hurt to break contact. However, she felt that since her primary relationship (with the father) was ended, it was pointless—and painful—to maintain contact with the daughter.

I must confess to a preference for Sharon's approach. Sharon encourages her children to maintain their own relationship with her former date, if they and he so choose. She will help by driving her children, but they must take the initiative in developing their own relationship with him.

YOU AND YOUR LONG-TERM RELATIONSHIPS

Living-Separately Arrangements (LSA)

Living-separately arrangements offer a blend of intimacy and independence, for each partner maintains his or her own dwelling. This is also a viable alternative for many single parents who feel that an LTA is morally or socially wrong and is—or could be—detrimental to their children's development.

Thelma, from Binghamton, New York, believes that an LSA leaves her daughter free of guilt when she establishes a relationship with someone or decides that she wants to leave home.

Judy, from Vestal, New York, finds an LSA to be convenient.

She enjoys both independence and security. The children seem to accept this. She believes they feel loved; yet they realize that she needs her time alone.

The most beautiful description of a successful LSA came from Harriet, in Potomac, Maryland, who commented, "My children are seeing a warm, loving relationship between a man and a woman that they did not see before. I have been open about going on trips with my 'partner,' and his spending the night. I have found it easy to discuss with my friends, family, and children. Because I am so comfortable with this arrangement, this attitude is accepted by others. My children reflect my own easy and loving attitude. They are happy with my 'partner' and his sons. There is surely more love in the house, more acceptance, and more respect."

Living-Together Arrangements (LTA)

An LTA arrangement offers the intimacy and shared living that is part of marriage but without a marriage's legal obligations or entanglements. The people with whom I talked felt that a special advantage of an LTA is that, since each partner is legally single, it is easier to end a bad relationship than if they were married. As a "single person" each partner can still participate in many activities of singles' and single-parent organizations, and thus retain the support of the single-parent community.

I was fortunate in having the opportunity to talk to two single parents who are currently involved in successful LTAs.

Peter, from a Washington, D.C., suburb, gave me a general overview of LTAs. He feels it is important to blend the two families, that is, get the children used to each other before beginning an LTA. Three potential problems that Peter discussed are

1. *One partner without child custody.* Unless it is dealt with, there will probably be rivalry between the children and the noncustodial parent for the time of the custodial parent.
2. *One partner without children.* This can be quite an adjustment for the nonparent, who has to learn to share the parent's time with the children.
3. *Two parents with different custody arrangements.* In a situation where

the children never see each other (if one partner is a custodial parent and the other is noncustodial), it can be difficult to achieve a completely satisfying blended family.

Peter said that his own situation presents the fourth type of difficulty: Both parents have custody of their children. Peter and Yona dated a lot, and got used to each other. As the children got used to each other, Peter and Yona told them that, "when we all live together, you'll be able to play together more."

Both partners share the discipline, but *all* the children accept discipline and praise more from Peter than from Yona.

Peter's daughter is 11; Yona's sons are 9 and 7.

The boys' father and Peter are friends for the sake of the children. To show the children that they are friends, the two men built a big wheel together. The boys' father also takes Peter's daughter when he picks up the boys.

Peter offers the following suggestions:

1. "Problems will occur in any family.
2. "In a blended family, there can be more structure than in a single-parent family—where it is too easy to compromise.
3. "Give your partner the feeling that your children are his or hers in practice, but do not impose on the child to accept your partner as his or her father or mother.
4. "Fairness is vital to children. Be equally fair to all children. It is easy to overcompensate. Reward and punish equally.
5. "Be honest, and criticize to another person's face (even if it is your partner or the children's other parent), rather than behind his back.
6. "Keep your promises. A promise is a big event, and a child looks forward to it. Don't promise unless you can keep it."

Sona and Stuart have been in an LTA for three years. Sona's son (age 6) and daughter (age 9) live with them. Stuart's former wife has custody of his 7-year-old son and his two daughters, ages 10 and 12. Sona explained:

"We were dating intensely. My children were two and five at the time. Stuart was sleeping over, but we were not letting the children know. Then, my mother said, 'Why not be open? You're lying to the kids. Why not live together? Your daughter already doesn't trust her father. Do you want her to stop trusting you too?'

"We were being secretive out of guilt and fear. It was not that long (one year) after my separation; and my daughter was going through pain, since her father hadn't seen her for a whole year.

"I believe that we worry too much about whether our children will accept and understand. Kids are much more flexible and resilient than we give them credit for. As a matter of fact, I have found that they are frequently more flexible and resilient than adults.

"There was an initial conflict between premature openness and dishonesty by omission.

"We anticipated the following problems," continued Sona,

1. *"Children's acceptance of their parent's partner.* Actually, they thought our living together was great. It gave them a sense of family. They thought it was 'neat' to have two homes. Stuart's children seem also to enjoy having a second home.
2. *"Social pressures.* There have been none.
3. "There is no way to describe their mother's relationship. This causes embarrassment, solely because there is no socially acceptable term to describe the person who lives with your parent.

"A positive aspect of our LTA relationship is that we have a better home life. My son has no recollection of living with his father. Stuart is a good male model for my son—but *not* another father. My son will accept another model, but not another father. My son has constant contact with his father. Stuart's children feel the same way about me as my son feels about Stuart.

"At first, the children of each were fearful of accepting their parent's friend, as they would feel they were negating their natural parent. As their relationship with their natural parent strengthened, so did their relationship with their parent's partner. After children have developed a strong relationship with their natural parent, then they can accept their natural parent's relationship, whatever it may be."

I asked Sona what she felt were the differences between an LTA and a remarriage. Sona mentioned the following differences:

1. *"Financial:* You pay less taxes if you are unmarried. Also, you can preserve your alimony if you are not married.

2. "You avoid legal hassles if you split up.
3. "Why ruin a good relationship by marriage? This way, you can still preserve your legal options if you separate, even though you will still probably experience emotional trauma.
4. "Marriage frequently has a negative connotation, especially if your first marriage failed. An LTA is an alternative that avoids these negative associations."

Asked if she had any suggestions to offer other single parents who were considering an LTA, Sona replied: "My suggestions would be primarily for those with young children who are considering an LTA.

1. "I recommend that anyone considering remarriage should live together first. You need the nitty-gritty experiences. Learn whether you can handle it. Can you adjust your schedules? Who goes to the bathroom first in the morning? Who does what for whom?
2. "Establish three financial accounts: yours, mine, and ours. It is important not to interfere with your partner's relationship (financial and otherwise) with his or her own children. You can discuss—but don't dictate. Having separate accounts avoids one partner saying to the other, 'You can't buy this for yourself or your kids.'
3. "How much control does the nonparent have over the children? Can he or she punish them? How? For example, I will not allow Stuart to hit my kids, but he can send them to their room.
4. "You need to agree on ground rules, such as what modes of punishment you should use. You need agreement, and an ability to work harmoniously as a team—with respect—to deal with present and/or potential problems in such a way that everyone's needs are considered and decisions have been reached by mutual agreements, rather than by dictatorship."

Remarriage

It is important, at this point, to restate the main point of this book: Being a single-parent family can be a satisfying and rewarding way of life for you and your children and does not have to be seen as merely a transition between marriages.

Recognizing that, it is important, also, to realize that many of us yearn to recapture that special feeling of family that can be obtained through a marriage. Many single parents are so desperate for closeness that they rush blindly into a second (or later) marriage before they are ready. Then, they wonder why they have problems, and possibly failure, in their remarriage or remarriages.

The Baltimore, Maryland, chapter of PWP (Chapter 1) offered a discussion that dealt with blending two families before a remarriage. The group agreed that several potential problems needed to be discussed before marriage. These included

1. Who disciplines whose children?
2. Whose home shall we live in? Will we move into a new home?
3. Should the wife do all the housework? Should both partners share this?
4. Should the wife give up her job or career?
5. How difficult will it be to adjust to each other's habits, such as cleanliness, neatness, or smoking?
6. Are your life styles harmonious? If not, what can you do to make them so?

The group also dealt with the problem of one noncustodial father who picked up his nine-year-old son for weekends. However, he spent all his time with his woman friend and her children. As a result, the boy got no time alone with his dad. Now the youngster feels hurt and resents his dad's woman friend. (The two are planning to marry soon.) He swears that he will never spend weekends with them. The answer to this problem, the group agreed, was for the father to arrange to spend time each weekend exclusively with his son.

The group had one recommendation for the person who is considering marrying a single parent: Don't try to be a substitute parent. You can be a caring friend and have your own close relationship. Treat the children as if they were cats—give them time to get used to you. Treat them as unique individuals, and with respect and consideration.

Joanne Small, psychiatric social worker, points out emphatically in her step-parent workshops that "in the original family, you build your own traditions, learn patterns of relating to each other, and develop your own unique family history. This all took time. It is this concept of family that many of us yearn to *instantly* recapture when we remarry. Furthermore, each of us brings previously acquired values, attitudes, traditions, and styles of parenting into the new family. Let's recognize that a family represents a beginning. It is important for parents and children in the step-family to be willing to recognize that they might need to make changes and build new traditions that are more appropriate to their new family."

Remarriage: Some Experiences

Here, three remarried couples from the Baltimore, Maryland, metropolitan area share with us their experiences and insights.

Lee and George

Lee and George have been remarried for three years. Lee has no children. George is the noncustodial parent of three sons (ages 14, 12, and 11) and a daughter (age 13). Before marrying Lee, George was a single parent for two years. I asked George the following questions:

Were there fears or concerns that you had about remarriage? How did you deal with them?
What problems, if any, involved the children? How did you deal with them?
Has your marriage helped or hurt your relationship with your children? How? Why?

George replied, "Being single gave me the chance to really know and spend time with my kids. It built a foundation of closeness and mutual trust that was vital. (I think this was helped by the fact that I never "put down," or criticized, their mother.) We have built on this closeness and trust to build a special (for us) extended family that includes my new wife, the kids, and myself.

"The fears and concerns that I had revolved around my children. I worried that they would not accept my wife. I dealt with this problem by informing my children that my new wife did not want to take their mother's place, but she would like to be a friend (someone whom they could talk to, if they had to).

"My marriage has helped my relationship with the children.

They realize that I am happy, and this happiness has rubbed off on them. We can discuss things more freely than before. I do more and more with each of them. Also, they now realize that their mother is much happier than before. They can understand more about love, happiness, and the feeling that's involved when two people really love each other.

"Before, the kids would wonder about reconciliation between their mother and myself. They now have seen that I can have a happy family life—even though not reconciled with their mom—that includes them. Even though they only see us on alternate weekends, we are closer and feel much more like a real family than when I was married to their mom.

"My suggestions would be, be honest and truthful with your children and try to explain exactly what happened, and possibly why (if there is an answer)."

Phil and Rose Marie

Phil and Rose Marie have been married since October 1977. Phil is the noncustodial father of a 17-year-old daughter and 16- and 15-year-old sons. Prior to his remarriage, Phil had been single for five years. Rose Marie's three daughters—ages 19, 17, and 15—have always lived with her. Before getting remarried, she had been a single parent for two years. I was especially fortunate in having an opportunity to talk to each partner individually, as well as to both together.

Phil

"I met Rose Marie through a divorced and separated Catholics' organization," Phil began. "I knew her for two years before I proposed. I didn't get scared until after she accepted. I had felt comfortable and secure as a single parent and was attracted by Rose Marie's honesty and her unusual sense of integrity.

"When Rose Marie said she would marry me, all my generalized fears about marriage came out. Some of the things that scared me were

1. "Possible loss of freedom.
2. "Financial responsibilities.

3. "Would our children get along?"

Phil continued, "The first year of marriage *was* difficult. I felt all alone in a household with four women, and I missed my privacy. I expected more frequent visits from my children. The boys have benefited from our blended family. My daughter chose to opt out, probably because of my commitment to Rose Marie and the potential rivalry of her three daughters.

"The positive aspects of our marriage have been special, as have the ways in which we have overcome our problems. Rose Marie provided a more stable home environment than when I was a bachelor. All of our children participated and saw our new house when we purchased it. None of the children were forced or rushed into a new relationship before they felt ready. We let them feel their own way.

"In August 1977 we had a joint camping trip with all the children. (We got married two months later.) The first few days, we had good will. I noticed it was the same with our first few months of marriage. At first, all of us tried super hard; then, we relaxed and related as real people.

"As a noncustodial parent, I spent a lot of money and time. Now, the boys come over and relax. A real key has been Rose Marie's ability to lay back and provide room in which she could get to know my boys.

"Two dangers I would caution single parents to watch out for are rushing and overwhelming their children and new wife or husband, rather than letting the relationship develop gradually, and a feeling of guilt and desperation that can drive people into second marriages before they are emotionally prepared to handle them."

Rose Marie

"I was exceptionally close to my girls, as a single parent," Rose Marie explained. "When I was single, we had a tradition that at 11:00 P.M. every night, we would talk over the day's events and get into each others feelings and concerns. The key was knowing about each other, and caring.

"I had my own fears about remarriage:

1. "Phil and I had different temperaments.
2. "Could we be close?

3. "As a single parent, I was in control; and didn't have to consult anyone.
4. "I was afraid Phil did not listen to me. I wanted a close relationship, with the ability to communicate.
5. "Cruelty—I soon realized this was an unfounded fear.

"My daughters had mixed feelings. They were glad for me but were apprehensive. They liked Phil but were scared at giving me up. My problem was to balance time between Phil and my kids. I was an arbiter between them and was constantly in the middle.

"Phil is not naturally open. He was unsure how to act with my daughters. Now, he's direct with them, gives them room, and tries to be interested in them. His concern shows. They in turn, give him room. This enables him to be kind and sympathetic."

Phil and Rose Marie Together

As with most couples, Phil and Rose Marie have their disagreements. Rose Marie's characteristic negative response is "Let's sell the house;" while Phil's is "Don't do things without my permission."

As a result of their remarriage, Rose Marie and Phil have found that

1. Their friendships with old and new single friends depend on the quality and the basis of the friendship.
2. They are more analytical than previously about how other marriages seem to work or not work, and why.
3. Each has a greater willingness and ability than before, to listen, be open and empathize, communicate, and work together.
4. Their second marriage is deeper than their previous marriages had been.

Rose Marie and Phil offered the following suggestions for single parents considering remarriage:

1. "A second marriage is deeper and more demanding than your first marriage.
2. "With children, a major caution needs to be 'Understand what you're getting into, and avoid unrealistic expectations.'

3. "Important keys are communication, space, and not forcing your own standards on your partner.
4. "The 'loner' (noncustodial parent, or nonparent) should sit back and get the feel of the territory.
5. "The custodial parent often is too used to caring for everyone and needs to remove herself (or himself) from the middle.
6. "Finally, you should ask yourself two key questions:
   Are you good companions?
   Can you, and do you, get along as friends?"

Saralee and Charles

Saralee has three children: two daughters (ages 18 and 16) and a son (age 10). She was divorced in 1975 and remarried in 1976. Saralee told her story thus:

"Charles did not ever cut into my time with my children. I would not have a relationship at my children's expense. When Charles was around, it was in a positive way—almost like a special grandparent. We did fun things together or had a special dinner. (Of course, I did the same for my children's special friends.) We did things together, such as baking a cake for Charles or my children's friends.

"When he wasn't around, I encouraged the children to use my perceptions of Charles to complement their own—for example, "we had a nice lunch together"—to show casually that being with Charles made me feel nice.

"I was not looking for someone and was satisfied with my life as a single parent. Charles did *not* 'rescue' me.

"During my first marriage, my children did not see sexual love or demonstrable affection. Within six months after meeting Charles, I was lighter, gayer, and more joyful. There was a new buoyancy, and an opportunity for the children to see a loving relationship.

"Seeing me in love has helped my daughters. They have lit up and bloomed more seeing me happy.

"Both my marriages had mutual support that the parents gave each other. The second also contains a 'feeling component.' My children have seen me grow, love, and be loved. They see things that I like but couldn't show before (such as returning to college). We have more fun in this marriage than I did in my first marriage. We still won't drag the kids to the museum if they don't want to go, but we can all go out and enjoy having a pizza together.

"*Integration* (or, getting used to the new situation gradually) has also been important. For example, I would pick up the children with Charles in the car. Then, Charles would drive and I'd go along. Finally, occasionally (even now), as they got used to seeing Charles, I would let Charles pick them up himself. If they asked, 'Why is Charles picking us up?' I could say I was doing dishes and he wanted to see the end of the game (if they were at a game).

"We also used *modeling* in developing our relationship. By this, I mean that we always moved slowly, gradually, and sequentially into a relationship."

Saralee continued, "The children still have a close relationship with Larry (their father). We have never hinted that Charles should replace Larry as their father.

"Larry and I have always supported each other as parents. We call each other mom or dad in front of the children (rather than your mother, or your father). This type of 'affectionate endearing address' helps the children feel that each parent is still important: both to the children, and to each other (as coparents and friends).

"Another strength that Charles and I have is that we have emerged as a strong unified couple. We—not the children—make the final decision. We *told* the children of our marriage. When we decided to move to Charles's house, we said, 'We will move because we think we'll be happy and enjoy growing together. When you grow up and leave, we will enjoy growing old here together.'

"We will not allow the children to come between us and are committed to a permanent growing relationship."

Saralee had three suggestions for noncustodial parents who are remarried and have poor communication with their former spouse:

1. "Use writing, instead of speech. Write about six weeks in advance, if you want them for a special time for visitation (for example, Thanksgiving).
2. "You need firm guidelines to deal with issues such as money and visitation. Deal with these problems in advance.
3. "If the custodial parent refuses you permission, you can let your children know that you cared enough to try to see them."

Resources for Remaried Parents

A list of resources for remarried parents can be found in Appendix C under both Remarried Parents' Groups and Step-parent Resources. A list of useful books may be found in Appendix D under Remarriage and Step-parenting.

SUMMARY

As you have seen, you have a variety of options available to you as a single parent. The most important suggestion I can offer is do what you are comfortable with, rather than what you think "everybody's doing." You may not want to do any dating, or possibly prefer only casual dating. You may want a long-term relationship. If so, you might want to reread the sections on LSA, LTA, and remarriage. Are you concerned about whether your children will be hurt by your dating several people, rather than having one permanent relationship? Other single parents have found that this does *not* have to be true. You might want to read, again, about the Montcosps dialogue that dealt with you, your relationships, and your children.

Although you do not "need" a remarriage or LTA in order to have a satisfying life as a person and single parent, both an LTA and remarriage are choices you might consider. Our final piece of advice, heard time and again from single parents: Before considering any relationship, learn to know, value, and appreciate yourself as a person. As you become more independent, you are far more likely to be able to handle a long-term relationship. It is far healthier for both partners if each enters the relationship because of independence, inner strength, and free choice, not desperation and need.

Chapter 8

You and the Nonsingle Community

We live in an increasingly fast-paced, impersonal metropolitan society. It is all-to-easy to feel—with some justification—that we have little
or no control over our lives. Our government, the high cost of living,
the boring nature of so many jobs, the pressures of child rearing, the
high mobility rate—which makes it difficult to rely on friends since
you are not sure they will still be around in a year or two—and the all
too frequent demands on what free time we have, these all combine to
give us a feeling of being trapped and foster a growing desire for
familiar routines. In such an atmosphere, it is difficult and time-
consuming to react to each new person as an individual. In sheer
self-defense, a natural reaction is to judge and evaluate people instantly, to fit them into categories, or "boxes," based on their job,
marital status, appearance, or whatever. It then becomes simple to sift
through the boxes, rejecting all members of boxes other than the one
to which we belong. Perhaps at work or in a social situation *you* are an
outgoing, friendly person. But remember the time when you met
someone who was shy, and how you might have mistaken that shyness
for snobbishness? Yet when you took the time to know the person,
you may have found that you enjoyed his or her company—perhaps
even becoming friends. Had you relied completely on your negative

first impression, you would probably have missed a valuable friendship.

Remember when you were a child or teenager? This tendency to "type" people, and reject those not in our group, is even more common with children and teenagers. However, if we take the time to reach out beyond labels and stereotypes, some really rewarding friendships, in which each person's differences contribute something special to the relationship, can develop. I remember one such example from my years in high school.

When I was in high school, I enjoyed music and the arts. "Of course," I was part of the "arts group." When I got to know Craig, a varsity basketball player, however, I realized that my stereotype of athletes was not necessarily true. Craig and I would go for walks and share interests such as classes, the future, ideas and values; we enjoyed each other's companionship. I came to understand and appreciate the hard work, comradeship, and special satisfaction that Craig received from his involvement in basketball. I believe that Craig (from what he told me) came to appreciate my ability to play the piano—with the special satisfaction I derived from my piano playing—and my love for literature.

As single parents, we are in a special situation. If we were married or, in some cases, in a long-term relationship outside marriage, when we were married, we became used to being part of a couple. Our friends were primarily other married couples—or, more likely, the marital partner of our own sex. While we might have kept up with some of our single friends, so often we tended to grow away from each other ("After all, they have their world, we have ours.") We were part of normal married society and were accepted and respected accordingly. Life was usually comfortable, familiar, and safe. Our relationships were usually limited (by geographical proximity and our general life style) to those in a similar stage of life—in short, to other married couples with children.

When we became single again, we had to discard our previously comfortable identity as a married person and develop a new, more appropriate identity as a single person and single parent. We no longer fitted comfortably into married society. As a *one* in a society of *twos*, we felt strange and different, and were frequently seen by our married friends as a potential threat to their marriage. Their initial sympathy too often turned to impatience and rejection. (From my observations and experiences in single-parent and singles' discussion groups, I have learned that this apparently is more true for newly single women than men.) The all-too-frequent attempts by our married friends to help us by playing matchmaker were often seen by us as an unwelcome intrusion.

We had to change the way we saw ourselves, from being part of a couple to being a single person. To achieve this, we, at that time, had to reject as no longer appropriate to our needs the married friends, organizations, and society to which we had become accustomed, and find clubs, organizations (such as Parents Without Partners), and other resources that could help us develop a new life and identity as a single person and single parent. (I have already discussed some of these resources, and how you can use them effectively, in Chapter 6.)

As time progressed, we became more accustomed to living as a single person. Singles' organizations and activities came to be "normal" to us. At the same time, friendships with married couples—either old friends or new people—came to appear unrealistic or undesirable, perhaps supported by our secret fear of being considered a second-rate parent because we are single. (Indeed, many people—including some to whom I have talked—get upset at the idea that the single-parent family can be positive or beneficial for its children and parent.) Just as newly married couples see themselves as growing away from, and ultimately rejecting many—if not all—of, their single friends, it is common and understandable for single parents to limit their friendships to other single people.

At this point, it might be worthwhile to reexamine your friendships with married couples. Do not forget that you were friends with many of these people when you were married. You probably shared some common values and interests. When you were newly single, you needed room in which to find yourself and grow. Your married friends probably felt strange too. They might well have asked themselves questions, such as the following:

> How do we stay friendly without taking sides?
> Will he or she want to stay friendly with us now that he or she is single?
> How can we help and not impose?
> If their marriage couldn't survive, how secure is ours?

When people become part of different groups, such as married couples and single parents, there are two choices. Either friendships can be limited to those in one's own group, or each friendship can be judged on its individual merits. I believe that opening yourself to friendships (both renewing old friendships and establishing new friendships) can be very satisfying for all of you and your children.

OTHER SINGLE PARENTS' EXPERIENCES

Phyllis, from Billings, Montana, made an important observation when she said, "The durability of my nonsingle relationships depends on the quality of the prior friendship."

Several single parents, such as Carol Ann (from Arnold, Maryland) and Julia (from Belen, New Mexico) are more friendly with one individual in the marriage (typically the wife) than the couple as such.

Hazel, from Erie, Pennsylvania, observed, "I have not been rejected by those people who have a security of themselves and their relationships with their mates. Only those who feel insecure reject me, as they feel I am a threat to their relationship. I don't consider them more than acquaintances."

I was surprised at the number of single parents who felt—or anticipated—rejection by their married friends, and sometimes by new couples they met. Some reasons were the difference in marital status and a belief that singles and marrieds have a completely different lifestyle and sharply differing values. These are some reasons why, at single-parent discussion groups, single parents so frequently reject the possibility of friendships with married couples and look to the single community for all their social needs.

THE ADVANTAGES OF FRIENDSHIPS BETWEEN SINGLE PARENTS AND MARRIED PEOPLE

There are several ways that single and married people alike can benefit from "single-married" friendships.

Married couples can offer stability, reliability, and a contrasting life style. With married friends, you can be yourself and relax from the dating scene, the need to impress other single people, and the often hectic pace and pressures that go with being a single parent. Since each partner, in a happy marriage, has more time to carry out his or her responsibilities and pursue individual interests, married friends can frequently offer helpful hints useful to you as a single parent. Your children can also benefit from the opportunity to get to know a two-parent family and recognize the many positive aspects of this type of family situation.

There is much that you as a single parent can bring to the friendship. It is all too easy for married couples to become locked in to familiar roles, routines, and habits. As a single parent, you have had to develop new skills and strengths, change and become more resourceful to deal with your new living situation. Since you have no full-time partner, you have had to adapt to a double responsibility in raising your children, frequently requiring more involvement and responsibility from your children than is the case in many two-parent, or nuclear, families. Through your involvement in single-parent or singles' organizations and discussions, and your role as a single parent, you have probably learned to look beyond traditional gender stereotypes, realize that men and women share many needs and concerns, and appreciate each new person as an individual. If you are a single mother, you have had to support yourself economically, compete in the job market, obtain training and gain at least some familiarity with household repairs, car maintenance, and other traditionally masculine pursuits. If you are a single father, you have had to learn (if you hadn't already) how to cook, clean a house, manage a household, and do laundry.

Thus, as a single parent relating to married friends, you can contribute openness to new ideas, change and flexibility, and a less tradition-bound life style.

Steve and Kathy: A Couple with Single-Parent Friends

Because the issue of single-parent friendships with married couples has seldom been addressed, I asked Steve and Kathy, a couple from the Baltimore, Maryland area, to comment on their own experiences and insights, and offer suggestions that might help both other married couples and single parents. In response to my questions, Steve commented, "We were friendly with one couple who split up. I met the wife through work; then, we became friendly as couples. When they separated, we wanted to continue the friendship. However, I sensed a defensiveness on the part of the husband when I met him at a festival. He acted embarrassed and defensive, as if he expected rejection. He acted as if he didn't want to be friendly. The wife wanted to continue the friendship. However, she continually played, with us at least, a 'happy-face mask.' She seemed all fun and games, as if she was really happy. However, we wanted and needed honesty, not pretense. We had—and probably still have—common interests with each of those two people, but dishonesty and defensiveness have ruined what could still be a rewarding friendship. I, for one, would have preferred honesty about their feelings, rather than an artificial approach as a basis for renewing our friendship."

I asked Steve if he had any suggestions for couples or single parents who find themselves in a situation such as the one described. Steve offered the following:

"I would encourage couples to assume a nonjudgmental, accepting attitude toward their newly single friends. Accept people first as human beings, and second as former marriage partners. This nurtures an attitude of honesty. Then, after the single parent feels he or she can say anything, this removes the barriers and the tremendous pressures, and eases up the friendship.

"Criticism, judgmental attitudes, and incomplete honesty (you can be both diplomatic and honest) are tremendous barriers to friendships.

"Think before you speak. This requires an attitude of trust.

"My advice to single parents in this situation would be don't project outdated cultural values (such as "all married couples think all single parents are failures in a second-class family"). Think of your married friends as individual human beings, rather than labeling them. Take the risk and be honest! If they reject you, ask yourself the question, 'Is this a friendship I really wish to pursue?' It's their loss. Don't put the burden of guilt upon yourself."

Steve and Kathy are also friends with two women, who are older than they (Steve and Kathy are in their late 20s), who are single parents. Steve commented, "We respect these people because they have already accepted themselves. This positive self-image makes it easy to see them as friends who happen to be single, rather than desperate divorcees. Each has several children. We all share the experience of being parents, and our differing perspectives add to the quality of our friendship."

In a friendship between single parents and married people, explains Steve, "an advantage to the married couple is a more realistic understanding of life's alternatives. By being more open to people in different situations than our own, we can see new situations (such as death or divorce) as less of a threat. The single parent can benefit by receiving support and understanding from the married friends."

Steve had the following advice:

"For married couples, I have observed that most married couples don't ask the single parent's children how they feel about their family. The children's response can give an honest idea of how the family actually works. I would encourage married couples to keep in touch, personally, with children of single-parent families.

"For single parents, I would mention that my single-parent friends have chosen to treat my wife and me first as individual human beings, and second, as a married couple."

HOW TO GET STARTED

We all have a fear of rejection. This is something we, as single people, have to routinely deal with.

Yet, we all know that if we don't try, we will never have a chance of meeting interesting people, getting a better job, or achieving any of our other goals in an area where the rewards can be great—but so can the risks. So, we swallow our fears and take the risk, realizing that even should we not achieve our goals, or have a good time, *lack of success doesn't necessarily mean that we are failures*. And, sometimes, we do meet an interesting new person to date, new friends, or achieve something else that we really want. Then, everything seems especially worthwhile, and we are glad that we took the risk.

The same can be true when we take the risk of contacting old friends. Even here, there is always the fear of rejection, but this says more about your friends than it does about you. There is always the very real possibility that your friends might also have been afraid to contact you, and they will be genuinely glad to hear from you.

I remember a strategy which I saw in Dale Carnegie's book *How to Stop Worrying and Start Living*. In Chapter 2 of his book, Carnegie discusses "A Magic Formula For Solving Worry Situations," which he learned from Willis Carrier, (former) director of the Carrier Corporation in New York. This formula consists of three parts:

1. "Ask yourself, 'What is the worst that can possibly happen?'
2. "Prepare to accept it if you have to.
3. "Then calmly proceed to improve on the worst."[1]

While no formula can solve all our problems, this approach has often helped give me the courage to take chances. After all, if we apply Carrier's method to developing nonsingle relationships, for example, we can realize

1. What is the worst that can possibly happen?
   Answer: That my efforts at friendship will be rejected.
2. Prepare to accept the worst.
   Answer: If that happens, I won't be any worse off than I already am. In addition, my uncertainty will be resolved; and I will be more free to concentrate on developing friendships with greater potential.
3. Calmly proceed to improve on the worst.
   Answer: If I don't try, I'll have the fears and uncertainty of not knowing where I stand; and I still won't have the friendship. *The only way I can achieve what I want is to take the risk and try.*

As I have said earlier, many married couples would like to maintain friendships with their single friends (whom they knew as part of a couple), but they are not sure how to deal with their friend's newly single status. Also (and this applies to both old friends and potential friends), there is an increasing tendency—especially among modern couples—to accept both divorce and single-parent families as a reality and be more concerned with a person's values and interests than his or her marital status.

Without question, single parents, married couples, and society as a whole will gain from closer friendships between single parents and married people.

Because of the charged emotion and frequent stereotyping by

[1]Dale Carnegie, *How to Stop Worrying and Start Living* (New York: Pocket Books, 1953, p. 32.

both married and single society, I have suggested a strategy which will help you develop, maintain (or evaluate and end) friendships with married people. You will see (1) how you can use your interests to find your kind of people, and (2) what you can do to overcome society's prejudice and negativity toward you as a single parent.

Proposed Strategy for Improving the Quality of Your Nonsingle Relationships

You Are a Special Person, and Your Friendship Has Value

As a single parent, you have had to overcome many obstacles in order to make a rewarding life for yourself and your children. You can be proud of yourself, and you can realize "I'm a worthwhile person, with a lot to offer in a friendship." Your experience as a single parent, your interests, your values, all add up to make you a pretty special person. People are not doing you a favor by being your friend; they are, like you, gaining some benefit from the relationship.

Base Your Friendships Around Common Interests and Values, Not Marital Status

I have found that my most lasting friendships have been based on common interests, whether my friends are single or married. Common interests can be children, sports, music, or any other area that all of you enjoy sharing.

One problem many of us who are single have come to face is that *many of our couple friends from our marriage were friends because of our marital status*. We did things together in pairs, just accepting and enjoying the companionship. When we became single, we ceased to be part of a couple; and the common bond with these married friends was no longer present. In such a situation, it is any wonder that our friendship generally disintegrates? If our friendships with our married friends (or married people we meet *after* we become single) are to survive and become meaningful for us, they need to be based on what we all can share *now*.

Don't Be Afraid to Take the Initiative

If you want to re-establish ties with old friends, or get to know new people, be prepared to take the first step and call. Many times, after a couple separates, their friends feel unsure of how they should act and are often reluctant to impose. A friendly call from you can help break the ice.

This also holds true for those married individuals and couples you meet after you have become single. Often, people get so involved with their own lives that they may not get around to calling you. If you give them a call, they will usually appreciate it—and if not, you are no worse off than if you had never called.

Don't Drain Your Friends or Expect More Than They Can Give

Each of us has only a limited amount of emotional energy. While friends can be a real help and support to us, it can be all too easy to drain them by our complaints and problems.

Let's face it: In most cases, our married friends can offer little real support in areas related to our singleness. They are not single; we are. Where they can help are in areas of mutual concern, areas such as jobs or careers; parenting; shared interests, values and frustrations; and those concerns common to us as human beings.

I have found that I am a far better and more caring friend when I do not rely on my friends to help me with all my problems. To accomplish this, I have found that Hotlines can be an effective, free, available, and safe place to release emotional tension.

For problems concerning your life as a single parent and single person, discussion groups (such as those offered through churches, community groups, and single-parent organizations) seem to be an ideal resource. In these groups, you can learn how other single parents and single nonparents have dealt with a common concern or problem. These discussion groups can be far more effective in dealing with problems concerning your single and single-parent status than can well-intentioned married friends, who can relate little, if at all, to this area of your concern.

By using Hotlines and singles' discussion groups effectively, we are better able to enjoy our friends in an unburdening situation.

Treat Your Friends As Individuals, Not Stereotypes, and Expect Them to Do the Same to You

Your friends are pretty special; otherwise, why would they be your friends? To have friends, you have to be a friend. This means trying to understand and appreciate their point of view—even if it is not always the same as yours. For example, don't expect your friends to pick you up or pay for you on social engagements, unless it is because *all of you* are comfortable with this arrangement. Empathize with and support your friends, even if their concerns are not always identical to your own. If you care, and understand their point of view, you will have a much more rewarding friendship than if you only concern yourself with your own needs.

This can be especially true if you are friendly with only one of the married partners. Recognize that there will be times when your friend will want to be with his or her spouse rather than you, accept it as a given part of the friendship, and appreciate those things that you can enjoy together. (After all, aren't there times when you would prefer to be with other single people, or on a date, rather than with married friends?) Your friendship can then be a mutually satisfying one.

It is also important that your friends treat you as an individual, rather than as an incomplete part of a couple. Married friends will sometimes offer to find you a date for times when you all go out together. Presumably, you will feel more comfortable as part of a couple, if only for a given occasion. I have found an effective response to be something like, "I really appreciate your concern, but I would much rather just enjoy your company. Our friendship is special to me just as it is."

Determine Whether the Friendship Is Meeting Your Needs, and Take Any Necessary Steps to Maintain, Modify, or Dissolve It

My first recommendation was that you appreciate and value yourself and your own worth as a friend. It is equally important to recognize the importance of fulfilling your needs in a friendship. A major value of being single is that we can choose our friendships on the basis of our feelings, without worrying about those of a partner. A test I periodically apply to each of my friendships is "Do I feel better when I am with this person than I would be if I didn't see him or her?" If the answer is yes, I don't worry about the friendship.

If the answer is no, I then determine why and try to decide whether I want to preserve this friendship with modifications or terminate it, since my needs are no longer being met.

If there are problems, I need to discuss them with the other people involved and try to work out a mutually satisfactory solution.

If this does not work, or if I conclude that the friendship is not worth saving, I then no longer devote my time and energy to this particular friendship, but move on to other relationships that meet my needs. When I tell my former friends that I "just don't have any free time these days," I mean it literally. My children, my interests, my job, and my need for time alone leave little time for any relationship that is not rewarding for me.

This of course also applies if my friends decide to end the friendship. I am disappointed and frequently hurt, but I have to realize that perhaps we are no longer right for each other. In any case, how much enjoyment could I gain from a friendship in which the other people are uncomfortable with the relationship?

Renewing a Friendship from the Married Period: A Personal Example

Most relationships with married people are adequately covered by my six previous recommendations. However, our relationships with our friends from our marriage can cause particular problems.

195

For this reason, it might be helpful to see how such a relationship was handled in one actual situation.

When I was married, my wife and I lived in Massachusetts. There, we became friendly with John and Linda. When my wife and I moved to Virginia, the four of us still got together during vacations. At the time of my separation, in late 1974, we had not seen Linda and John for two years.

Linda's birthday was approximately one month after our separation. I sent her a birthday card and added that my wife and I were now separated. When I never received a reply, I felt rejected. This added to my overall feelings of insecurity and failure at marriage. However, I learned to deal with my new single status and to accept and value myself. Through counseling, and some of the resources discussed earlier, I became more appreciative of my own worth and, as a result, better able to listen to and appreciate other people, without always concentrating on my own problems.

Finally, 11 months after my separation, I felt ready to contact old friends. I called John and Linda. When I mentioned our friendship, they told me they weren't sure how to act but invited me to visit them at Christmas. In December 1975 I visited Linda and John, and we all had a really great time. This was so for several reasons. First, I was there because I wanted to be, not because I felt a social obligation. Second, I felt good about myself and had already dealt with my emotional tension by using hotlines and single-parent discussion groups. Since I knew that these resources would again be available when I returned, I was free to listen to, and get to know, John and Linda as friends—rather than as amateur therapists or referees in arguments between my former wife and me.

A year and a half later, my children came to live with me. At that time, we went to visit Linda and John and their two children. Because of my tension with my children, John's attending summer school, and Linda's working, there was little opportunity for any of us to relax. On our last night together, John, Linda, and I went to see a play; and we were all finally able to relax and enjoy each other. During intermission, Linda told me how nice it was to see me calm, because my continual tension had made them wonder whether they could be comfortable with our friendship.

After returning home, I thought about what Linda had said. I finally wrote a letter, telling Linda and John what our friendship meant to me, suggesting that perhaps we had all felt a great deal of tension at the time. What did they think? When I called, several weeks later, they told me that they agreed with my description of the problem.

My willingness to risk rejection by calling Linda and John initially—and to work out my personal problems by using more appropriate resources—made it possible to develop our friendship. Once I took the first step, the rest was up to the three of us. Our honesty, willingness to share our concerns by working together to resolve and anticipate problems, and our enjoyment and appreciation of each other as individuals have added greatly to the quality of our friendship. I consider my friendship with John and Linda (as individuals and as a couple) to be one of the deepest and most satisfying friendships that I now have.

Your Interests: One Key to a More Rewarding Life

One of the truest sayings I know is, To thine own self be true. This applies very much to our relationships. While we can meet our "type" of people anywhere, we have the greatest opportunity if we pursue our own interests. If you love music, join a chorus or a band. If you enjoy the outdoors, clubs such as the Sierra Club offer what you want. The list is endless. The only thing that is unique is you and your individual interests. When you attend activities related to your own interests, you *know* you have at least one thing in common with the other people who are there (whether they are single or married): your shared interests. Developing relationships then just becomes a matter of finding other people with whom you feel comfortable. Even if you do not make any new friends, you can still have fun doing something you enjoy.

Overcoming Prejudice and Negativity Toward You As a Single Parent

Since single parents are a minority in today's society, we often encounter some hostility from businesses, employers, and community groups.

I have found that it is important to understand what these

groups are saying. Some of their concerns *are* valid. Single parents are not usually as free to travel as nuclear-family parents; single parents typically do not have as much free time or extra income as their married counterparts; and single-parent families are still—all too frequently—seen as an undesirable alternative to nuclear families.

It can often be helpful to empathize with the critic and then state that the type of situation he or she describes is *not always true*. You are an individual and wish to be treated as such. If you are told that single parents are not reliable workers, you might reply that you cannot speak for other single parents, but your job means a lot to you, as it offers an opportunity for involvement and accomplishment away from your family. At the same time, you have had to develop flexibility, interpersonal techniques, inner resources, control of time, and leadership ability to succeed in managing a household, holding a job, and still have time for a life of your own. These qualities, plus your seriousness of purpose, can be advantageous to your (prospective) employer, if the two of you can work together to achieve your common goals.

This approach can be used with businesses, community groups, and other organizations or individuals with negative feelings toward single parents. If you try to understand the organization's or the individual's situation, if you try to step into their shoes and through empathy create a common bond, you have won half the battle. Your most important step is to refuse to be *the* representative for all single parents. Just as you should treat the other person as an individual, you too deserve to be considered as an individual. You can then more effectively win the other party's respect, simultaneously increasing your chances of achieving your goals. Thus, you can also help to create a better understanding and appreciation of single parents, and single-parent families, in our society.

SUMMARY

The following reviews, in brief, the recommendations for improving your nonsingle relationships.

1. Remember that you are a special person and your friendship has value.
2. Base your friendships around common interests and values, not marital status.

3. Don't be afraid to take the initiative; don't wait for the other person to make the first move.
4. Don't drain your friends or expect more than they can give. Rather, investigate and take advantage of other resources such as Hotlines and single-parent discussion groups.
5. Treat your friends as individuals, not stereotypes; and expect them to treat you the same way.
6. Determine whether the friendship is meeting your needs and take any necessary steps to maintain, modify, or dissolve it.

In addition, listed here are the suggestions to help you overcome prejudice and negativity toward you as a single parent.

1. Emphathize with the other party and try to understand his point of view. (Put yourself in the other person's position, and imagine how you might feel in the present situation.)
2. Refuse, preferably in a tactful way, to be *the* representative for all single parents.
3. Expect and ask to be treated as an individual—and extend the same courtesy to the other party.
4. Help the other party find areas of common interest, and use these as a basis for achieving a mutually satisfactory agreement.

Chapter 9

Making It As a Single Parent

Throughout this book, we have shared much together. You have seen that being a single parent can be a rewarding and positive way of life for both parent and children; and you have heard from other single parents how they have succeeded in progressing from the initial shock of separation or divorce, of death or desertion, to building a stable and fulfilling family life for their children and themselves. We have examined the day-to-day problems of single parenting and learned about the special concerns of individual groups of single parents (such as widows and widowers, never-marrieds, and gays and lesbians). Joint custody and divided custody are alternatives for raising children as a single parent.

Being a single parent can sometimes seem a lonely and difficult way of life. However, as you recall from Chapter 6, if you are aware of what resources are available—and how you and your children can use them most effectively—you do not have to do everything alone. You can get valuable help, support, and advice in a variety of areas. It is vital that you accept yourself as a single person and learn to enjoy living with yourself.

We have explored together a variety of potential relationships—ranging from each partner having his or her separate home, to remarriage (and arrangements that fall in the middle)—and seen that there does not have to be an irreconcilable conflict between your children and your other relationships.

Finally, as suggested, you can gain real benefits from friendships that extend beyond the single community. Developing relationships that transcend group boundaries not only gives you, your children, and married couples a broader perspective than you otherwise would have, but it creates a basis for mutual understanding and appreciation that can go a long way in eliminating the prejudice, hostility, and distrust that frequently separate single parents and their children from our society as a whole.

If you are a single parent (custodial or noncustodial), this book has shown you that single parenting can work—and, in fact, *is working* for countless other single parents. Explore your individual situation, feelings, and needs; reread some of the ideas and suggestions that have worked for other single parents; then develop your own system. If you trust yourself, are flexible and open to new approaches, are willing to learn from others—to seek help, when necessary—are not afraid to make mistakes, and can come to view single parenting as a special opportunity for personal and family growth, then you *can and will* succeed in single parenting.

If you are not a single parent, you have seen in this book some of the positive aspects of single-parent families, and how single-parent families can be—and, in fact, are—a beneficial influence on each of their members. Understanding how single-parent families *do* work has perhaps helped you to realize that the successful single-parent family is *not* the same as a broken home, but a positive and unique type of family. If you can use this awareness to help single parents and their children to build on and appreciate the special strengths of their one-parent family (instead of lamenting the "tragic break up of the two-parent family"), you will be performing a much-needed service for not only single parents and their children but society as a whole.

If there is one question I would like to leave you, my single parent readers, with, it is this, "How does your present relationship with your children compare with your prior relationship with them, when you were married?" Perhaps, this is the ultimate test of how well the single-parent family serves the needs of its members. If—as virtually all the single parents whom I contacted for this book found—the parent-child relationship, custodial or noncustodial, has improved since the end of the marriage, then the single-parent family can indeed be and is a positive and beneficial influence on its members.

I do not see "a tragic breakup of the family." Rather, I am encouraged by the fact that if and when existing nuclear families fail to meet the needs of their members, parents are willing to try alternatives such as single-parent families—rather than give up on the family. The successful single-parent family has shown that by providing an alternative family foundation which encourages and supports its parent and children in their efforts to fulfill their potential as human beings, it meets the needs of not only its individual members but society as a whole.

FOR RELEASE: September 19, 1979

APPENDIX A: KENTUCKY FRIED CHICKEN TIME OUT INSTITUTE SINGLE PARENT STUDY©

SYNOPSIS

BACKGROUND

Founded in 1977 by Kentucky Fried Chicken, the Time Out Institute was established to examine the changing role of today's American women and to contribute to the information available about their problems, attitudes, needs and concerns. The 1979 Institute focus on single parenting reflects the fact that 84% of all single parents are women. To promote better understanding of this group, Kentucky Fried Chicken has underwritten national research about single parents.[1]

Research objectives were two-fold: 1) to determine the impact of becoming a single parent in terms of attitudes and feelings, financial and employment status, and 2) to understand childrens' feelings and changes in their attitudes.

© KFC National Co-op, 1979
[1]conducted by National Family Opinion, Inc.

Two self-administered mail questionnaires were sent to a nationally projectable sample of single parent households. Responding were 768 single parents and 483 children of single parent homes (ages 10 to 17).

For purposes of this study, single parents are defined as: a mother or a father with one or more of their own children under age 18 residing in their home. Based on this definition, since 1970, the number of single parent mothers has increased 62%; of single fathers 38%; of total single parent families 60%; and of total families 10%.

CONCLUSIONS

1) Family life is adapting to the needs of the 20th century.
   - 75% of single parent families are doing well and the kids know it.
   - The children are well-adjusted.
   - The institution of the family is resilient enough to survive new lifestyles.
   - You can go it alone and do fine.
2) When the non-custodial parent remains involved, the single parent families do well.
3) *Unhappy parents (25%) have troubled children.*
4) *To be well-adjusted, single parents need to be employed.*
   Working is the critical factor;
   - they need the money
   - they need a sense of independence and capability
   - they need adult friends, social life

HIGHLIGHTS

I. Single Parents' Feelings

A. The Upside

Seventy percent of single parent respondents answered YES to the statement "I basically like being a single parent." How do they do it?

1) a network of support. Eighty-four percent say they receive emotional support from friends; 75% say they receive such support from family.
2) feeling of control. Seventy-nine percent say they have gained more control over their own life since becoming a single parent.
3) satisfactory living arrangements. Seventy-seven percent are proud of the fact that they were able to maintain the same or comparable living quarters—which gives them a feeling of security for themselves and their children.

B. The Downside

Single parents expressed surprisingly few strong negative attitudes toward their role. Only 28% of the single parents surveyed feel their children are emotionally deprived; 24% feel their children are resentful; 24% that children limit dating opportunities; and a very low 6% feel they have failed in life.

II. Identified Changes Since Becoming a Single Parent

A. Lifestyle Changes

Although 64% say they feel more capable of handling *all* responsibilities, the majority of perceived lifestyle changes center around the children. Sixty-six percent feel they are closer to their children; 54% say they go and do more with the children; 53% spend more time with their children and 53% feel they are doing a more effective job with the children.

B. Economic Changes

Keeping in mind that, according to the U.S. Census, the median income for all families is $14,816 and the median income for female-headed single parent families is $6,844, the survey of these single parents' source of income (own job, government aid, monies from other parent) shows that single parents *must* work in order to earn in excess of the median income.

Seventy-four percent of the single parents surveyed are currently employed, 26% are not currently employed and 33% changed their work status since becoming a single parent.

To the single parent, employment means: being a happier person (63%), being a more interesting person (60%), and having more friends (44%).

Ten percent of all single parents stopped working after becoming a single parent because they felt their children needed them at home. In fact, 54% of those who stopped working sought professional counsel for their kids; 32% consulted with other parents. However, even those who stopped feel that working is better than not working for the single parent.

III. Attitude Segment—Parents and Children

For attitude segments emerged from the survey data analysis. Each group shares similar feelings and holds similar attitudes toward their single parent status. These segments indicate that 75% of single parents have made, by their own standards, a satisfactory adjustment to single parenthood. The unhappy segment of single parents felt marriage was a better alternative than being single. These four groups are identified below by the shared attitudes indicated:

Parents:

1) Doing OK—(28% of all single parents)

The most significant reason for coping given by this group is the fact that they have enough money. They are characterized as "managing."

of these 28%:
61% feel they have an active social life
58% feel free to spend money on themselves
67% feel free to spend money on their kids
69% have more time for their own interests

2) Full Life—(24% of all single parents)

This group is coping in the fullest. They touch base with all aspects of life: employment, finances, their children and their personal life.

of these 24%:
70% feel they have opportunities to do fun things
69% feel they are doing an effective job as a parent
80% say they have become more interesting people

3) Child Oriented—(23% of all single parents)

Relative to the segments these single parents are most concerned with their children. They see themselves as coping and handling all responsibilities.

of these 23%:
81% feel they are capable of handling all responsibilities
69% feel they are doing an effective job as parents
74% say they spend time with their children

4) Unhappy in Every Way—(25% of all single parents)

of these 25%:
67% say they became irritable
75% say they had to cut out extras
78% feel they have limited opportunities to meet the other sex
49% feel people are critical of them
58% say they receive unsolicited advice on how to run their own lives
50% resent fulfilling the responsibilities of both parents

Children:

1) If the parent is "doing OK":

62% of the kids feel closer to the parent they live with

2) If the parent is leading "a full life":

48% of the children feel more loved now that they live with one parent
48% said the parent they live with spends more time with them
67% feel closer to the parent they live with
53% get more attention from the parent they live with

3) If the parent is "child-oriented":

72% of the kids feel closer to the parent they live with
60% get more attention from the parent they live with
36% are more interested in their custodial parents' work

4) If the parent is unhappy in every way:

32% of the kids feel different from other children because they live with one parent
27% feel more lonely
41% talk more to adults other than their parents
39% get angrier; have more quarrels with custodial parent
43% get upset more easily

APPENDIX B: QUESTIONNAIRE FOR MAKING IT AS A SINGLE PARENT

1. Please describe your own parental status:
   □Custodial Mother □Non-Custodial Mother □Joint-Custody Mother □Co-Parenting Mother □Divided Custody Mother □Custodial Father □Non-Custodial Father □Joint-Custody Father □Co-Parenting Father □Divided Custody Father □Other (describe)
2. Please give the ages and sex of your children, and how long you have been a single parent.
3. Please check *only if A, B, or C applies to you*:
   □A) Never married single parent
   □B) Widow or Widower who is a single parent
   □C) Single Parent who has adopted children
4. As a single parent, have you in the past, are you presently, or are you considering:
   A— Living with a member of the opposite sex
       □Past □Presently □Considering
   B— Remarriage
       □Past □Presently □Considering
   C— Having an intimate relationship, where you and your partner spend extended periods of time together, but maintain separate dwellings.
       □Past □Presently □Considering

5. How have you found each type of living situation in #4 affects (or, how do you believe it could affect):
   A— *Yourself*
   B— *Your Children*
   C— Your relationship with your children, and the quality of your family life

6. As a single parent, do you feel that you have been able to build a family structure and living situation that is comfortable for both yourself and your children?
   □Yes □No

7. If you answered yes to Question 6, how have you and your children been able to achieve this and how does your family work now? Please also mention whether either or both of the following have played an important role in developing a rewarding life for you and your children:
   A— Family Rituals and Traditions
   B— Daily Schedules and Continuity

8. What suggestions might you offer another single parent with reference to questions 4–7?

9. Have you encountered any discrimination because you are a single parent, for example: finding employment, at your present job, individuals or organizations in your community, etc. How have you dealt with it?

10. Have your children encountered any discrimination because they have only one full-time parent? How have they tried to deal with this?

11. How have you reconciled your needs and interests with those of your children?

12. Have you experienced any unusual problems with your children in any of the following categories:
    □Infant/Toddler □Grade School □High School □Young Adult/Adult
    What are they? How have you dealt with them?

13. Please discuss how your family deals with the following areas, and how effective it is:
    A— Problem-Solving
    B— Discipline
    C— Giving your children responsibility, independence, and security.
    D— Values

14. If question 3A, 3B, or 3C applied to you, please describe any special problems you have encountered. How have you dealt with them? Any suggestions for others?

15. Please answer this question *only if one of the following applies to you*:
    I) Custodial Father
    II) Non-Custodial Mother
    III) Joint or Divided Custody, or Co-Parenting Arrangement (give details)
    A— Why did you decide on this type of arrangement?
    B— What have you found to be the benefits?
    C— What problems have you encountered because of your custodial situation?
    D— Have you any suggestions for others in the same custodial situation?

16. Are there other special problems you have experienced and dealt with, for example: handicapped children and/or parents, retarded children etc.?

17. How have you and your children benefited or failed to benefit from:
    A— PWP and other single parent groups (please describe)
    B— Community groups such as scouts, athletic teams, community activities, etc.
    C— Church and religious organizations
    D— Social Welfare, Special Classes, Career Counseling, Other Community Resources
    E— Resources that you and your friends have begun, such as food-co-ops, baby-sitting co-ops, communal living situations, interest groups, etc.

18. Have you and your former spouse been able to work *together* for your children's benefit? If so, how have you achieved this? Have you any suggestions for others?

19. If you have negative opinions about your former spouse, how do you believe this should be handled with your children? What have you done, and how has it worked?

20. How have the following types of relationships been affected by your single parent status, and how do they affect you and your children?
    A— Your Family (*Your* Parents, Brothers, Sisters, etc.)
    B— Your Former Spouse's Family
    C— Your Single Friends of Both Sexes

D— Your Dates and Ongoing Relationships
E— Your Former Single Friends Who Have Gotten Remarried
F— Your Non-Single Friends:
    I) From your married period
    II) Since you've been single again
21. Please answer this question only if you are, or have been, a non-custodial parent:
    A— How do you gain and maintain your children's love when you see them without "buying" it?
    B— "I love my children, but it hurts." Do you find it more painful to see them for a short period than not see them at all? How have you coped with this?
    C— Have you experienced distance, hostility (of your children and/or former spouse) or other special problems as a non-custodial single parent? What have you done?
    D— How (if at all) have you been able to create a "second home" that is comfortable for both your children and yourself?
    E— How has your relationship with your children affected and been affected by your other relationships?
    F— How have you and your children been able to benefit from your non-custodial relationship?
    G— Are there resources that you have found helpful to you and your children?
    H— Are there suggestions or recommendations that you could offer non-custodial single parents, or those considering becoming non-custodial single parents?

PLEASE USE THIS PAGE TO ANSWER ANY QUESTIONS FOR WHICH YOU DID NOT HAVE SPACE ON PAGES 1-6.

If you wish, you may write your first name and today's date

(Last name, only if you want!) May we use your first name in the book? May we contact you for more information, if needed? Yes   No
THE INFORMATION YOU SUPPLY WILL BE USED IN WRITING THE BOOK: *SINGLE PARENTING*, AND THUS HELP SINGLE PARENTS THROUGHOUT THE NATION. *NO NAMES* (EXCEPT FICTITIOUS) WILL BE USED UNLESS YOU GIVE YOUR FIRST NAME, AND PERMISSION TO USE IT (SEE ABOVE). THE SAME FOR LAST NAMES.

APPENDIX C: RESOURCES WHICH CAN HELP SINGLE PARENTS AND THEIR CHILDREN

Adoptions By Single Parents or Single People

The following agencies can offer help in this area:

Committee for Single Adoptive Parents
P.O. Box 4074
Washington, D.C. 20015

New York Council on Adoptable Children
125 East 23rd St.
New York, New York 10010

North American Council on Adoptable Children
c/o Linda Donn
250 East Blaine St.
Riverside, California 92507

This group deals with both Canada and the United States.

Black Unmarried Mothers

Sisterhood of Black Single Mothers
P.O. Box 155
Brooklyn, New York 11203
212/638-0413

Counseling for Families and Individuals

Family Service Association of America (FSAA)
44 East 23rd Street
New York, New York 10010
212/674-6100

The FSAA has member agencies throughout the United States. These agencies provide counseling and other such services to individuals and families. Frequently, there are support groups and other special services for single parents and their children. The fees are generally adjusted according to your income, number of dependents, and expenses. You can call FSAA's New York office to find out which of their member agencies serves your area.

Education, Continuing

> CAEL (Center for the Assessment of Experiential Learning)
> American City Building, Suite 212
> Columbia, Maryland 21044
> 800/638-7813—Toll-free, except in Maryland
> 301/730-9188 or 301/596-6799 in Maryland

This organization will tell you about colleges in your area that allow college credit for your work outside the classroom. (The term for this is *experiential learning*.) Just call their toll-free number, (or one of their two Maryland numbers).

Education: You and Your Children's School

> National Committee For Citizens In Education (NCCE)
> Wilde Lake Village Green
> Columbia, Maryland 21044
> 800/638-9675—except in Maryland
> 301/997-9300—in Maryland

The NCCE serves as an advocate and resource group for parents of school-age children. Their single-parent project has dealt with identifying the needs and problems of single parents. The NCCE can provide help and advice concerning problems and other concerns that you or your children may experience. I highly recommend their monthly magazine, *Network*.

Family Mediation

Family mediators work with both parents and children to provide a solution to conflicts that meets the needs of each party. It is frequently an alternative to bitter and expensive legal battles. For more informa tion about family mediation, and to find out about qualified family mediators in your area, you may contact

Dr. Mark R. Lohman
P.O. Box 103
Great Falls, Virginia 22066
703/759-9610

Fathers

Single Dad's Lifestyle
P.O. Box 4842
Scottsdale, Arizona 85258
602/998-0980

A magazine for dads, whether single or unmarried, who live with their children, want to gain custody, or simply want to enjoy more meaningful visitation experiences. ($12 per year, $1 for a single copy)

Fathers' Rights Groups

National Council of Marriage and Divorce Law
Reform and Justice Organizations
P.O. Box 60
Broomall, Pa. 19008

This organization can send you their directory of fathers' rights organizations throughout the United States.

Fathers United for Equal Rights
P.O. Box 9751
Baltimore, Maryland 21204

Financial and Budget Counseling, and Debt Payments

National Foundation for Consumer Credit
Suite 510, 1819 H St., N.W.
Washington, D.C. 20006
202/223-2040

The foundation is the accrediting body and national headquarters for over 200 Consumer Credit Counseling Service (CCCS) non-profit agencies throughout the United States. Typically, a CCCS agency offers free budget counseling and, for a low fee (to cover bookkeeping), can set up programs to help you pay off creditors at monthly rates you can afford. You can call the foundation's Washington office to find out which of its agencies is most convenient to you.

Four states have no CCCS agencies. Unfortunately, Alaska has no family service association. However, Arkansas, Delaware, and Mississippi have family service agencies that provide financial counseling. Their addresses are:

ARKANSAS:
Family Service Agency of Central Arkansas
North Little Rock Community Center Building
P.O. Box 500
North Little Rock, Arkansas 72115

DELAWARE:
Family Service of Northern Delaware
809 Washington Street
Wilmington, Delaware 19801

MISSISSIPPI:
Family Service Association of Greater Jackson
1510 North State Street, Suite 201
Jackson, Mississippi 39202

Gay and Lesbian Parents'
Organizations   *(Also See:* PARENTS
OF GAY AND LESBIAN CHILDREN)

For a complete and up-to-date list contact either

National Gay Task Force
85th Avenue, Suite 1601
New York, New York 10011
212-741-5800

or

Call your local Gay Switchboard
listed in your telephone directory.

Job Readiness for Displaced Homemakers

Displaced Homemakers Network
755 8th St., N.W.
Washington, D.C. 20001
202/347-0522

Displaced Homemakers is a national network, designed to help women (and men, if they qualify) who are at least 35 years old and are full-time homemakers who have suffered a loss in income due to separation, divorce, disability, or the death of a spouse. The Displaced Homemakers Center offers job-readiness training, help in finding a career, training, and placement. For more information and to find the location of the center serving your area, contact the national headquarters of the Displaced Homemakers Network.

Men

Free Men
P.O. Box 920
Columbia, Maryland 21044

A resource group for men who want to examine alternatives to traditional stereotypical male roles, Free Men is a national organization that, according to its brochure, is "founded on the premise that society assigns men, as well as women, limiting roles in which they are expected to perform, regardless of their individual abilities, interests, and physical or emotional constitutions."

Free Men "seeks to promote awareness in men and women of how these gender-based roles limit men legally, socially, emotionally, and sexually—and to provide support and assistance for men who choose to break free of gender-based limitations."

Free Men offers workshops and support groups, and publishes a monthly newsletter. (Write to the group for dues and membership information.)

Parenting Groups

American Guidance Services, Inc.
Circle Pines, Minnesota 55014

This publishing company developed the STEP (Systematic Training in Effective Parenting) method that is used by many PWP chapters. Unlike some other parenting programs, STEP requires that only one parent participate in the program. Kits and a textbook are available from the publisher.

American Society of Adlerian Psychology
159 Dearborn Street
Chicago, Illinois 60601

The Society sponsors parent-education centers throughout the United States and has excellent educational materials. Their approach is based on the teaching of Rudolf Dreikurs.

Effectiveness Training Associates
110 South Euclid Ave.
Pasadena, California 91101

This organization teaches Dr. Thomas Gordon's Parent Effectiveness Training (PET) method and has parent groups in most cities.

Parents Anonymous (PA)
National Office
2230 Hawthorne Boulevard, Suite 208
Torrance, California 90505
Toll-free (except in California): 800/421-0353
Toll-free in California: 800/352-0386

Parents Anonymous helps parents deal constructively with their anger, frustration, and other feelings about their children. Their object is to help parents stop beating or otherwise abusing their children. The group is supportive, charges no dues, and has chapters in each state. Each state has a 24-hour hotline, and each chapter has weekly meetings, where baby sitting is usually provided free.

Parents of Gay and Lesbian Children

National Federation of Parents and Friends of Gays
P.O. Box 24528
Los Angeles, California 90024
213/472-8952

Parents of Gays has groups in many parts of the United States and Canada (the national headquarters can give more details). The local groups are self-help and educational groups, where parents first share their feelings and experiences when they discover their child is gay. These groups promote a positive attitude toward homosexuality by providing accurate information—through good reading material and outside speakers—and by the opportunity to meet a variety of gay women and men, as well as activities. (Its publications and other recommended reading are listed in the Bibliography.)

Religion and Single Parents

North American Conference of Separated
and Divorced Catholics (NACSDC)
5 Park Street
Boston, Mass. 02108
617/742-4461

This is the national organization for separated and divorced Catholics' groups throughout the United States.

Remarried Parents' Groups *(Also*
See: STEP-PARENTING)

Remarrieds Inc.
Box 742
Santa Ana, California 92702

This national group has chapters throughout the United States.

Remarried Parents, Inc.
175 5th Ave.
New York, New York 10010

A New York City–based group. You can ask them if they have chapters in other areas.

Single-Parent Organizations

Montgomery County Single Parents (Montcosps)
c/o John Holl

8807 Arliss Street
Silver Spring, Maryland 20901
301-587-6973

A Washington, D.C., area single parents' club. Members must have at least one child under 18. The dialogues (discussions) are exceptional, as is the club's special sense of single-parent community. Montcosps also has social events and family activities.

Parents Without Partners, Inc.
International Headquarters
7910 Woodmont Ave., Suite 1000
Washington, D.C. 20014
301/654-8850

This is the largest single-parent organization in the United States and Canada. (There is also an autonomous chapter in Australia.) The National Headquarters publishes a monthly magazine, *The Single Parent*, and several excellent bibliographies and resource guides; it maintains an extensive information center, which contains books and materials relating to single parents and their children; and it serves as an advocate for single parents and their children before national and state governments, and elsewhere.

Local chapters offer discussions, educational programs, family activities, and adult social activities, as well as organizations for young people.

For information about the local chapter in your area, and membership requirements, contact PWP Headquarters.

I would especially recommend that you ask PWP to send you a list of their pamphlets and booklets relating to separation and divorce, widows and widowers, remarriage, fathers and other issues. A single copy is free, and generally lists books and resource groups that can help you.

Single Parents on Campus and Community (SPOC)
University Memorial Center
University of Colorado
Boulder, Colorado 80309

A support group for single parents that includes a drop-in center, a big-brother, big-sister program which uses student volunteers, an emergency locator service for locating a single parent on campus in the event of an emergency involving his or her child, special programs for university-age children of single parents, and rap sessions and panel discussions.

Three other organizations are listed below. You may contact them directly for more information about their programs.

Single Parent Resource Center
10 West 23rd Street
New York, New York 10010
212/620-0755

Single Parent Project
5715 Lindo Paseo
San Diego, California 92115
714/286-9472

Single Parent Resource Center
3896 24th Street
San Francisco, California 94114
415/821-7058

Singles' and Single-Again Resources

The Beginning Experience
4503 Bridge Street
Fort Worth, Texas 76103
817/429-2920

This program, available in many states (ask the national head-quarters for specific locations), consists of a weekend experience which attempts to help separated, widowed, or divorced persons who are past the initial stage make a new start in life. This program, comparable to Marriage Encounter, is designed by and for Catholics but is open to members of all faiths.

The weekend features presentations by a trained team, followed by private personal reflection, and then dialogue in small groups. The leaders include widowed and divorced people, as well as others with experience in life renewal.

The Beginning Experience is an alternative to estrangement from the Church.

The program's brochure recommends that participants be beyond the initial stage of anger and despair, and ready to make a new start.

Solo
1822 N.W. Broadway
Portland, Oregon 97232
503/287-0642

This is a resource group and center for single people that offers a variety of workshops and programs relating to concerns of single people. The group also has some programs especially for single parents.

Step-Parent Resources   *(See Also*
REMARRIED PARENTS' GROUPS)

The Stepfamily Foundation, Inc.
333 West End Ave.
New York, New York 10023
212/877-3244

This is a nonprofit foundation that serves as a resource and educational center for issues and concerns relating to step-parenting. For one dollar (to cover postage and handling), the Stepfamily Foundation will send you a wealth of current information (you can write periodically), including such things as where to get additional help and information, articles relating to step-parenting, tips for step-parents, programs and groups in your area, and the foundation and its programs. The foundation also offers workshops and seminars for step-parents, and trains social workers and other professionals who work with step-families. It also seeks to inform the public about the special needs and concerns of step-families.

Women

FOCUS (For Our Children and Us)
c/o Fran Mattera
P.O. Box 325
Levittown, New York 11756

FOCUS consults with legislators, works to promote changes in the court system, and educates women. You can start a group in your own area. FOCUS will help you and even accompany you to court, if necessary.

NEXUS
P.O. Box 176
Garden City, New York 11530
516/248-0043

NEXUS offers the newly separated, divorced, or widowed woman mutual support, provides her a haven after a breakup, and helps her in her new life style. Groups usually have 25 to 30 members. NEXUS has recently published a manual to help women, throughout the U.S., start their own NEXUS groups.

Youth and Children

Big Brother/Big Sister
117 South 17th Street, Suite 1200
Philadelphia, Pa. 19103
215/567-2748

This national program arranges for a volunteer of the same sex as a.child to spend time with the child and befriend him or her, while providing a positive role model. The organization is a valuable aid to single parents; however, some of its groups still might think of a single-parent family primarily as a broken home.

International Youth Council (IYC)
c/o Parents Without Partners
International Headquarters
7910 Woodmont Ave., Suite 1000
Washington, D.C. 20014
301/654-8850

The IYC provides teenage children of single parents their own counterpart in PWP. Many PWP chapters have affiliated IYCs. Membership in IYC is open to any teenager who has at least one parent still single. The parent does *not* have to be a member of PWP.

The IYC chapters offer both discussion—where young people

can gain the support of others in the same situation—and social events.

Contact PWP headquarters to find out if your local PWP chapter has an IYC and, if not, how you can start one.

APPENDIX D: ANNOTATED BIBLIOGRAPHY

I want to express my special thanks to Elizabeth Hormann, book reviewer for *The Single Parent*, for taking the time to recommend several recent books that I did not have the time to read. These books are indicated by an asterisk (*).

Adoptions by Single Persons or Single Parents

SCHLESINGER, BENJAMIN. "Single Parent Adoptions, A Review." *The One-Parent Family.* 4th ed. rev. pp. 68–74. Toronto: University of Toronto Press, 1978.

A short discussion of the success that single parents have had in adopting and raising children. A short bibliography and list of resources adds to the usefulness of this article.

Communication

BACH, DR. GEORGE R., AND DEUTSCH, RONALD M. *Pairing*. New York: Peter H. Wyden, 1970; Avon (paperback), 1971.

A helpful guide which demonstrates ways in which single adults can establish communication and build intimate relationships.

FAST, JULIUS. *Body Language*. New York: M. Evans, 1970; Pocket Books, 1970.

An excellent guide to nonverbal communication and how it affects our relationships with other people.

Custody

WOOLEY, PERSIA. *The Custody Handbook*. New York: Summit Books, 1979.

This beautiful and stirring book is an outstanding resource guide to alternatives to traditional maternal custody. This book is unusual in its in-depth discussion of the feelings of both divorced mothers and fathers in terms each can relate to and understand.

I highly recommend this book for any single parent who is concerned with finding a long-term custodial alternative that meets the needs of the children and *both* parents.

Day Care

COLLINS, ALICE H., AND WATSON, EUNICE L. *Family Day Care: A Practical Guide for Parents, Caregivers, and Professionals*. Boston: Beacon Press, 1976.

Useful for its description of family day care, child-care co-ops, informal day-care arrangements for working parents, and information and referral systems, this book is a helpful guide to day care in a home setting.

MITCHELL, GRACE. *The Day Care Book*. Briarcliff Manor, N.Y.: Stein and Day, 1979.

This is a recent book written for working parents by a parent who has also had years of experience in running a day-care center. There is plenty of good advice: both about what to consider in choosing a day-care center and about other problems and concerns of working parents. The author discusses preparing children for day care, dealing with the guilt parents frequently feel about leaving their youngsters at a day-care center, and includes many personal examples. Highly recommended for its thorough coverage of *all* aspects of day care.

Discipline

DODSON, DR. FITZHUGH. *How to Discipline with Love.* New York: Signet (paperback), 1978.

An exceptional book that discusses ways that you can use discipline to help your children. In addition, his chapter on the single parent is one of the few chapters in any book which does *not* assume that a single-parent home is unhealthy for a child.

Divorce

GETTLEMAN, SUSAN, AND MARKOWITZ, JANET. *The Courage to Divorce.* New York: Simon & Schuster, 1974; Ballantine (paperback), 1974.

The authors see divorce as a healthy, constructive, fulfilling beginning of a new purposeful life for both parents and children.

KRANTZLER, MEL. *Creative Divorce.* New York: M. Evans, 1973; Signet (paperback), 1975.

This classic work explains how divorce can be the beginning of a healthy new life and discusses feelings, problems, and solutions. Essential for any person who is either contemplating divorce, or is newly divorced.

Divorce and Children

BERGER, TERRY. *How Does It Feel When Your Parents Get Divorced?* New York: Julian Messner, 1977.

A poignant book, written as a storybook, on a child's level. Highly recommended for helping young children (through second grade) understand their feelings and come to peace with themselves and their lives.

BERNSTEIN, JOANNE E. *Books to Help Children Cope with Separation and Loss.* New York: R.R. Bowker, 1977.

A resource guide for using books to help children deal with death, divorce, and the question of "who will take care of me?"

GARDNER, RICHARD. *The Boys and Girls Book about Divorce.* New York: Bantam (paperback), 1970.

Excellent for helping children understand and cope with *their* feelings, fears, and concerns.

SALK, LEE. *What Every Child Would Like Parents to Know About Divorce.* New York: Harper & Row, 1978; Warner Books (paperback), 1979.

This book, written by an internationally recognized child psychologist who is also a single parent with custody of his children, offers a convenient question-and-answer format which covers many of your concerns about how divorce can affect your children and what you can do about it.

*SARAH, BONNET STEIN. *On Divorce.* Open Family Living Series. New York: Walker, 1979.

This book's unusual format has one side for first graders and the other for parents. The child's side features large pictures, with a few lines of large print. The parent's side has small print. The book can be read by parent and child together. The parent's guide suggests ideas and questions to help your child understand and cope with the new situation.

Divorce and Teenagers

RICHARDS, ARLENE, AND WILLIS, IRENE. *How to Get It Together When Your Parents Are Coming Apart*. New York: David McKay, 1976; Bantam (paperback), 1977.

Highly recommended as a practical resource guide for adolescents and those who work with them.

Education

BLAZE, WAYNE; HERTZBERG, BILL; KRANTZ, ROY; AND LEHRKE, AL. *A Guide to Alternative Colleges and Universities*. Boston: Beacon Press, 1974.

This book lists campus-based B.A. programs, two-year A.A. (Associate of Arts) programs, external degree programs (where students spend little or no time on campus), special programs, and free universities. Unfortunately, the fact that it was written in 1974 may limit the book's usefulness. Verify all information with the individual school mentioned.

Family

HENDRICKS, GAY. *The Family Centering Book: Awareness Activities the Whole Family Can Do Together*. Englewood Cliffs, New Jersey: Prentice-Hall, 1979.

An unusual book that shows how communications and mediation exercises can be used to bring a family closer together. Good examples and exercises that you and your children can do together.

Fathers

SHEPARD, MORRIS A., AND GOLDMAN, GERALD. *Divorced Dads; Their Kids, Ex-Wives, and New Lives*. Radnor, Pa.: Chilton, 1979.

Excellent down-to-earth advice by two divorced fathers. This book discusses how to build a close relationship with your children, how you can be involved in your children's everyday lives—even if you're not there—sharing your children with the other parent, and remarriage and other relationships as these relate to the children. If I were to recommend one book for divorced fathers, this would be it! See also Appendix C under "Fathers."

VICTOR, IRA, AND WINKLER, WIN ANN. *Fathers and Custody.* New York: Hawthorn, 1977.

This resource guide, for fathers considering custody, discusses fathers' custodial alternatives in terms that single fathers and other interested persons can relate to. Particularly useful are three Appendices: "Divorced Fathers Groups," "Single Parent and Child Help Groups," and "Legal Advice Referral."

Financial and Budget Management

FELDMAN, FRANCES. *The Family and Today's Money World.* New York: Family Service Association of America, no date available.

This book, highly recommended by Patricia Nurse, MEd, education consultant to the National Foundation for Consumer Credit, is available (check for price) from

Family Service Association of America
44 East 23rd Street
New York, New York 10010

Gay and Lesbian Single Parents

The following books and articles were reviewed by A. Billy S. Jones, founder of Parents Who Are Gay, and author of the selection in Chapter 6: "Gay Fathers and Lesbian Mothers."

BERZON, BETTY, AND LEIGHTON, ROBERT. *Positively Gay.* Millbare, California: Celestial Arts, 1979.

Two chapters (pp. 112–129)—"Being A Gay Father," and "Being A Lesbian Mother"—consist of gay and lesbian parents sharing insights about their personal experiences and relationships, and their reflections and insights concerning how their personal and family lives have been affected by this.

MILLER, BRIAN. "Gay Fathers And Their Children." *The Family Coordinator*, 28, no. 4 (October 1979) 544–552.

Available from

National Council of Family Relations
1219 University Ave., S.E.
Minneapolis, Minnesota 55419

This study demonstrates that gay fathers have the ability to raise their children.

STEVENS, MARY. "Lesbian Mothers in Transition." In *Our Right To Love*, by Ginny Vida, pp. 207–211. Englewood Cliffs, New Jersey: Prentice-Hall, 1978.

Excellent advice for the mother who is moving from a heterosexual relationship to a single-parent situation—or shared-parenting situation—as a lesbian mother.

Gay and Lesbian Children, and Their Parents

Answers to a Parent's Questions About Homosexuality and *Twenty Questions About Homosexuality*. Available free from

National Gay Task Force
80 Fifth Ave., Suite 1601
New York, New York 10011

FAIRCHILD, BETTY, AND HAYWARD, NANCY. *Now That You Know: What Every Parent Should Know about Homosexuality*. New York: Harcourt Brace Jovanovich, Inc., 1979.

This is a chatty, easy-to-read guidebook for parents by parents. It includes personal experiences of the authors, other parents of gays, and gay men and women.

SILVERSTEIN, CHARLES. *A Family Matter: A Parent's Guide to Homosexuality.* New York: McGraw-Hill, 1977.

This insightful book, written by a psychologist, who is also a sex therapist, can be valuable to any parent who has, or thinks he or she has, a gay or lesbian child.

Joint Custody and Coparenting

GALPER, MIRIAM. *Co-Parenting: A Source Book for the Separated or Divorced Family.* Philadelphia: Running Press, 1978.

A positive yet realistic view of joint custody, as experienced by the author, her former husband, and other single parents. Essential reading for any single parent who is considering joint custody or coparenting.

Lesbian Single Parents   *(Also See:* GAY AND LESBIAN SINGLE PARENTS)

Parenting

BARUTH, LEROY. *A Single Parent's Survival Guide: How to Raise the Children.* Dubuque, Iowa: Kendall/Hunt, 1979.

A concise practical guide that applies Dreikurs' parenting techniques to the problems and concerns of single parents. This book is based on the belief that children raised in a single-parent home can be as happy and well adjusted as those in two-parent families. It is a book recommended for single parents by Ann Parks, information coordinator for PWP, Inc.

The Princeton Center for Infancy. *The Parenting Advisor.* Edited by
Frank Caplan. Garden City, New York: Anchor Press, 1977;
Doubleday (paperback), 1977.

A useful child-development encyclopedia, for those with infants
or toddlers, to put next to your Dr. Spock.

DREIKURS, RUDOLF, M.D. *Children: The Challenge.* New York: Hawthorn, 1964.

The classic book that is the basis for the Dreikurs-Adlerian approach to parenting.

GORDON, THOMAS. *Parent Effectiveness Training: A Tested New Way to
Raise Responsible Children.* New York: New American Library,
1975.

This outstanding book is the basis for the well-known PET system of parenting.

SCHENK, QUENTIN F., AND SCHENK, EMMY LOU. *Pulling up Roots: For
Young Adults and Their Parents–Letting Go and Getting Free.* Englewood Cliffs, New Jersey: Prentice-Hall, 1978.

A thorough and down-to-earth guide to young adults, and their
parents, this book offers valuable advice on how parents can help
their children to achieve independence. Recommended for single
parents with teenage or young-adult children.

Remarriage and Step-Parenting

KRANTZLER, MEL. *Learning to Love Again: Beyond Creative Divorce.* New
York: Thomas Y. Crowell, 1977; Signet (paperback), 1979.

A personal account of the author's remarriage, this book discusses problems and strategies which may help single parents. Highly recommended.

*NOBLE, JUNE AND WILLIAM. *How to Live with Other People's Children*. New York: Hawthorn Books, 1977.

This informal and down-to-earth book is valuable as a practical guide for step-parents. It is highly recommended by Elizabeth Hormann, book reviewer for *The Single Parent*.

ROOSEVELT, RUTH, AND LOFAS, JEANNETTE. *Living in Step*. Briarcliffe Manor, N.Y.: Stein & Day, 1976.

This and the Nobles' book are the best resource guides for step-parents and those considering step-parenthood. This book discusses adjusting, concerns of stepmothers and stepfathers, growing up in a step-relationship, noncustodial parents, and parents with custody. Written by the founder of the Step Family Foundation (Ms. Lofas) and another step-parent, this book is a *must* for any single parent considering remarriage.

WESTOFF, LESLIE ALDRIDGE. *The Second Time Around: Remarriage in America*. New York: Viking, 1977.

This highly recommended book is by a remarried parent who has interviewed other people in various stages of remarriage. A candid discussion of the joys and problems of remarriage, with special sections dealing with children. This is basically a remarried equivalent to *Single Parenting*.

Resources

TANSEY, ANNE M. *Where to Get Help for Your Family: A Directory of 157 Agencies That Can Serve You in Time of Need*. St. Meinrad, Indiana: Abbey Press, 1977.

A useful guide to agencies throughout the United States. Especially helpful are the listings under Children, Family, and Youth.

Resources, Children

FASSLER, JOAN. *Helping Children Cope.* New York: The Free Press, 1978.

A child psychologist shows how books and stories can be used to help reduce fears and anxieties, help children grow, and initiate open, honest communication.

Singleness as a Way of Life

EDWARDS, MARIE, AND HOOVER, ELEANOR. *The Challenge of Being Single.* New York: Signet (paperback), 1974.

This highly recommended book shows how being single can be a satisfying and richly rewarding way of life.

JOHNSON, DR. STEPHEN M. *First Person Singular: Living the Good Life Alone.* Philadelphia: Lippincott, 1977; New York: Signet (paperback), 1977.

An exciting book which shows vividly how single life can be a rewarding and desirable lifestyle. Particularly valuable are the sections on developing friendships, meeting people, and building intimate relationships.

Single-Parent Families

DESPERT, J. LOUISE, M.D. *Children of Divorce.* New York: Doubleday, 1962.

The classic study that shows how single parent families can be beneficial to children.

The Single Parent. A magazine published ten times a year by Parents Without Partners, Inc., 7910 Woodmont Ave., Washington, D.C. 20014.

Included as a part of PWP membership, and available to non-members for a subscription rate of $7.50 per year.

The magazine for single parents. There are excellent articles and features pertaining to all aspects of single-parent life. I strongly recommend that all public and academic libraries, and all persons who work with single parents and/or their children, as well as all single parents, should subscribe to this magazine.

Time and Life Management

LAKEIN, ALAN. *How to Get Control of Your Time and Your Life.* New York: Peter H. Wyden, 1973; New American Library (paperback), 1974.

A valuable and highly recommended guide as to how you can make the most effective use of your time—while ensuring that you still have time to do the things that you enjoy.

Widowed Single Parents

CAINE, LYNNE. *Widow.* New York: Bantam (paperback), 1975.

A personal account by a widow, who is a single parent, which is recommended as the single most useful book for widows by both widowed single parents with whom I talked and Ann Parks, PWP's information specialist.

*COHN, JANE B. AND WILLARD K. *The Widower.* Boston: Beacon Press, 1979.

The authors (a husband-and-wife team) are a widower, and a sociologist. The husband gives his story of how he became widowed and raised his six daughters. There are two sections. His autobiography is followed by his second wife's commentary on the broader implications of his experiences. The book shows the father's struggles in learning to parent alone; and it combines a warm and moving personal account with broader analysis.

GROLLMAN, EARL A. *Talking About Death: A Dialogue between Parent and Child.* Rev. Ed: Boston: Beacon Press, 1976.

Outstanding both for its parents' guide for explaining death to your children and its children's read-along which can help your child in terms that he or she can understand. There is an excellent guide to resources that can help you and your children deal with death, and suggestions for further reading.

*TEMES, ROBERTA. *Living with an Empty Chair: A Guide through Grief.* Amherst, Mass: Mandala Press, 1977.

This brief guide touches on the various stages of grief in a very personal way. The author writes directly to each reader.

Women

NAPOLITANE, CATHERINE, AND PELLEGRINE, VICTORIA. *Living and Loving after Divorce.* New York: Rawson and Associates, 1977.

A practical and compassionate guide for divorced women that helps women in their transition from newly single to fulfilled single. Especially helpful is the discussion of eight steps to recover from the shock of divorce. Ms. Napolitane is the founder of NEXUS (listed in Appendix C).

Index